LINCOLN CHRISTIAN COLLEGE AND SEMINARY

P9-CRU-027

UIC Library of the
UNIVERSITY OF ILLINOIS
AT CHICAGO Health Sciences - Chicago
UNIVERSITY LIBRARY

REC'D JAN 3 0 2014

http://library.uic.edu/lhs-chicago
312 996-9163

Praise for *Terrify No More*

This book will shock you, upset you, inspire you, and challenge you as it tells the story of how some people of God struggle against one of the most obscene forms of oppression in the world today. The book is only a micro-picture of a macro-problem that we have tried to pretend isn't there.

Tony Campolo, Ph.D.
Professor Emeritus, Eastern University

A shocking glimpse into the unimaginably perverse world of 'sex tourists' who abuse children trapped in the international sex trade. This is an important step toward unmasking and prosecuting the thousands of crimes against children committed by American citizens abroad each year. A compelling read.

Rich Stearns
President, World Vision U.S.

For those of us who embrace the fact that the Lord's desire and pleasure is upon those who are advocates for justice in an unjust world (Micah 6:8), this book is a must-read. As a proven practitioner in the enterprise of bringing God's justice to the plight of the oppressed, my friend Gary writes with unusual clarity and con-viction. But, reader beware, *Terrify No More* will relentlessly tug at your heart and show you how you too can join the growing number of followers of Christ who are taking seriously His desire to grace our treacherous world with freedom from the enslavement and bondage in which millions are hopelessly lost.

Dr. Joseph M. Stowell
President, Moody Bible Institute

I have never read anything as moving and inspiring. I felt my heart racing as I was given a front row seat looking at the real heroes of our day. If these accounts of suffering and redemption do not provoke you to find your place in the fight against injustice . . . nothing will. In these pages are the wild, unpredictable, high-risk exhibits of true worship through service that the modern church, so preoc-cupied with safety, needs to drink in deeply. Thank you, IJM!

Dan Haseltine
Jars of Clay/Blood:Water Mission

Terrify No More communicates with clarity the pain and sufering I've witnessed first-hand working among the poor. It is a compelling tale of lawyers and investigators using their finely honed skills to bring justice to victims of oppression. A must-read for any person who believes it's possible to change the world.

Millard Fuller
Founder & President, Habitat for Humanity

TERRIFY NO MORE

GARY A. HAUGEN
PRESIDENT OF INTERNATIONAL JUSTICE MISSION

WITH GREGG HUNTER

W PUBLISHING GROUP
A Division of Thomas Nelson Publishers
Since 1798

www.wpublishinggroup.com

In memory of Vera Shaw,
who still thought God was good,
and now knows.

Copyright © 2005 International Justice Mission

All rights reserved. No portion of this book may be reproduced, stored in a retrieval system, or transmitted in any form or by any means—electronic, mechanical, photocopy, recording, or any other—except for brief quotations in printed reviews, without the prior written permission of the publisher.

Published by W Publishing Group, a Division of Thomas Nelson, Inc., P.O. Box 141000, Nashville, Tennessee, 37214.

W Publishing Group books may be purchased in bulk for educational, business, fundraising, or sales promotional use. For information, please email SpecialMarkets@ThomasNelson.com.

All Scripture quotations, unless otherwise indicated, are taken from The New King James Version (NKJV), copyright © 1979, 1980, 1982, Thomas Nelson, Inc. Publishers.

Other Scripture references are from the following sources:

The Holy Bible, New International Version (NIV). Copyright © 1973, 1978, 1984. International Bible Society. Used by permission of Zondervan Bible Publishers.

The New Revised Standard Version Bible (NRSV), copyright © 1989 by the Division of Christian Education of the National Council of the Churches of Christ in the USA.

Editorial Staff: Kate Etue (Associate Acquisitions Editor), Evelyn Bence, Deborah Wiseman, Lauren Weller
Cover Design: AJ Buffington, Washington, D.C.
Page Design: Stacy Clark, Book & Graphic Design, Nashville, Tennessee

Photos courtesy of Ted Haddock © International Justice Mission, except where otherwise noted.

Library of Congress Cataloging-in-Publication Data is available

ISBN 0-8499-1838-3

Printed in the United States of America

04 05 06 07 08 QW 9 8 7 6 5 4 3 2 1

CONTENTS

ACKNOWLEDGMENTS

My deepest gratitude is extended to my IJM colleagues who do the work and make the life choices that give us these stories to tell. The true depth of their courage and generosity is seen only in secret by their Maker; but in these years, I have been granted sufficient glimpses of such authentic goodness and glory that I now hold a storehouse of stories for my grandchildren of when I walked with real, flesh-and-blood heroes. I am very grateful for their sacrifice of time in helping recover these narratives and for all my colleagues who helped assemble the facts and artifacts of memory with characteristic rigor, insight, and inspiration. I am deeply indebted to my collaborator, Gregg Hunter, who did all the heavy lifting in pulling these stories together, and did so with extraordinary sensitivity, intelligence, kindness, and skill. Given the relentless press of IJM's daily operational demands, this story simply would not have been rendered without Gregg stepping forward to make it happen. I am also so very grateful to Ted Haddock for the photographs that tell us what words are too poor to say, and to Penny Hunter and Dan Raines, who shepherded this project so faithfully and relentlessly with excellence. Thank you to David Moberg and Kate Etue of W Publishing Group, who believed in this book from the beginning and have courageously committed to introduce the world to the victims of oppression; and to Jeanie Kaserman from Creative Trust for the counsel she provided. I must also express my earnest thanks to the thousands of friends and supporters of IJM who make it concretely possible to render service to those in desperate need—those who cannot, on their own, afford the advocacy they deserve. To a small circle of friends who took special care to make sure that IJM had the resources to conduct these operations in Cambodia; this generosity, too, has been seen by our Father in secret. To Jan and the kids, thank you for making this an offering we can give together— with joy.

—Gary Haugen

Thank you to the IJM staff who spent so many hours telling the stories captured in this book: Sharon Cohn, Bob Mosier, Robert Earle, Will Henry, John Richmond, Sean Litton, Kristen Romens, Chris Livingstone, and others. You are my heroes, and you inspire me. The mountain of facts, names, dates, and places in this book are correct because of the wonderful service of Becca Kipe, who answered endless questions quickly and graciously. Also, special thanks to Ted Haddock for sharing intimate reflections from his personal journals, including some of the very words used to tell these stories.

Thank you, Darlene Howell, for reading the early manuscript and giving thoughtful input that made the book better.

To my wife, Penny, whose idea this book was, and who not only managed the process but also provided necessary encouragement along the way: This wouldn't have happened without you. Zach and Nate, thank you for giving the sacrifice of your dad's time so that others may know the truth about oppression in the world. And to Gary Haugen, thank you for the trust you've shown me and for your generosity in allowing me to work with you, one of the best communicators I've ever known. You've opened my eyes to God's heart for the oppressed in ways I never would have imagined.

—Gregg Hunter

INTRODUCTION

You're about to embark on a journey into a world of injustice. It's a world my colleagues live in every day—a place of darkness, fear, bondage, and oppression. As you walk with my friends and see their display of God's love for the oppressed—along with their diligence in addressing evil head-on— you will also be ushered into refreshing places of hope, courage, freedom, and justice.

Because of the nature of the work we do at International Justice Mission, we must be vague in some of our geographic references. Our work requires careful bridge building with foreign governments and others in influence. For us to continue to set captives free, to seek justice, we must maintain positive relationships with many in power. So, rather than name specific countries, we've been more general at times. And many of the names we use are pseudonyms—aliases to protect the identity of victims, our staff members, and operatives who may be at risk if their names appear in these pages.

Some of the stories in this book may be more graphic than what you are used to, but I am convinced that any serious contest with evil requires a painful confrontation with the truth. The greatest and most shameful regrets of history are always about the truth we failed to tell, the evil we failed to name. The greatest enemy in our struggle to stop oppression and injustice is always the insidious etiquette of silence.

And so, I ask you to stick with us through the discomfort caused by some of the subject matter. For in the pain, there is promise; in the hurting, there is hope. And our God is the God of justice, who does not turn a deaf ear to the cries of the oppressed. He alone empowers us as we confront the dark world of injustice and experience the joy of rescue, relief, and grace given to those who are suffering. We join him in the rescues we work so hard to obtain, so "that man, who is of the earth, may terrify no more" (Psalm 10:18 NIV).

CHAPTER 1

WHAT IF?

What if one of the pimps pulls a gun on the bus full of children? I thought as I stared at the operational diagram on the wall. After all, we can't check the bad guys for weapons before they get on the bus with all the kids. I began to picture the scene in my mind. The pimp on Bus 1 gets nervous. He pulls out a gun. The kids all start screaming. The pimp yells at the bus driver. The bus driver starts to panic. Chaos. Screaming kids. A gun flailing in the air. A bus careening down the highway.

"What's the plan if something goes wrong on Bus 1 on the way to Bravo?" I asked Bob Mosier, the operation's tactical leader, now giving our team its final briefing.

This was game time, and the last chance to visualize the operation step by step and picture everything that might go horribly wrong. You can't always stop things from turning bad, but you don't want to be thinking about the problem for the first time when dozens of kids are suddenly screaming and someone is waving around a loaded pistol.

And there wasn't much time left. My colleagues had meticulously planned the operation for seven months and now we were here, early on a Saturday morning in March 2003, huddled in a small hotel meeting room in Phnom Penh, Cambodia, with the pale green blinds pulled shut. We had made the decision to push our barrel over the falls; having set the operation in motion, we were gearing up for our free fall toward the water, or rocks, or oblivion ahead. Within hours our team of professional investigators, lawyers, and other strategic staff members planned to raid a series of nasty and dangerous brothels where scores of very young girls were being sold for sex in an open market. We had been in the country for nearly two weeks dealing with delay after

1

delay, to the point that our lead investigator's life was now in danger and the rescue of the brutalized little girls was gravely at risk.

As International Justice Mission colleagues, we shared a vision for rescuing victims of violence, sexual exploitation, slavery, and other forms of oppression and abuse. Headquartered in Washington, D.C., our young human rights organization, best known as IJM, had established offices around the globe. Working with local police, we'd carried out many rescue operations over the last several years. We'd learned some hard lessons. With our impending move into the brothel community of Svay Pak, eleven kilometers outside Phnom Penh, only hours away, it was my job to ask all the questions I might one day desperately wish I had asked ahead of time.

It was 6:00 A.M. as we sipped coffee, shifted in our thin, black-lacquered chairs, and passed around copies of the operational plan, maps, checklists, and extra cell-phone cards. Most of us hadn't slept more than a few hours for days, and some not at all. But in such final moments of preparation, a restrained but fierce adrenaline rush provides intense clarity. My colleagues are extremely good at what they do, and as the briefing proceeded, I noticed their steely confidence and immovable courage. With anticipation and awe, I sensed I was about to see, by the grace of God, something of extraordinarily rare beauty—an authentic miracle of passionate goodness, pure courage, and the most excellent love.

Bob and the security team walked us through escape routes and contingency plans for each person involved, in case crowds of onlookers became hostile mobs ready to unleash their anger upon anyone who threatened their livelihood. And we hoped to do precisely that—to threaten, disrupt, and shut down the business they were conducting at the expense of innocent girls.

Our investigators had set up a ruse to convince the brothel keepers to allow us to transport as many child victims and perpetrators as possible on a bus to an offsite party, where the girls' services would be needed. Once at the safe house, location "Bravo," the girls would be rescued and the perpetrators arrested by a squad of Cambodian National Police.

Bob Mosier, a former SWAT team and criminal investigations division commander, coolly answered my question with characteristic precision. He explained that if a pimp had a gun on the bus, we would move into standard police response and neutralize the threat.

"We will request that the police have checkpoints along route 598, so that officers will be available to follow the bus or stop the bus and assist the victims and staff if something goes wrong," Mosier said.

He then outlined a reasonable scenario in which the local police authorities could be called upon to aid in capturing or eliminating such a threat to the safety of children, IJM staff, and our operatives.

"What if a mob gathers and threatens the safety of IJM staff? Does everyone know the exit strategy?" Mosier quizzed us.

Though he was certain everyone did, Mosier started at the beginning: "First, anyone in danger should call or radio Will Henry immediately. He will have temporary command over two buses of Cambodian National Police waiting here on the main road outside the village," he said, pointing to the map. "He will direct the police to your location in the village at any moment you feel you're in imminent danger.

"In a few minutes I will hand out a more detailed emergency evacuation strategy, including what happens if we need to evacuate Bravo. But, the most important thing to remember is this: Don't panic; we will get you out."

CHAPTER 2

THE GIRLS OF SVAY PAK

We had first learned about Svay Pak nearly three years earlier, in 2000, from a contact in Southeast Asia who passed along rumors of a small, lawless village where scores of girls, including very young girls, were sold on an open market to be molested and abused by sex tourists. My colleagues were well experienced in infiltrating and fighting the shadowy underworld of the commercial sex trade around the globe, but we had never seen anything like this. There were just so many very young girls being sold and abused—tiny, elementary-school-age girls. Perhaps most shockingly, the whole cesspool of rape, sadism, and child molestation was held out openly to the public, in broad daylight, with brutal arrogance. Yes, in recent months the brothel owners had taken some steps to ensure they wouldn't get caught; but behind the thin veil of cover, their sexual exploitation of innocent victims was operating as usual.

Other than a small fishing industry, the whole village of Svay Pak was built around the sex trade; any other form of business conducted there was either a thin cover of legitimacy behind which the brothel owners hid or a place that provided amenities to brothel customers, such as bars or cafés. Scores of children and young women were held against their wills in Svay Pak, forced to serve sex customers in dingy cubicles as small as six by eight feet, a space often shared with one or more other girls. What would look like very small bedrooms or walk-in closets to most Western kids—with posters hung on the walls and stuffed animals in a corner—were the pens where customers came to exploit them. When Western tourists in Phnom Penh asked a moto-taxi driver for a ride to Svay Pak, the driver knew immediately the tourist was looking for sex with minors.

Most of these drivers made a profit from the business by collecting a commission from the brothel keeper for every customer brought in. It's part of the growing web of protection around a despicable industry: The more people who profit from it, the more acceptance it gains as a legitimate business, the more normalized it becomes within a community and a culture until finally it becomes "just the way things are." I wouldn't have believed it if I hadn't seen it so many times before, but, amazingly, a massive and routine business of raping and molesting children can become "just the way things are," even among people of goodwill in the community.

Our mission was to break that deadly cycle of resignation and despair and to demonstrate that it was possible to unravel the web, rescue the children, and get the perpetrators sent to jail. It would take committed operations over many years to clean up a place like Svay Pak, but our immediate mission was to stop the abuse of these kids and change the calculation about what was possible. Of course that is always the toughest step. If people thought it was "possible" to rescue these kids and bring the bad guys to justice, it would have happened a long time ago. But the darkness had grown too thick, so thick that dozens of children could be openly sold off to pedophiles and sadists and there was just "nothing that could be done about it." And, truth be told, there was a lot more evidence to support that conclusion than there was to challenge it.

But again and again we were confronted with two unrelenting facts: First, the children were being horrifically abused before our eyes. Second, we all professed a faith that there was a God who loved these children and called us to do for them what we would want done for our own children. This was not a clever quiz on an ethics exam or a contrived piece of sensationalism for a shocking marketing campaign. This was the world as it really was, right in our faces. This was put up or shut up. It was time to fasten our chin straps or get out of the uniform.

CHAPTER 3

A FORCE OF NATURE

How do I describe Bob Mosier, our vice president of investigations? He's a force of nature. I'm sure that sounds dramatic and overdone, but the people who have worked with Mosier in the field know what I am talking about. A force of nature changes weather and landscape, shadows and lighting, and then when you step back to explain why it happened, you can't. Words and rational explanations fail. Similarly, for years I've watched Mosier deployed on IJM missions into the darkest corners of the fallen world, and when it's all over, the young girl in Thailand is out of the brothel; the families in South Asia are set free from bonded slavery; the innocent child in the Ivory Coast is released from prison; the pastor in Bolivia is rescued from the torture chamber; the bad guys are in jail, and the local authorities are buying Mosier dinner and naming their children after him. And why did all that happen?

You could say that Mosier is a highly trained criminal investigator with tremendous experience who works very, very hard. But that's a bit like saying erosion caused the Grand Canyon or Einstein studied math or Mozart loved music. It just doesn't get you very far in explaining the phenomenon.

The fact is, almost all of the tactical investigative operations that IJM has become best known for were pioneered by one guy: a former sheriff's deputy from a rural county in Virginia named Bob Mosier. It's one thing for IJM colleagues around the world to have the courage and skill to execute the infiltration, the surveillance, the sting, or the undercover operation they've been trained to do; it's quite another thing to be the first one to prove that such operations were even possible in the contexts where we work. But that's what Mosier did.

Travel with Mosier in the field, and you sense he was invented by his

Maker to catch the bad guys—to lure them in, expose their lies, and bring their brutality into the light of day. It's easy to caricature Mosier as this one-dimensional Sergeant Friday from Central Casting because, frankly, he is. No one else shows up to meetings at our headquarters with the coffee mug that reads, "Life is simple: Eat. Sleep. Fight crime."

But none of that gets you very far in explaining the mystery of why you can plop Mosier down in any spot on the globe and watch the local weather begin to change. Indeed, when you meet Mosier, your first impression gives you few hints of what you are up against. When I first met him in 1997, only one clue registered with me—the lingering force of his handshake. Everything else about him blended into the crowd: average height, average weight, guy-next-door looks. And that's exactly what makes him so effective. Mosier has developed a persona that allows him to fade into the background, to appear nonthreatening. But actually he's vacuuming up information for storage and processing.

Even when portraying a pedophile, Mosier moves into and out of character with ease. Sometimes people don't understand how guys like him can stomach the charade. They ask, "How can you make yourself act like you want to abuse little girls or little boys? Doesn't that mess with your mind after a while?"

Without hesitating, Mosier, the former cop, replies, "No. I used to pose as a drug dealer to catch drug dealers. It's what I had to do to capture the bad guys. That's all I'm doing in this job, too. A good investigator must have a solid strategy and keep the goal in mind at all times, refusing to become distracted.

"Sure, if it would work I would just walk up to a criminal and say, 'I'm really a nice guy, and I'm wondering if you sell small children for sex, because if you do, I'll have you arrested.' Unfortunately, it doesn't work that way."

"How do you deal with all the atrocities against children you've seen?" someone asked him once.

"How do I *not* deal with it?" Mosier replied. "What am I supposed to do, curl up in the fetal position and surrender when I see cruel abuse? How would that help to get more victims set free? What they need is a rescuer. We must be prepared to be that rescuer, regardless of the repulsive situations we find victims in."

As a trained investigative expert, Mosier has mastered some fundamental skills. One of his greatest strengths is his ability to get people to talk and to gather whatever information he needs—even if the person he's talking with doesn't mean to give it. After meeting with Mosier for about an hour, a writer once told me, "By the time we were done, I felt like he was reading my mind." And he probably was.

On one trip to South Asia, Mosier used this skill to take him all the way to the top of an organization that used large numbers of slaves to roll cigarettes. He had started at the bottom and asked to talk with that person's boss, then his boss, then his boss, until he reached the top dog.

"I have seven hundred slaves, about three hundred of them children," the man bragged as he showed Mosier his whole operation with the same kind of pride you might see in an American businessman conducting a tour of his factory and showing off the latest manufacturing equipment. Almost as an afterthought, he paused, looked at Mosier, and asked, "Was it okay for me to tell you all this? You're not going to get me in any trouble, are you?" But by then it was too late. The proverbial cat was way out of the bag, and Mosier had it by the tail.

Mosier's skills and experience as a police officer took him on a United Nations mission to Bosnia-Herzegovina as part of an elite International Police Task Force in 1996 and 1997 with the U.S. Department of State's peacekeeping efforts. The understanding he gained about conducting international police work within other governmental and legal systems has proved extremely valuable to IJM as we developed our standard practices for international investigations. We were paving the way in this area of human rights work, and Mosier was our pioneer.

Traditional human rights investigations have generally been conducted by civil rights lawyers, academics, and journalists, with a heavy emphasis on victim interviews, documents, and friendly, sympathetic sources. Mosier took IJM a step further by emphasizing the evidence that comes from getting close to the perpetrators themselves. But Mosier not only got us inside—the brothels, the prisons, the police stations, or sweatshops—he also came back out with the ugly truth captured on videotape for the whole world to see. For the first time, people could actually see what previously only the victims could see. Bob introduced the use of sophisticated undercover surveillance technologies that allowed us to show the world what it really looks like when an eight-year-old girl is being sold for sex, when a police officer extorts his bribe, when the police officer beats the street kid with his baton, or when the prisoner languishes in a jail without charge or trial. I've testified in a number of congressional hearings where everything was proceeding with clinical dullness, until members of Congress saw Mosier's undercover videos. The infinite distance between the dignified setting in which we talk about the gross brutalization of people and the places where it actually happens suddenly collapsed when the sights and sounds of evil incarnate filled the room.

As a result we've come to equip our investigators with top-of-the-line undercover technology; in our line of work, we can't afford to miss the evidence due to equipment failure. And in a situation where we don't have actual footage of a crime being committed—when it's just our word against theirs—the legal system in some countries often supports the criminal, not the victim.

I've been awed many times by the way Bob Mosier does his job. One prime example illustrates his dogged determination to not quit until the goal is reached. Accompanied by a crew from *60 Minutes II,* we went to India to research bonded slavery issues, investigating cases of kids who were forced to roll cigarettes twelve to fourteen hours a day. We hoped we could link this slave labor to the use of these tobacco products by kids in the United States, which would make the story more relevant to Americans. We wanted the world to know how these slave children were being treated and that somebody was willing to do something about it.

We had been doing an enormous amount of work in extremely remote areas of India for several days, driving to and from small villages on horrible roads. As usual, Bob had been out front, leading the charge, establishing relationships with operatives, supervising their investigations. We were on a mission that seemed nearly impossible: to try to find where child slaves were working, to identify specific kids and specific locations, to complete comprehensive documentation of those kids so we could use it in securing their freedom—and to do it all in living color with a huge camera crew from the United States in tow. But Mosier led the way logistically, making all the arrangements in advance.

We finally arrived at our destination and were able to nail down with perfect clarity the suffering of these kids and trace the story all the way to the wholesale group at the end of the production chain of this slave labor. Bob had been working eighteen-hour days, day after day, in stifling heat to complete this investigation.

The crew from *60 Minutes II* had everything they needed, except for a critical link between the wholesalers and the export of their products to the United

States. They needed to establish an absolute connection between the U.S. market and these cigarettes produced by the hands of child slaves. The producer needed this thread in the story to connect with U.S. viewers, because American viewers can be rather narrow: *If it doesn't pertain to me or my people, I'm not interested.*

Without this link, it looked as if the whole story might collapse, and with it our opportunity to bring accountability to the larger business interests involved in the use of these slave-produced products. We saw this story, and our cooperation in it, as a significant way to get the word out. Now the story was unraveling before our eyes.

It was around 11:00 P.M., and Bob had been working all day in blistering heat when this story started to fall apart. As we brainstormed our options, we discovered from our operative that the same cigarette manufacturer had a similar operation running in the west-coast village of Mysore. So Bob said, "Well, I guess we need to go to Mysore"—a line that has become synonymous with Bob Mosier and getting the job done.

To make this as precise as it needed to be, Bob would hit the road with an operative immediately, heading to a place he'd never been before, driving through the night and catching a flight to the opposite coast—all this set up via a few phone contacts with people he didn't even know—simply because it needed to be done. And when Mosier sees something that needs to be done, he does it, whether it's emptying the trash, getting water for our staff people so they don't get dehydrated, or wrestling with a pimp who is trying to escape from a brothel. Bob will make the important things happen. It was no surprise, then, that eighteen hours later I received a call from Bob, saying, "Yep, we got the children rolling cigarettes for the manufacturer, being shipped to the United States. Connection made. Mission accomplished. Not a problem." Then as an added punctuation mark, the fruit of his mission was realized as the children he documented were released from slavery.

I don't say it often, because I know what I'm invoking when I do, but there are those occasional intense moments when I have to turn to Bob and simply ask him to "get it done." With amazing regularity, it just gets done. Not in the way you might think, by cutting ethical corners, exploiting people, or compromising on proper restraints, but by the relentless application of mental focus, courage, creativity, hard work, and faith.

There are times when he just can't make it happen. But over these years I have seen Mosier head into the darkness where people are being crushed, and then I've seen the unexplainable and the indescribable occur. I have seen the waters part and the beaten and abused walk to safety and dignity. And at the end of the day, I think the most powerful force at work has been faith.

The Scriptures describe faith as "the assurance of things hoped for, the conviction of things not seen" (Hebrews 11:1 NRSV), and Mosier has core convictions about some things he cannot see. He believes that he was made by a God who exists and can be known. He believes this God cares about him and has given him work to do in the world—the work of helping people in desperate need. And, finally, he believes that God—the ancient and almighty God who made the universe—is on his side in this work and will help him do it.

I am willing to assert that he believes these things for one simple reason: He acts as if these things are true. Mosier is a great example of what Dallas Willard has written so clearly about regarding the nature of faith (amplifying, of course, what the New Testament epistle of James said long ago): Namely, we believe something not when we *say* we do or even when we *believe* we do, but when we *act* as if we do.

The seventeenth-century philosopher John Locke noted that we Christians *say* we believe the most marvelous, earth-shattering, and revolutionary things: that we are fully loved by a good and all-powerful God who will never fail to secure us in life and death, that we are therefore free to experience and exhibit selfless love and courage and joy every day, no matter what, for eternity. But how many of us live as if these things are true? John Locke estimated not one in ten thousand, and that sounds about right to me. But I think I have seen a sheriff's deputy from rural Virginia who lives as if these things are true—and in a brutal world of darkness and evil, he moves like a force of nature.

If ever we needed such a force of nature at work, if ever we needed a "conviction of things unseen," it was here in Svay Pak. Because what we could see seemed utterly brutal and hopeless.

CHAPTER 4

TESTING THE WATERS

Perhaps the greatest challenge in confronting evil is simply getting started. How do you take that first step into the abyss? Sometimes you start with what you are given, and our first chance to test the waters in getting some kids out of Svay Pak came in May 2002. An opening appeared, and we tried to seize it.

Sharon Cohn, our vice president for interventions, and Will Henry, investigative specialist, were in Southeast Asia concluding a rescue operation that had ultimately freed five girls from a brothel. One of those girls placed in an aftercare facility was Dacie, whose story would profoundly touch my own life—but we'll return to her later.

Their work completed on that case, Will was ready to head back to the States. Homesick after being away from his family for three weeks, he packed his bags and was thirty minutes from leaving for the airport. However, Sharon had just been on the phone with Mosier at headquarters; while they were already in Asia, maybe Will and Sharon should make a trip to Svay Pak to continue the investigation.

Bob and I discussed the options and decided that yes, Sharon and Will should go to Cambodia, into Svay Pak, to refresh evidence gathered on previous trips and continue our efforts to mobilize the Cambodian authorities to take action against the horrific abuse of children. Mosier talked with Will on the phone, outlining the mission that would delay his reunion with his family.

Mosier then quickly wrote up a mission order detailing the objectives of this three-day operation:

1. Conduct investigations to identify victims of child forced prostitution.

2. Conduct operations to encourage Cambodian police to commit law enforcement actions that result in release of victims of child forced prostitution.

3. Conduct operations to encourage Cambodian law enforcement to commit legal actions that result in the arrest and prosecution of suspects identified as having been involved in ongoing criminal activity.

4. Obtain cooperation from the government in securing placement of any rescued victims in an approved aftercare facility.

This was an opportunity for us to present some solid, living evidence that would compel the Cambodian government to cooperate. We had been in Svay Pak on three occasions before May 2002, and we had submitted intervention reports detailing abuses to the government each time—with no visible results. First in October 2000, then in July and September 2001, we had delivered to governmental officials our documentation and videotaped evidence, along with the request for police action that would result in the release of victims and the prosecution of perpetrators. Each time we had received no response.

Imagine what would happen if you walked into your local police station with videotapes of elementary-school-age children in your community being openly sold to customers for sex. What if you gave them pictures, names, and addresses of those who were running the child-sex business, along with little maps on how to find them? What would you expect to happen? In Cambodia we gave this information to the highest law enforcement authorities in the country, who sat in offices not twenty miles away from where the child-sex-ring was operating, and nothing happened. Nothing at all.

This time we decided to take a different angle, employ a different strategy. Mosier had given specific orders to Henry to secure the "release of victims of child forced prostitution"—to get some kids out. Then we would present their cases as evidence to the authorities and say, "Here's living proof that the problem exists. Now it's up to you to help take care of these girls." We wanted to give the authorities in Cambodia the clearest possible opportunity to do the right thing. We wanted to make it very hard for them to turn away. We wanted to get some kids out of that hellhole and walk the Cambodian authorities through a concrete opportunity to bring some of the perpetrators to justice, hoping that such an action might send a signal through Svay Pak that the open-market sale of children to sexual predators just wasn't going to be tolerated.

You have to get started somewhere, and once you start, you'd better be prepared to finish.

CHAPTER 5

CONFIDENCE EARNED THE HARD WAY

Will Henry boarded the airplane to Phnom Penh equipped with all the gear of his trade—small undercover camera, lenses, microphones, cables, tapes, and batteries—everything he would need to record crimes of forced child prostitution and to build a compelling case for the authorities. Henry, a veteran of sixteen years on a state police force, had three and a half years of undercover experience and two years in deep cover.

Deep cover, in Will's words, is where an officer "lives the life of a scumbag, befriends other scumbags, and then betrays them." On these assignments, he would check into a seedy motel or a cheap apartment, develop a dubious identity, check in with his handler once a week, and otherwise build a case against the perpetrators of various crimes from the inside.

His last deep-cover mission as a cop was a costly one. While posing as a college student, Will was shot during a gunfight that broke out between two guys he was talking with and one of their enemies. "I walked away when I should have run, and I got caught by a stray bullet," he said. It hit him like a leaded baseball bat in the back of the left leg and would cause him to be out of action for about nine months as he recovered.

Will's instincts for undercover work were honed in the real world where split-second decisions can make all the difference. He is also highly trained and deeply experienced in security operations, especially in the area of executive protection. He would need all these skills for where he was going.

Will and Sharon landed in Cambodia at dusk on May 7, 2002, descending over acres and acres of charred fields, probably burned deliberately to clear unwanted brush but giving the landscape an ominous look, as though scorched by war. Neither had been to Cambodia before. Together they navigated the crowded roads filled with out-of-control motorcycles, cars, bicycles, and pedestrians. The smell of garlic and spices hung heavy over the scene of controlled chaos.

They checked into their rooms on the third floor of a cheap hotel, and Will called their operative, Sky, who had arranged their accommodations.

"We've arrived at the hotel," Will said. "Shall we meet for dinner?"

"Yes, I'll come and pick you up," Sky answered. "But I will take you first to get some things you'll need for this trip, including your cell phones."

Operating in the developing world has its challenges, even if you are not trying to infiltrate a dangerous child sex-trafficking ring. The general lawlessness that allows such brutalities to thrive in places like Svay Pak also permits a high level of overall street crime. In fact, Will's pulse got a little elevated on that first night in Phnom Penh, when he heard distant gunfire in the streets and when it briefly appeared that the moto-taxi driver was diverting Sharon away from the direction of the hotel and into dark and dicey side streets. Drawing on experience and basic awareness skills, Will quickly secured the situation.

This was not the first time Will and Sharon had worked together in the developing world; they had acquired a seasoned mutual trust in navigating such circumstances—a confidence earned the hard way.

In November 2001 Sharon and Will had met with the governor of a Nigerian state to talk about the horrendous problem there with sex trafficking. The governor had admitted that 70 to 80 percent of the trafficking victims in Nigeria came from his state, quite a dubious history that the governor was hoping to rewrite.

After meeting with him and missing their appointed flight, Will and Sharon had hired a car to drive them across remote Nigerian terrain to catch the next flight out of the country. Exhausted from the long trip, Will had fallen asleep while Sharon watched the drab, brown landscape pass by.

Suddenly she tensed up, noticing that cars in the adjacent lane of the four-lane divided highway were heading toward them, coming the wrong way. That in itself was not uncommon in Nigeria, where drivers on a bad stretch of road would jump onto smoother lanes heading the other way. But something was clearly wrong here. Drivers and passengers leaned out the windows of the oncoming cars, waving their arms. "Armed bandits! Armed bandits!" they shouted.

Will woke up as their driver made a quick U-turn, flowing quickly into the stream of escaping autos. They sped away en masse for a few miles, until many pulled over at a wide spot in the road adjacent to a village. The hope was that the bandits—if they were still pursuing this group—would forgo a stop here, avoiding a gathering of so many people. It looked like some strange high-school pep-rally competition as occupants of all the vehicles—including Will and Sharon—bailed out of their cars, arms and legs flying, running for shelter behind one of the nearby buildings.

As gunfire, whoops, and shouts grew closer, the travelers hardly breathed. *Shall we flee into the jungle?* Will wondered. But what did he know of jungle survival? No, they remained in the village and prayed that God would send angels to protect them. Though they saw no otherworldly manifestation, they think the bandits did. At the village, their van stopped for a second and then sped away, out onto the open road, weapons firing as if something were chasing them.

And that was Sharon's first trip for IJM, just her fourth week on the job.

As the attorney leading our intervention efforts and specializing in sex-trafficking cases, Sharon had lead responsibility for the Svay Pak operations. She was ultimately responsible for getting the kids out, bringing the perpetrators to justice, and getting the kids to safe aftercare. This was her first exploratory operation into Svay Pak.

Her top priority was—and always is—the victims whom Will was planning to draw out of the darkness of the brothels and into the bright light of freedom. Sharon would need to make contact quickly with nongovernmental agencies that would take several girls into aftercare on very short notice. She would also try to contact top-level officials in Cambodia in preparation for a larger operation that would secure the freedom of perhaps dozens of girls.

CHAPTER 6

IT'S ALL ABOUT "THE ONE"

I had first met Sharon a few years earlier in a setting rather far from the poverty and desperation of small Cambodian villages. We met at a reception in Washington, D.C., for Harvard alums who had been active in Christian ministry at the university. I had just started my work with IJM and was making the rounds, talking about our work and inviting people to support us. In such settings I was also constantly on the lookout for talent I might recruit to IJM, especially people with topflight legal training and some experience working in the developing world—not a common combination.

Sharon was a graduate of Harvard Law School, was at a top firm in town, and had worked for the witness protection program at the U.S. Department of Justice. That last bit certainly got my attention, and we started to chat. What a delight. Sharon is blazingly smart and funny. It takes only a few minutes before you realize she speaks full paragraphs of the kind of perfect prose it would take me an afternoon to compose. Her offhand reference to traveling in the developing world on service projects made me file the introduction away in my mental keep-track-of-this-one folder. I subsequently found myself remembering and repeating several comments Sharon had made in this brief encounter, even though I didn't see her again until she turned up for an interview in our offices a couple of years later.

With Sharon, the raw intellectual horsepower under the hood manifests itself in the precision and power of her articulation. She sometimes seems to have an entirely different energy about her, as if her mind is working on two different planes at once, maybe more. In conversation, it's obvious that she's there with you, participating, witty, and engaging. But sometimes she quickly detaches and leaves the conversation abruptly in order to get on to the next thing—always with the sense of accomplishing one more important task.

Sharon's intellectual energy seems to flow from her beating heart—a heart of compassion, hung out and hurting for the pain and humiliation of others. In contrast to an overdeveloped intellect that seems to shrink and harden the heart, it seems that Sharon's generous and passionate heart is the boiler room that fires the pistons of her mind with extraordinary force, precision, and speed.

Considering her legal talents, Sharon could work anywhere. In fact, she left a lucrative career with one of the largest Washington, D.C., law firms and came to work with IJM because she wanted to do work that "really mattered." She had always wanted to get involved with casework or policy work.

"I wanted to get to know the victims and *see* the actual output of what I was pouring my life into," she said. "There aren't a lot of legal jobs, or jobs anywhere, where you get to do that."

In her role as head of our sex-trafficking casework, her compassion and tender heart act as a magnet for the girls and women she champions. So many times rescued young girls cling to Sharon as they are released from the brothels where they were held captive. I think they sense, as kids often do better than adults, Sharon's warmth and caring coupled with her tenacity and courage. She has the perfect blend of gifts to be exactly what those kids need at that moment: bold defender, compassionate caregiver, and friend.

In a speech Sharon prepared to deliver at the White House when she was recognized by President George W. Bush, she painted such a clear picture of her compassion for the victims she meets and her commitment to the scores she hasn't yet met. "While there are millions of girls and women victimized every day, our work will always be about the one. The one girl deceived. The one girl kidnapped. The one girl raped. The one girl infected with AIDS. The one girl needing a rescuer. To succumb to the enormity of the problem is to fail the one. And more is required of us."

Another time, as Sharon told the story of a rescued victim named Elisabeth, she addressed the same issue from a different angle. "When weary Washingtonians say, 'So you rescued one; there are millions of others. What's the point?' I say, 'I think Elisabeth understands the point. Elisabeth *is* the point.'"

Sharon exhibits an absolute, unwavering commitment to the truth. She knows that the ultimate power of freedom comes from the prevailing power of truth. Like Mosier, Sharon believes that the work of justice and freedom is the work of God, into which human beings are invited to participate. And in that work, the single most powerful tool we are granted is *truth*.

In fact, the ultimate vulnerability of abusers and oppressors is manifested in their overwhelming need to lie. If you think about it, why do abusive police, sex traffickers, slave traders, and torturers always have to lie about what they are doing? Because they know that they never have enough power or force or violence to withstand even a fraction of what people of goodwill could bring to bear against them; and so they must hide behind lies. This is why Aleksander Solzhenitsyn, the famous Soviet dissident and Nobel Prize winner for literature, wrote:

> Violence does not live alone and is not capable of living alone: it is necessarily interwoven with falsehood. Between them lies the most intimate, the deepest of natural bonds. Violence finds its only refuge in falsehood, falsehood its only support in violence. . . . At its birth violence acts openly and even with pride. But no sooner does it become strong, firmly established, than it senses the rarefaction of the air around it and cannot exist without descending into a fog of lies.

Likewise, Sharon knows that the most powerful tool for bringing freedom to the victims in Svay Pak, and in all our casework around the world, is the prevailing power of the proven fact, the fact that cannot be denied. Truth compels people of goodwill to act; and because all that is necessary for the triumph of evil is for good people to do nothing, the end is near for the perpetrators of injustice when the truth compels good people to do something, especially good people in places of power. We have seen this work again and again in the face of all kinds of evil.

CHAPTER 7

BODY-CRUSHING TOIL

In the fall of 2003, *National Geographic* brought to the attention of the world the hidden reality of modern-day slavery. The magazine made the case that there are approximately twenty-seven million slaves in our world today—not metaphorical slaves, but actual slaves. That's more slaves in our world today than were extracted from Africa during four hundred years of the transatlantic slave trade. Many of these slaves are held in South Asia, and I have met hundreds of them. Such slavery is completely against the law—as is child sex slavery in Cambodia. But the poor frequently don't get the benefit of law enforcement, and so millions find themselves in slavery.

I've seen them—men, women, and children—toiling away, six or seven days a week, ten to sixteen hours a day, never free to leave their owner's service. They spend their entire lives in mind-numbing, body-crushing toil—breaking rocks by hand in quarries, making bricks, rolling cigarettes, weaving carpets, milling rice, plowing fields. Again, it's completely against the law; but in the vast and remote regions of South Asia, there frequently is no one to painstakingly take the truth of what's going on to the officials who have the power to stop it. That's why IJM sends its investigators out into these abandoned communities to infiltrate the slave works. We bring the evidence to magistrates who have the power to release the slaves and bring the owners to justice. The truth has a transforming and liberating power, but the bad guys generally don't sit idly by. You must be prepared for the way a bully cornered by the truth will ratchet up the demands of the game.

In fact, I remember when we started getting word at IJM's headquarters in Washington, D.C., that IJM informants warned of brewing violent resistance to our rescue work in a small town in South Asia. Eventually the threat began to come into focus for our local team and the urgency of the situation at one particular brick factory became acute. Two weeks earlier, IJM had liberated forty-nine slaves from a separate brick kiln and now, as our staff moved in on a second operation at a nearby kiln, the owners of the second kiln were gaining support from those in the surrounding area.

These brickmaking operations are big business in several developing nations. Usually resembling a rustic fortress, most are surrounded by walls seven or eight feet high—to keep brick poachers out, and to keep slave laborers in. They have a dark, otherworldly presence to them because of the dust and smoke that hang constantly in the air, coating everything within the walls with gray-red dust and soot.

Many brick factories have actual kilns inside the walls—coal-fired ovens where the bricks are baked to harden more firmly and quickly than they would in the sun alone. While most people refer to these facilities as "kilns" whether or not they have the baking ovens, the true status symbol is the chimney—which stands as an indication to passersby that this is a sophisticated operation using the best techniques available to make quality bricks. Much more so if you have more than one chimney.

Naturally, the kilns require extra labor, because someone has to stoke the charcoal fires constantly to keep them at their optimum temperature. This is one of the worst jobs in an operation defined by awful jobs—excruciatingly hot, dirty, and sticky, the workers covered with charcoal dust that mixes with the dust of clay and dirt until sweat-soaked skin begins to harden and crack.

Before the bricks are ready for the kiln, they must be shaped and predried in the sun. All day long, slaves perform the backbreaking labor of packing wet clay and straw into molds that form the bricks. They slap the clay into the molds forming row after row, then other workers, usually children, carry the bricks on their heads to set them out in the sun to dry. When they are dry enough to fire, the slaves carry them to the kiln to be baked. Hour after hour, day after day, weeks that flow into months, months that fade into years . . . some of these slaves have been at this dirty, tedious, painful work for decades with no relief in sight. Until now.

With the cooperation of local police, our staff conducted a raid of this second facility that started peacefully enough. In any raid, our objectives are to get victims out and keep criminals from escaping. Since we have little or no authority in most jurisdictions where we work, we need to rely on local law enforcement authorities to conduct the operation in a way that accomplishes our objectives and theirs. But we don't just leave it to chance.

Most often, our staff conducts investigations, including covert interviews and inspections, so we can draw up complete and accurate maps for the police to use. Lawyers on staff study the existing laws, evaluate the feasibility of the intervention, and craft a plan for ensuring positive outcomes for victims and punitive action for perpetrators. We freely and respectfully offer our advice and opinions about what might work best when conducting the raid, which always benefits from the element of surprise. We uncover facts about the facilities and those who operate them, then pass those items along to the police as well; facts such as how many floors in each building, number and location of exits, profiles on owners and operators, details about how many staff or managers are on shift at the time we propose conducting the raid. We'll even make recommendations about the number and skill set of officers who should be included in the raid and, quite often, our suggestions are taken seriously.

Once police have assigned the appropriate personnel to the raid and the time has been set, we move forward with prayer and determination in our effort to set the captives free. In this particular brick kiln, we were able to secure the area in question fairly quickly and easily, ensuring that the slaves were not quickly stolen away to another location. But, apparently, not all the perpetrators were caught inside the police net.

After the area was secured, IJM staff set up an area inside the walls of the brickworks in which to begin documenting each case of bonded slavery, one by one. This long process gave the owners time to contact dozens of cronies, servants, and family members to disrupt the release, coerce the slaves back into the brickworks, and scare off our staff. Shortly, a crowd began to accumulate and nearly one hundred people stood outside the interview area, milling about, growing louder in their shouts and taunts of IJM staff. Tensions escalated, and what began as an uphill battle for freedom became imminently dangerous for our team of rescuers. The angry mob broke through the halfhearted police security and rushed toward the IJM staff, looking for someone from whom to extract some revenge.

In the crush, the slaves froze, unsure what to do next. These people— whole families of children, women, and men—daily bore the weight of their oppression under dreadful conditions, physically as well as emotionally. Out of convenience, the kiln owners had enslaved many low-caste, tribal people. Now, the slaves that IJM sought to free braced themselves against retaliation and against the larger fear that nothing would ever change, that freedom was simply unattainable for them.

In this region, another large-scale release of slaves would send a seismic shift through the very underpinnings of the oppressive system. So, surrounding the slaves and IJM staff, the mob began to beat our staff members with their fists, threatening to kill them if they didn't stop the raid and leave immediately. (Fortunately for the slaves, the aggressors in the mob left them alone during the attack and concentrated their energies on our staff.) While shielding themselves and weathering the angry blows, IJM staff managed to ferry a total of thirty-four people from the kiln to a small bus and drive them to freedom.

Later that day, in the safety of another town, the former kiln slaves wore unbounded smiles of gratitude and awe, amazed that IJM staff would put themselves in harm's way and suffer physical pain for people they didn't even know. The IJM field director later wrote, "I wondered how they could be so happy while we were all in shock. Then it dawned on me that this was nothing new for them. They got threatened and hit on a regular basis. This was the status quo. We were just joining them in their world."

Standing with the oppressed, even in the face of personal danger, is simply the only effective strategy for securing change and bringing to life the deep hope that freedom is possible.

CHAPTER 8

SIGNATURES

In late 2003, Thangavel had taken about as much as he could bear. He and several family members, along with eleven other families, were held as slaves in a rock quarry under a brutal owner who treated them worse than civilized people would treat their animals. So one night Thangavel, one of the only people in the quarry who could actually read and write, sat down to compose a letter to the leading government official in his district.

> *Sir,*
>
> *We are 30 individuals, 12 families belonging to Chetty Savadi, Kannankuruchi Village, living as bonded slaves for the past five years under our mudalalis, Mr. Kharbanda and Naseeruddin. We are not paid appropriately for the stones we break. We are paid [U.S. $2.22] for every load of the broken stones. We could not fill a load even if three persons jointly break stones for one whole day. So we do not even get [U.S. $.55] per day. If we challenge this, we are threatened, beaten, and tortured. We asked to be sent back to our native place, for which they said, "Pay back the money that you owe and then you can leave; if not, we will lock you up in a room." With this they harass us every day. We are not paid enough even for food. We are harassed a lot. So, we humbly request that you free and rescue us from bonded slavery.*
>
> *Yours truly,*
>
> *Thangavel*

The most moving part of Thangavel's well-written letter was not his words but the signatures of the other victims on the reverse side of the document. Actually, they weren't really signatures. Because they didn't know how to sign their names, these slaves had used their thumbprints instead of pen and ink as their endorsement of Thangavel's plea for freedom.

Seeing those thumbprints somehow made their plight more real, more tangible to me than a simple list of signatures on a letter of appeal. I could imagine them gathered quietly, after dark, in the hut of one of their co-laborers, first placing one rough, work-worn thumb on an ink pad made by spilling the contents of a ballpoint pen on another piece of paper, then touching that wet thumb to the back of Thangavel's letter. Sometimes the great emotional weight of years of suffering turning toward hope is conveyed in such simple acts. These oppressed laborers were "signing" with the mark of their unique identity, which, for me, packed more than the swipe of a pen across the back of a piece of paper. It seemed to carry the embodiment of their struggle made, literally, by the tool of their trade—their bare hands.

And I'm sure many asked themselves, even as they pressed thumb to paper, "Could this be the letter that sets me free, or could this thumbprint get me beaten or killed?"

A few days after he wrote the letter, Thangavel heard that IJM staff members were in the village to pick up a witness for another bonded labor trial. He secretly left the quarry and approached the IJM staffers, gave them the letter and asked if they could rescue him and his coworkers from their bondage. They told Thangavel they would do whatever they could to help him, then returned to the office and wrote up a report with the recommendation to document the victims.

Within a couple of weeks, an IJM investigative team arrived at the quarry where Thangavel and the others were held as slaves. As they turned off the main road onto the driveway of the quarry, they saw four people standing next to a small concrete building. Operating undercover, two team members, John and Pragati, approached the group and engaged them in conversation. The owner of the quarry, Mr. Kharbanda, agreed to tour the group around his operation and let them take a look at his rock crusher.

As Kharbanda led the majority of the crew on a tour, three of our team members slowly eased away from the group, pretending to pick up rock samples. They made their way toward the huts of the laborers, hoping to gather more information. They spoke with a few of the workers for several minutes and determined that they were not perpetrators in this case. The honk of the truck's horn told them the IJM group was leaving, so they quickly said good-bye and joined the others.

———

Over the next few weeks, IJM staff and operatives continued gathering information until they convinced police to conduct a raid on this quarry. The raid was successful, and, in the end, our team helped to secure the rescue of the thirty brave slaves who had signed Thangavel's letter with their thumbprints, along with twenty-four others from the same quarry.

CHAPTER 9

WHERE WERE YOU?

I grew up with a great love for reading history, and I used to wonder, *How would I have fared in the great moral struggles of the past? Would I have been on the right side? Would I have acted with courage? Would I have made my grandchildren proud?*

Would I have been a supporter and confidant of William Wilberforce and his Clapham sect in fighting the British slave trade, or would I have been part of the detached and oblivious middle-class masses who said and did nothing?

Would I have stood shoulder to shoulder with Harriet Tubman in secreting slaves to freedom on the Underground Railroad, or would I have been left flatfooted with apathy, moral neutrality, or fear?

Would I have walked with Dietrich Bonhoeffer in a journey of costly discipleship during the Nazi era in Europe, and would I have been known as a righteous Gentile during the Holocaust? Or would I have been immobilized by confusion and fright, or perhaps preoccupied with smaller things?

In many respects such speculation feels idle. Who knows what we would have done?

Besides, it feels as if history has perhaps passed us by. The great struggles of good and evil, right and wrong, seem to be of a bygone era. All the great and heroic battles have already been fought, haven't they? In the twenty-first century we are left with only petty battles in gray areas, certainly nothing our grandchildren will ask us about. Right?

This perspective was shattered for me about ten years ago.

Early in 1994, I lived in Washington, D.C., with my wife, minding my own business, employed as a civil rights attorney for the U.S. Department of Justice. I was trying to assemble cribs for our expected twin daughters. I was trying to trade in our Honda Civic for a Taurus station wagon. I was trying to match wits (and losing) with the boys in my sixth-grade Sunday school class. I was enjoying an occasional jog around the monuments on the Mall. And I was denying that I had ever watched *Melrose Place*.

Then in April, small news stories began to appear about the outbreak of ethnic conflict in an African country I had hardly heard of, Rwanda. Before long the news carried pictures of bloated corpses choking the rivers of Rwanda, and commentators used the word *genocide*. It seemed thousands, maybe millions, of Tutsis were being slaughtered by their Hutu neighbors in a genocidal hysteria sweeping across the country. But like much of the global ugliness transported by television into my living room, it just didn't seem real; it seemed true, but not real—the way descriptions of life in ancient Rome seem true, but not real. Or reports about how many stars there are in the Milky Way—all true enough, but not real. Not real like my kids when they are sick. Not real like my job when I'm falling further behind in my work. Not real like my neighbor when she has been in a car accident.

But within a few months it became all too real as I found my own feet slipping in the mud of a mass grave in Rwanda. In September 1994, immediately after the genocide had exhausted itself, I was put on loan from the Department of Justice to be the director of the United Nations genocide investigation in Rwanda.

All murder investigations begin with the location of the bodies, so I was given a list of one hundred mass graves and massacre sites and began my journey there.

As we would soon learn, approximately eight hundred thousand people were murdered in the short span of about eight weeks. Slipping in the mud of that mass grave, I stopped wondering how I might have fared in the great moral struggles of history. It there became abundantly clear that such struggles are not matters for idle speculation; such struggles are now.

Since then, this conviction has been powerfully reinforced in my work with International Justice Mission. In 1997 I left the U.S. Department of Justice and founded IJM, which is a collection of lawyers and law enforcement officers that takes case referrals from faith-based organizations serving among the poor overseas.

What have I found? Massive man-made disasters of epic proportions that are not of a distant era; they are the tragedies of history taking place on our watch. Among the most common disasters are global sex trafficking (the massive business of rape for profit), slavery, illegal detention, and sexual violence. Though certainly not all-inclusive, these are four disasters I have seen with my own eyes, four disasters that will end up crushing more lives than the Rwandan genocide.

In the face of such massive suffering, one has to ask: Why does such great evil triumph in the world?

Having seen much of this suffering in the world firsthand, I believe one of the greatest insights was articulated by Edmund Burke about two hundred years ago: "All that is necessary for the triumph of evil is that good men do nothing."

This was certainly true for the Rwandan genocide. The histories now written make one thing clear: It could have been stopped. And we missed it.

All that is necessary for the triumph of evil is that good men do nothing.

If this is true, then why do good men and good women do nothing?

As I consider this question, I find three deep sources of poverty that conspire to keep me and my good neighbors on the sidelines in the great struggle against evil: a poverty of compassion, a poverty of purpose, and a poverty of hope.

I am frequently amazed at my own shrunken circle of compassion, especially when I come from a faith tradition that teaches again and again of God's great compassion—and passion—for the world. To be honest, do you know what I'm passionate about every day? Me. I am enamored with the shriveled world of me and mine. Most often, my first thought in the morning and my final thought as I drift off to sleep at night revolve around me. I have a poverty of compassion.

Aleksander Solzhenitsyn said there are two standards by which we judge events in the world: near or far. If it is near to us, we care about it. If an event is happening on the other side of the world, I have a hard time working up concern or compassion about it. It's how overwhelming tragedies such as Rwanda become tolerable disasters of bearable proportions. It's how little girls in Cambodia who have been robbed of their childhood innocence can suffer without the Western world taking notice.

It was the simple and clear teachings of Jesus of Nazareth that challenged me on the narrowness of my circle of compassion. In Luke 10 he said, "Love the Lord your God with all your heart, and with all your soul, and with all your strength, and with all your mind; and your neighbor as yourself" (v. 27 NRSV).

Then a lawyer, who wanted to make it complicated, as we often do, asked, "And who is my neighbor?"

In response Jesus told the parable of the Good Samaritan. The application of that parable makes me ask myself, *Which way are the borders of my heart heading, inward or outward?* Do I find them shrinking more and more tightly around me, closing out an increasing percentage of the world's problems?

Or am I touched by the stories I hear of suffering in other parts of the world? Do I find my heart softening when confronted with troubling stories of the suffering and oppression of people from other countries, different cultures?

As I expand my exposure to other peoples, other traditions, other problems, I better identify with the pain in others' lives and develop a more magnanimous compassion. I am discovering the mysterious joy of opening my heart to the world.

The second poverty that causes me and other good people to do nothing is a poverty of purpose.

I marvel at the way forces conspire to bend the purpose of my life toward increasingly petty things and away from the grander purposes outside myself for which I sense I was truly fashioned by my Maker. I am amazed at my capacity to be distracted by small and unworthy things. It is sobering to look at the headlines that were competing with the Rwandan genocide ten years ago. How much impact, comparatively, did those other things have upon mankind?

I am equally amazed at my capacity to wage scorched-earth war over the petty things—battles that diminish others even as they diminish me. Jesus rebuked the leaders of his day, especially the religious leaders, for neglecting the weightier matters of the law—justice, mercy, and the love of God. That stings me.

C. S. Lewis once wrote, "We must picture Hell as a state where everyone is perpetually concerned about his own dignity and advancement, where everyone has a grievance, and where everyone lives the deadly serious passions of envy, self-importance, and resentment."

Who in the midst of the preoccupations of that hell would have the energy and generosity for the larger battles?

This leads me back to a self-audit of small and unworthy things. What might it mean to our country if the readers of this book resolved to abandon every petty, small, and unworthy battle this year? What if they resolved to give themselves fully to larger things that matter, to things of God and his kingdom?

In fact, in a world of so much acute suffering, hurt, and need, for what purpose have you and I been granted so much?

A third reason good men and good women do nothing in their time of history's testing is a poverty of hope.

In the face of overwhelming evil and injustice, we often feel powerless. And that powerlessness paralyzes us and steals our hope. When the problems are so big and so bad, can we really make a difference anyway? When police officers in Svay Pak are part of the problem and many barriers stand in our way, can we even hope to bring rescue to the victims? Should we even try?

We are paralyzed in a poverty of hope because, first, we underestimate the value of what God has given us to transform lives. Second, we underestimate the value of a single life. And third, we underestimate God's determination to rescue us from a trivial existence if we will just free up our hands and our hearts from unworthy distractions and apply them to matters that make a difference in someone else's life.

Perhaps the saddest part of this story for those of us who have the ability to set a powerful example for others is not our own poverty of compassion, of purpose, of hope, but rather the way we end up leading others into or along the path of poverty.

What would this nation and world look like if we began to lead with riches of compassion, grandness of purpose, and an abundance of hope? Indeed, I think the God of history takes attendance. And he convenes a tribunal of our grandchildren, who will someday ask us, "Where were you?"

"Where were you, Grandpa, when the Jews were fleeing Nazi Germany and seeking safety on our shores?"

"Where were you, Grandma, when they were marching our Japanese neighbors off to internment camps?"

"Where were you, Grandpa, when our African-American neighbors were being beaten for registering to vote?"

Likewise when our grandchildren ask us where we were when the weak and the voiceless and the vulnerable of our era needed a leader of compassion and purpose and hope—I hope we can say that we showed up, and that we showed up on time. And that the very God of history might say, "Well done, good and faithful servant."

CHAPTER 10

SEEK JUSTICE

In former jobs, I had traveled the world, witnessing the results of injustice, from abusive and murderous police and soldiers in the Philippines to South African apartheid to genocide in Rwanda. I had frequent conversations with attorney friends from church about a gap that existed in the great humanitarian efforts established worldwide. Wonderful organizations addressed many needs of the poor—providing comfort, housing, medical care, and food. But an obvious question emerged: Why don't we rescue them when they are being abused?

There were, for instance, efforts in Cambodia to feed the hungry, heal the sick, shelter the homeless, and preach the gospel; some of these ministrations were offered within yards of the brothels in Svay Pak. Although some of these efforts might reduce the risk of some children being sold as sex slaves, what about the kids who were inside the brothels and getting abused now? Who was going to go in and get *them* out? And who was going to do the most powerful thing to prevent it from happening again; that is, who was going to bring the perpetrators of these crimes to justice? What were we doing when the poor suffered because of the abuse and oppression of other people?

This question became even more acute as I considered the commitments of my community of faith, and especially as I considered the teachings of Scripture on the matter. When I was directing the UN's genocide investigation in Rwanda, it became clear in the aftermath of those massacres that at the point of most critical need, as blood-hungry mobs circled the churches in which victims huddled, those victims were not crying out for food, medicine, or housing. They were crying out for someone to restrain the hand of the oppressor. And likewise for the girls in the brothels of Svay Pak; their very souls were crying out for someone to rescue them from the hands of those who, day by day, abused them in ways that cannot be described in polite company. Who was going to respond to that need and see that the purveyors of such brutality were actually made to pay a price for their crimes?

This mandate to respond directly to the needs of the victims of abuse came home to me as a conviction of faith in Rwanda when I discovered the powerful words of Psalm 10 (NIV), a psalm that held little meaning for me before I had been forced to sort through the carnage of mass graves.

> Why, O Lord, do you stand far off?
>> Why do you hide yourself in times of trouble?
> In his arrogance the wicked man hunts down the weak,
>> who are caught in the schemes he devises.
> He boasts of the cravings of his heart;
>> he blesses the greedy and reviles the Lord.
> In his pride the wicked does not seek him;
>> in all his thoughts there is no room for God.
> His ways are always prosperous;
>> he is haughty and your laws are far from him;
>> he sneers at all his enemies.
> He says to himself, "Nothing will shake me;
>> I'll always be happy and never have trouble."
> His mouth is full of curses and lies and threats;
>> trouble and evil are under his tongue.
> He lies in wait near the villages;
>> from ambush he murders the innocent,
>> watching in secret for his victims.
> He lies in wait like a lion in cover;
>> he lies in wait to catch the helpless;
>> he catches the helpless and drags them off in his net.
> His victims are crushed, they collapse;
>> they fall under his strength.
> He says to himself, "God has forgotten;
>> he covers his face and never sees."
> Arise, Lord! Lift up your hand, O God.
>> Do not forget the helpless.

> Why does the wicked man revile God?
>> Why does he say to himself,
>> "He won't call me to account"?
> But you, O God, do see trouble and grief;
>> you consider it to take it in hand.
> The victim commits himself to you;
>> you are the helper of the fatherless.
> Break the arm of the wicked and evil man;
>> call him to account for his wickedness
>> that would not be found out.
> The LORD is King forever and ever;
>> the nations will perish from his land.
> You hear, O LORD, the desire of the afflicted;
>> you encourage them, and you listen to their cry,
> defending the fatherless and the oppressed,
>> in order that man, who is of the earth, may terrify no more.

It was abundantly clear that God was passionate about the work of rescuing the oppressed and bringing the perpetrators to justice, and it was equally clear that God had given to humans the *work* of rescue and justice in this world:

> Seek justice,
>> rescue the oppressed,
> defend the orphan,
>> plead for the widow. (Isaiah 1:17 NRSV)

Out of such a conviction, International Justice Mission was established with a clear and precise mission: to help people suffering injustice and oppression who cannot rely on local authorities for relief. The agency documents and monitors conditions of abuse and oppression, educates the church and public about the abuses, and mobilizes intervention on behalf of the victims.

The work we do is very simple to categorize: (1) Free the victims; (2) prosecute the perpetrators; (3) secure places of safe aftercare for victims; and (4) transform communities so the injustice isn't acceptable any longer.

These objectives combine to form a comprehensive approach to the abuse of power in a community. As we work to accomplish one of these objectives, we're almost always working to accomplish all four. If we're planning a raid to free a family of slaves from backbreaking work in a rock quarry, we're simultaneously gathering evidence that will cause the perpetrators to have to pay for their crimes. As we're working to free the victims, we also endeavor to secure the next step in their new lives of freedom by connecting them with caring people who can support them. And when the bad guys pay for their crimes, other slave owners see that their future is in jeopardy if they continue in their ways, causing a change in the community of quarry owners.

It's important to realize that we are lawyers, not cowboys; law enforcement professionals and investigators, not vigilantes. Sometimes, for added hype, the media will portray IJM workers as a bunch of "Rambos" cavalierly busting into the bad guys' fortress in a foreign country and dramatically rescuing victims, like action heroes without regard for local law. That may make good TV, but nothing could be farther from the truth. Wherever IJM works, we always support local authorities in the simple enforcement of their own laws. In fact, it is the power of local law that ends up being our most powerful tool for motivating local authorities to bring rescue to the victims of oppression. Truth be told, we don't have the power to do anything apart from using the power of truth to motivate local authorities to enforce their own laws.

Certainly there is drama in what we do, because the abuses being suffered are horrific and the perpetrators are brutal. Having said that, the work we do is tediously careful, professionally precise, and built on endless hours of monotonous preparation. And that was certainly the case with Svay Pak. What was happening to the children in that slum was completely against Cambodian law, and we were simply on a mission to document meticulously the reality of those abuses with such excruciating clarity that the authorities would have little choice but to act. It wasn't going to be easy; in fact, it felt impossible. But the fundamentals of our methods were the same, and we had seen these principles work time and again around the world. On the other hand, this was Cambodia, a country with a unique culture and society and a devastating history.

CHAPTER 11

HOW CAN THIS POSSIBLY BE?

From our earliest investigations in Cambodia, we realized we needed to learn a lot about the country, the government, and the culture before we could hope to be effective in our mission. Fortunately we had a vast array of local contacts who could bring us up to speed, coach us through the fog, point out the pitfalls, and direct us to the openings. We also enlisted a strong team of local operatives who understood the way things worked in Cambodia, on the surface and behind the scenes.

When people look at video footage of small children being sold to sexual deviants for pleasure, they often ask, "How can this possibly be?" There were many reasons why the child sex trade in Cambodia had grown uncontrollably. These reasons rose up as roadblocks in our efforts to shut down Svay Pak.

As a result of years of war and social turbulence, Cambodia's legal system was left staggering and weak. In many ways it resembles a newly formed nation starting from scratch. During the rule of the Khmer Rouge through the 1970s, 1980s, and part of the 1990s, most of the country's intellectuals were killed, including experienced, high-level legal professionals. Those in charge of the government at the time eliminated potential leaders—people smart enough to put together any sort of resistance or change public thinking about what the Khmer Rouge was doing. (When the United Nations set up the democratic government in 1993, there were only about five lawyers left in this country of seven million people, according to the *New York Times*.)

The rule of law still has not been fully restored in Cambodia. Enormous political intrigue is ongoing, with many subplots and undercurrents that remind me of a man standing on the top rung of a tall stepladder. Although the ladder may be stable for the moment, the political scene gives the sense that the delicate balance could be disrupted with little effort and without warning.

Working within a system like this to get support for our rescue efforts would require a great deal of sensitivity, intelligence, and finesse—and for that we would need a lot of help.

Not only is the system weak, there is also a profound shortage of those who would act as legal advocates for innocent victims. Cambodia has fewer lawyers than there were in one room when I spoke at a gathering of the San Diego chapter of the California State Bar Association! Our abundance of legal advocates is something we take for granted in North America, something many even joke about. But it's no laughing matter for victims of heinous crimes who wish someone would come to their defense, to bring justice to their tortured existence by taking legal action against their captors.

Because of inconsistent training, there are virtually no legal experts in Cambodia when it comes to the sexual exploitation of children. However, the people are willing to learn and have set up an impressive system to attack sex trafficking. The weakness lies in the implementation of that system.

The role of the police is an ongoing challenge in developing countries. Most Westerners have an image of cops as good guys. We would prepare our children for the possibility of getting lost in a big city by saying, "If we get separated, find a police officer and give the officer the card in your pocket. It has my cell-phone number on it, and we'll be back together in no time."

In some places, however, people learn to run *from*, not *to*, police officers. Because police power is often corrupt and unchecked, citizens become victims of police abuse of many kinds. For brothel owners, the primary source of their protection is the local police. Officers cut deals with the criminals and make extra cash by tipping off their contacts when a raid is imminent. Time after time, our people around the world have convinced police authorities to accompany us on a brothel raid, only to find the place empty when we arrive. There is little for the corrupt officers to fear, little to keep them accountable, and even less motivation to do what's right. So rather than stop the evil, police protect the evil, creating a huge barrier to freedom for innocent victims and the prosecution of criminals.

Forced prostitution thrives in the world *only* where it is protected by the local police. And this evil does, indeed, thrive in the world, to the tune of a million child victims a year, according to UNICEF. But a statistic like that is hard for me to grasp. It took meeting a girl named Dacie for me to concretely, clearly, and painfully understand the massive and brutal connection between child prostitution and police corruption.

CHAPTER 12

GOODNESS AND INNOCENCE MOCKED

Fourteen years old and on her school break, Dacie began looking for a summer job with her friend Diadra, so they could earn money to help their families. Maybe they could even keep a little of the money to spend on things teenage girls like to have: clothes, makeup, perfume.

One day a woman Dacie's mom knew came by and said Dacie could make good money working in a noodle shop in a neighboring country. Dacie eagerly discussed the opportunity with her family. Because they trusted the woman, and because she would be escorting Dacie and Diadra across the border herself, they all agreed it sounded too good for the girls to pass up.

So Dacie and Diadra packed their essential belongings and left, carrying with them great expectations. They had no idea of the horrors that awaited them. When they approached the border, the woman met up with a stranger, a man wearing police-uniform pants. The hometown escort helped transfer their things into his car, which was equipped with a police radio.

The man drove them across the border and into town, pulling up to a restaurant. He took the girls inside and introduced them to the female manager, who showed them to their room and immediately gave them new clothes to wear: string tops and short skirts.

When Dacie asked about the clothing, the manager said they needed to look sexy for the men who came here, because they would be having sex with them.

Dacie and Diadra protested and said they wanted to go home.

The manager insisted they had no choice in the matter; their freedom had been purchased from the man who had delivered them, and they must pay that debt back by earning money from customers for sex.

The brothel manager then performed a horrible and amateur gynecological exam on Dacie to determine that she was a virgin.

Now the woman saw before her not an innocent young girl terrified by the thought of having sex with strangers. Instead, she saw an opportunity to make extra cash from the customer who would pay a premium to rape Dacie for the first time. The woman was delighted at her good fortune. She put the word out that she was offering a virgin at her establishment for anyone who would pay the required price, more than seven hundred U.S. dollars.

Unfortunately for Dacie, they found a willing customer that very night for this fourteen-year-old who later told our investigator she had never even kissed anyone before. Shaking with fear, Dacie was taken into a room where the customer waited. When the man began to rape her, Dacie cried out so loudly in pain that the man complained about the service. The brothel keeper came in and strapped tape over Dacie's mouth to silence her screams so they wouldn't interfere with the customer's pleasure while he finished with her. But the tragic night wasn't over. Dacie was forced to have sex with seven more strangers that night.

We met Dacie less than a month later when our investigators working an area in Southeast Asia heard about this brothel offering very young girls. Two investigators posed as customers and went to the brothel, pretending to want the youngest girls in the place for the night. There were about seven minors in the brothel at the time, and the IJM investigators asked the brothel keeper if they could take Dacie to their hotel for the evening. She agreed.

The investigators had set up two undercover cameras in the room to record their conversation with Dacie. As lawyers and law enforcement officers, we see over and over again the importance of collecting this type of firsthand evidence. Every time we turn on a recorder or a camera, we believe it may provide the ticket out for the victim. It's the power of truth to set people free.

The brothel manager wouldn't let Dacie go to the hotel alone with our investigators. Dacie had been there only three weeks, and they didn't know if they could yet trust her to not run away. So the manager drove Dacie to the hotel for her rendezvous. As one investigator took the manager into the lounge, the other took Dacie to a room and interviewed her. How had she come to be at the brothel? Did she like what she did? Did she want to get out and go home?

Dacie said she hated working in the brothel. She wanted to get out so badly that she and a friend were going to try to escape. The IJM investigator told Dacie he didn't want to exploit her; he wanted to be her friend and get to know her. Though he wanted to give her some kind of hope, he couldn't reveal any of their plans to her, because they didn't know what she might do with the information. If the brothel keeper began a threatening inquisition regarding her time with her customer, he didn't want her to have information that would jeopardize her safety.

On another night, both investigators interviewed Dacie and Simla, a girl who had worked at the brothel for two and a half years, to gain information about others held in the brothel: how many, their ages, where they were being kept, how many brothel keepers there were, how the building was laid out in terms of rooms, hallways, and exits. They still didn't tell the girls they were planning a raid, nor did the investigators conduct these interviews like an interrogation. They simply and carefully gathered the information they needed in the flow of normal conversation.

When the girls were not sexually exploited, they grew nervous about the brothel manager's reaction. Before leaving the hotel that night, Simla asked the investigators, "Will you please tell the brothel manager that I was good? She beats me when a customer says I was not good."

"Really? Has that happened before?"

"Yes. The worst beating I ever got was after a policeman complained that I didn't smile when he finished with me," Simla explained. "Please say I was good."

The investigators promised to give a good report and encouraged the girls to not worry.

After the information gathering was completed, Sharon Cohn traveled to this country to participate in Dacie and Simla's rescue. The team quickly put together a report to take to the police. The documents included a map of the brothel though not its location, for fear of a tip-off, and a written account of the girls' accusations, complete with names and photographs of the victims. They knew it might take the full power of all this information to secure police cooperation in conducting a raid to get Dacie, Simla, and the other girls out.

A representative from another nongovernmental organization acted as the liaison between IJM and the police, securing an appointment to meet by assuring the authorities that IJM had a solid case that the police would want to pursue. The NGO representative was from that country and so was fluent in the language, whereas the IJM staffers were native English speakers, some of whom were learning the native tongue.

Through their translator, IJM staff members explained the case and asked the police official for the officers needed to conduct an intervention and get the girls out.

There were very few questions from the police lieutenant, and he surprised our team by pledging his full cooperation and agreeing to assign officers to conduct the raid that evening. Then an IJM investigator went over some of the logistics of the raid, spelling out that two of our people would go to the brothel approximately twenty minutes before the predetermined raid time and pose as customers, to be on site to help when the police arrived.

About twenty officers lined up in front of their motorcycles at the police station that evening, saluted their commanding officer, and took off for the brothel. They would actually gather at another location nearer the brothel and wait for the call to begin the raid. Sharon and the other IJM team members followed in a separate car along with eight other social workers who had been called in by IJM. There were forty girls in that brothel, so we saw a great need to have support staff on hand who could care for them after the raid. These social workers carried a variety of experience, including knowledge of tribal languages and dialects that could prove to be essential in communicating with the girls.

On the way to the raid, Sharon received word that the two IJM staff-members—supposed customers—arrived at the brothel, only to discover it closed.

Later, Dacie and Simla told Sharon that the brothel manager received a tip-off call: *The police are coming.* Managers quickly loaded the girls into the back of a flatbed truck, covered them with blankets, and drove to another part of town. By our team's calculations, the call came ten to fifteen minutes before IJM staff arrived with the police.

After the tip-off, the IJM team and police went into the empty brothel and saw where forty girls were forced to have sex with customers. Walking through the dark building, they noted the girls' possessions, including a little Mickey Mouse notebook—a journal in which one girl kept records of all the customers she was forced to be with. The girls are usually meticulous about documentation, because they are told that when they earn a certain amount of money they will be allowed to go free. They write the information in ledgers and on the walls, in hope that these details will be enough to earn their liberty one day. Of course these little ledgers are all part of the big lie; no one is ever let out until the brothel keeper is finished with them.

That night and the next day, the team went back and talked to the authorities, asking for their help in getting the documented minors released, along with the other minors they knew were being held there.

In a very unusual turn of events, the police called our staff two days later, saying that six of the girls, including Dacie and Simla, were at the police station, ready to be picked up if we wanted to take them.

Dacie and Simla explained that the brothel keeper had taken all the girls to a temporary location and had said they were going to board a bus that would take them to their home country. Afraid she'd lose track of the few possessions back in her room, Dacie spoke up. "I want my cell phone and my jewelry." The brothel keeper disappeared soon after that. It's possible there was another tip-off, because shortly after the woman left the girls, the police showed up at the bus stop and took them all back to the police station.

The day the girls were rescued, the police let our team take Dacie and Simla to an aftercare facility, though four other minor girls were forced to remain in jail on immigration violations. Sharon stayed with the four in jail for several hours and received assurances from the jailer that they would be kept unharmed in a cell separated from the other prisoners. Dacie and Simla were allowed to go with Sharon because they were the two whose photographs were included in the report filed earlier with police. The team continued to work with another nongovernmental agency and the authorities to secure the release of the others as well, and they were released the following afternoon.

When Sharon took all six girls to an aftercare facility where they would be cared for, the girls were very concerned that their possessions were still in the brothel. Everything they owned was in the building under lock and key, secured by the police after the failed raid. And though Dacie had been in the brothel only about four weeks, some of the girls had been there for several years. They really wanted to get their belongings out. So the team worked with the police to arrange a trip to pick up their things. Accompanied by a social worker, Sharon and others escorted the girls back into the brothel where they had been exploited.

"It was really quite extraordinary to hold their hands and walk with them into the rooms where men had sexually abused them day after day," Sharon said. "It had an eerie, evil feeling about it, but it also felt like the evil had died, had been defeated.

"One of the places we walked through in that brothel was a spot where customers would stand behind a wall with a peephole cut out of it. On the other side of the wall was a bench where all the girls were forced to file out and sit down so the customer could view them and make his selection. If the man didn't want to embarrass himself in front of the girls, he could look through the hole in the wall, then identify to the brothel keeper the girl he wanted; the keeper then brought him to her room. Day and night the girls were forced to line up and sit on the bench. Most customers came at night, but if one came during the day, when the girls were permitted a few hours of sleep, they were all forced to line up again so that he could make his choice."

As they went through the girls' rooms, Sharon saw that these kids had tried to create some sense of normal teenage life, even in the midst of horrific abuse. Some of them had shelves full of clothes, because this was not only where they worked, it was also where they lived. They had books, posters of rock stars on the walls, teddy bears, a favorite pair of shoes, and little kitty pencils; one of them even had a CD player.

"They were just normal possessions you would expect to find in the messy room of a fourteen- or fifteen-year-old," Sharon said. "It was interesting to watch the girls make their choices of what to take and what to leave behind. Simla had been in the brothel the longest, so she had a lot of stuff. But I saw her selecting her clothes carefully, taking out only the casual, play-type clothes, and leaving the sexy, sultry clothes on the hangers."

After Sharon and the girls collected in large garbage bags everything they wanted to keep, they walked out. The door was locked behind them. None of them would ever have to return to that horrible place again.

Reflecting back on that day, Sharon said, "When you walk into a brothel holding the hand of a little girl, the power of evil will nearly knock you down. But when you walk out of a brothel holding the hand of a little girl, the power of God will send you to your knees in worship."

As we debriefed following her trip, Sharon said: "When I talked to Dacie and her friends, I was shocked at the depth of their suffering. I still find it hard to believe that people would actually *do* these things to these young girls, that they would *pay* to do these things and would take pleasure in doing these things. You can't imagine what was going through Dacie's mind as these things were happening to her. Not just during a sexual assault, but the thought that it was going to happen day after day after day, and there was no expectation that it would ever stop happening.

"I have been with girls who have been stuck in the brothels for years," Sharon said. "They knew that every day was going to be just like the day before, and that the abuse would just continue far into the foreseeable future. When you look at kids like this, you can't believe their resilience—that they could even survive these situations—and the sorrow that must be in them, the sense of desolation."

That sorrow and desolation were clearly manifested in one of the girls rescued from the brothel where Dacie had been held. While Dacie and the others were furious with the woman for the pain and suffering she had forced them to endure, this girl wasn't as eager as the other five to give evidence against the brothel manager. The manager had been arrested and was being held at the same jail where the girls would come to give testimony to the police. Every time Dacie was called in to give more testimony, she would grab Sharon's hand and insist on going downstairs to where the suspect was being held, to see that she was still locked up, still being held accountable for her actions, that justice was being served.

This sixth girl, however, was the only one who didn't want to give evidence against the manager. The social worker asked, "Why don't you want to say what this woman has done to you?"

Her answer was one of the saddest statements I've ever heard: "Well, I'm not very pretty," she said, "so I don't have to be with very many men. It's not that bad."

It reminds me of what a brutal crime this is against the girls. Yes, certainly what happens to them physically is deplorable, but what it does to their sense of self and what gives them value is equally criminal. This girl had decided that because she didn't get beaten that often, and didn't have to be with that many men, that it just wasn't that bad. In her eyes, she was a loser either way—if she were prettier, she'd have to serve more customers; but since she wasn't pretty enough to make men want to abuse her, life in a brothel was okay.

———

"It gave me an understanding of the violation that's done to these girls on every level—physical, intellectual, and spiritual," Sharon said. "More than any other human rights abuse I can think of, forced prostitution—rape for profit—tears down the person completely, just strips away who they are."

Sharon was able to spend some time with Dacie, Simla, and the other girls over the next several weeks. She helped place Dacie and the others in an after-care center that would provide education, medical care, and counseling.

Dacie and her friends and Sharon were also able to go out on several trips after the rescue, including to the movies and the zoo. I was visiting one of our offices in Southeast Asia and had the enormous privilege of joining Sharon when she took Dacie and Simla to the zoo. It was wonderful to see these girls laughing and goofing around like the young teenagers they were. The fact is, they had been forced to see the worst the world had to offer, but they had never been to the zoo before. If these girls had ever had the childish joy of laughing at a monkey's antics, it would only have been because they could see them in the trees in the rural villages where they grew up.

One of the nightmarish evils of the commercial sex business is the way they take these utterly innocent and inexperienced girls from rural areas and plunge them into the red-neon darkness of the meanest big cities—a world of the ugliest sexual cynicism where all goodness and innocence are mocked, brutalized, and crushed. There these young girls, who yearn like any other for goodness and kindness and love, are painted and dressed up like world-weary prostitutes. It's actually nauseating to see what can be done with makeup and dress to make a childish fourteen-year-old tribal girl from the rural hill country look like a hardened, twenty-six-year-old sexual veteran. But let them scrub off the ugly lie and let them have their simple teenage outfits back, and you again recognize the face of fresh curiosity, silliness, delight, love, and tenderness. As Dacie and Simla and the other rescued girls hollered at, laughed at, and imitated the monkeys at the zoo, they looked a lot more like my nine-year-old twin daughters than anything else.

There's another dramatic part of Dacie's story—a family connection. Dacie had been in the brothel for about four weeks, but three weeks into her time there, her family got worried because they hadn't heard from her in the noodle shop. So the same woman who had betrayed Dacie went to the family and offered to take her older sister, Danja, down to the noodle shop to check up on Dacie.

When Danja arrived, she was told that she would also have to have sex with customers. She was similarly held against her will for three nights while the brothel keeper searched for a customer who would pay the highest price for her virginity. But during this time, police and IJM conducted the raid that in effect shut down the brothel. Though we did not secure the rescue of the girls that night, it was enough to let the brothel keeper know we were onto her, and that we were intent upon our mission.

We believe our presence and persistence at the police station prompted her to attempt to escape town, cut her losses and run, and abandon the girls at a bus stop, which is when the police located the girls. Because of this timing, Danja was saved from the horrible abuse Dacie suffered in the brothel her first night and every night until her rescue.

What is so devastating about Dacie's story is not just what it means to Dacie and what was done to her, but the fact that there are millions of Dacies all over the world being brutalized by this industry. I could write story after story of the girls with whom we have sat and wept, listening to their tales and sharing in their grief.

I could write the stories about girls who have cried out to us, "Where were you three years ago when I was brought to this place? Why didn't you rescue me then when it would have mattered?" I could write stories of girls crying out for help month after month, girls who ran away and were hunted down, brought back to the brothels, and beaten like animals.

That's the kind of urgency attached to this whole issue of sex trafficking. As we wait day after day, more and more girls are being exploited. It isn't just those girls who are being exploited *now*. If someone can go after the brothel keepers and traffickers and shut them down, then all the other Dacies and the Danjas who haven't yet been exploited can be prevented from being exploited just by someone doing the work, and *soon*. It isn't one of those issues that can wait.

But there's good news: Six months after the raid, IJM went back to the same town to see if minor girls were available for sexual exploitation. "No, no," the brothel keepers told our investigators. "We don't have young girls. Police don't let us keep young girls."

In Dacie's case, two of the three perpetrators were arrested, including the brothel manager. The brothel keeper was a very high-level and influential person who escaped, but at this writing there is a warrant out for her arrest.

CHAPTER 13

DETOUR TO SVAY PAK

Following this mission to secure Dacie's release, Will Henry changed his plans to return home, so he and Sharon could travel to Cambodia for three days to investigate Svay Pak Village and possibly effect a rescue.

After checking into their hotel rooms and meeting Sky, the operative, my colleagues went to sleep hoping and praying for the success of their mission. The next morning Will located Sky, a highly placed military officer, who brought one of his trusted men along. Together the three made the journey into Svay Pak.

Occasionally throughout the day Will would call Sharon as she conducted her own research on aftercare around Phnom Penh, still in character—*always in character*—he as the perverted boss, she as the obedient, naive secretary: "Did you send those faxes to Jim and John like I asked you? Good. What about the e-mails to Bob and Gary? Okay. Well, I've found a few great places here where I've located some girls, young ones, just like I like 'em. I may not be back for a while."

Later that morning, Sharon called Will for a prescheduled check-in. In a bar frequented by pedophiles, he sat with the two operatives and a couple of other customers they had just met when the phone rang. "Just checking in to see if you need anything," Sharon said pleasantly.

"Just shut up and do your job," Will answered, playing his role fully. "Everything's fine."

Then he hung up on her. For the guys he was with, Will was now developing the image of a confident, if arrogant, Westerner whose secretary was overly protective and intrusive. But the purpose of the call had been accomplished. Sharon knew Will was okay, and she could go about her tasks in Phnom Penh without worrying until the next check-in time. After the call he continued his investigation, visiting brothels, gathering names and images on undercover video that could be used later in prosecuting criminals.

As Will walked across the street, he made eye contact with a stocky Westerner approaching him with a distinctive duck-like waddle. Will struck up a conversation with the man, asking him for advice in locating young girls.

"This your first time here?" the man asked.

"Yeah," Will answered.

"Step over here for a minute," the man suggested and moved to a less-busy part of the street. He then gave Will advice about how to avoid suspicion from friends and colleagues back in the U.S. and how to make a deal with the brothel keepers to take more than one girl back to the hotel for the night. They were words he would soon regret, as they were recorded by undercover camera and would be played one day for millions to hear.

When the conversation ended, Will proceeded down the street, following the man's recommendation. Later that day, he called Sharon back. "You're going to need to make some arrangements, because I have four guests coming back to the hotel tonight," he said. "Two at seven, two at eight."

They didn't know anyone at aftercare facilities in Cambodia, but Sharon had a list of places our friends in another country had given her. So she began frantically calling people to see who could take four girls on short notice if their operation was successful and they needed safe harbor that night.

After making connections with some helpful, caring people, Sharon located a place that had a night shelter for girls brought out of forced prostitution. She made arrangements, so that even if she were to call at midnight, they would take the girls immediately.

In the meantime Will had checked into a room at another Phnom Penh hotel, which Sky had identified as a brothel-friendly facility. The brothel owner agreed it was a good choice—where Will could take several girls. Will called Sharon and told her where he was and which room he was in. Then Sharon arrived at the hotel as a tourist, asking to see a number of rooms, pretending to care about the specific room, the floor, the view, until she chose the room directly across the hall from Will's. It was important that the hotel not know the two IJM team members were together.

Will had scheduled two girls to be brought to the hotel at 7:00 P.M. and two to come at 8:00 P.M., driven by pimps. He had requested some of the younger girls he had met, but the smaller ones were not allowed to be taken out of the village of Svay Pak. The ones he subsequently selected were quite young anyway: an eleven-year-old, two twelve-year-olds, and a thirteen-year-old, though it was clear from the way they acted and their language that they were not new to what was happening to them.

The first two girls arrived shortly after seven. They came into Will's hotel room, which was being monitored by two undercover cameras to record everything that happened there from two different points of view. The girls immediately went into the bathroom to change into the pink baby-doll pajamas their mamasan had sent with them. While they were changing, Will quickly went across the hall to bring in Sharon and the lead operative, who spoke the girls' native language and would act as an interpreter.

"Tell them we didn't bring them here to have sex with them," Will said when the girls came out of the bathroom. "We just want to talk to them and get to know them."

The interpreter relayed the message, and Will began asking questions, such as, "How long have you been in the brothel? How did you come to be at the brothel? Do you like doing what you do?" All this ultimately leading up to the most important question: "Would you like to go someplace else so you don't have to go back to the brothel?"

"Yes, we'd like to leave that place!" they answered enthusiastically.

Sharon took the girls across the hall to her room to kill time, so Will and the interpreter could prepare for the second pair of girls, expected in about thirty minutes. Sharon had bought a portable video-game player that day, which Will called "the best purchase IJM ever made." So the girls played video games and watched cartoons while they waited to be taken to their new home. Sharon tried several times to get them to eat something, but they repeatedly refused food; she surmised they had been warned against taking food from people outside the brothel for fear of drugging or poisoning.

When the second pair of girls arrived at Will's room, he and Sharon interviewed them, while another IJM contact stayed with the others in Sharon's room. These two new girls also said they wanted to leave the brothel and go to live somewhere else, a safe place where they wouldn't have to have sex with strangers.

"Now," Will warned, "we have to be very careful getting the girls out of the hotel and safely to the aftercare facility."

The security challenge was to get the girls downstairs to waiting cars without being questioned by hotel staff who might tip off the brothel keepers. Will used his cell phone to call down to the street, where he had stationed a third operative to watch for a pimp lookout.

"Yeah, he's still here," the operative answered. "The guy who brought the second two girls. He's hanging around outside near the street."

Though Will had "rented" the girls until seven in the morning, he didn't expect the lookout to stay all night, just late enough to assure himself that the customer wasn't going to take the girls away. If Will was spotted trying to secret the girls away now, things could turn ugly in a hurry. It turned into a waiting game.

The girls either dozed with the TV on or played video games until 11:45 P.M., when Will's phone rang. It was the operative, informing Will that the pimp standing guard had just left.

"Great. Call three taxicabs to the front door. Have them pull up close to the covered entrance, as close as possible, then call me when they get there."

Soon the three cars were waiting, bumper to bumper, at the front door. Will and Sharon ushered the girls out of the rooms, into the elevator, and out to the waiting cars without incident. Two of the girls went with Will and the operative in the lead car. Sharon took the other two girls in the second car. Sky, in the third car, acted as a blocker, directing their moves from the rear and keeping watch for anyone following.

Sky gave instructions from his vantage point at the rear of the convoy to drive around the city for a while, ensuring they were not followed. When he was convinced they were not being tailed, he directed the lead car to the after-care facility. When they arrived, Will and Sharon ensured that the four girls were checked in safely, then left. I wonder how long it had been since those four girls went to sleep at night without the ever-present knowledge that they could be awakened at any moment to parade before a customer.

All that night Will and Sharon stayed up writing intervention reports that requested the government to intervene based on the information they had gathered on the girls they rescued and fifteen other victims Will had encountered in his undercover investigation.

Transitions are often very difficult for rescued girls. One would hope that victims would adapt easily to their regained freedom, that they would appreciate a clean place to sleep and not being forced to have sex with strangers sev-

quest date:1/25/2014 04:00 PM
quest ID: 44076
Number:306 742 H3714
Barcode:

hor: Haugen, Gary A.
e: Terrify no more / Gary A. Haugen with Gr
meration:c.1Year:
ron Name:XIXI ZHAO
ron Barcode:

ron comment:

quest number:

te to:
are Library:

ary Pick Up Location:

Islip Request   1/27/2014 2:15:39 PM

quest date 1/25/2014 04:00 PM
quest ID 44026
Number 305 242 H3714
Barcode

hor. Haugen, Gary A
Terity no more! Gary A. Haugen with Gr
iteration c 1Year
ion Name XIXI ZHAO
ron Barcode

no comment

quest number

ute to
nate Library

rary Pick Up Location

eral times a day. But many times the victims' equilibrium is thrown off by the dramatic change in their environment, and they don't respond well. This time, there were problems.

Sharon's phone rang in the very early morning hours as she and Will put the finishing touches on the intervention reports. It was the aftercare provider.

"You're going to have to come and pick up these girls," the woman said.

"Why?" Sharon asked. "What's wrong?"

"We can't keep girls who don't want to stay here, and these girls are asking to leave. Right now they are yelling and throwing things and making a big scene."

Somehow there had been a breach in security. One of the girls had snuck the use of a phone or been allowed to make a call. One of the head brothel keepers from Svay Pak Village, named Mao, had shown up at the aftercare facility demanding to take the girls back with her right then. Mao's driver was none other than a police officer who had been in the anti-trafficking operations division. His superiors had learned about his involvement with the brothel keeper and had suspended him from duty—a wise decision, as evidenced by his role in coming with Mao to steal the children back to the brothel. This was a clear indicator of the reality in which we were operating and a bracing sign of what we were up against. Fortunately, the aftercare provider was bold enough to stand up to the brothel keeper and her escort.

For the rest of the day, Will and one of the operatives provided security for the aftercare facility. At one point, while Mao was still at the house trying to get her girls back, she and Will made eye contact. She knew he was the one who had rented the girls out, and now she knew it was he who had brought them here. Eventually, Mao left the facility, but Will would see her again one day soon, up close and personal.

When they finished the intervention reports, Will went to the police station to deliver the documents to the appropriate authorities. These reports contained all the information Will and Sharon had gathered from the four girls just rescued: names, ages, locations of the brothels where they worked, names of brothel owners and managers, and photographs of the victims. As Will dropped off the reports, his cell phone rang.

The voice on the other end of the line delivered a shocking message: "Will, I'm packing your bags right now. If you don't leave right away, you'll be dead by morning."

It was Sky, and Will could tell he was serious.

"Everything's fine," Will replied. "What are you worried about?"

"I'm telling you, you've got to go, or you'll be dead by morning."

"It's fine. I'm with the police. We'll be okay."

Sky told him it didn't matter whom he was with; they wouldn't be able to protect him against this threat.

Will hung up and called Sharon on her cell phone. He told her they needed to get out of the country right away, that she should head straight for the airport. He had to stay and write an affidavit to go along with the intervention report, but he told Sharon she needed to leave immediately.

At first, Sharon didn't want to go. In fact, she refused to leave and told Will to go without her. There was too much to be done to secure ongoing care for the rescued girls.

"Sky called and said that our lives will be in jeopardy if we stay," Will told her. "I need to go back to my room and pick up my camera equipment. Please take my undercover tapes with you, so I don't have them at airport security," Will said.

Sharon made several intense calls to governmental officials and received promises that the girls would remain in aftercare, then she headed for the airport back through the same crowded streets by which they had arrived.

One primary objective for aftercare facilities is creating a peaceful, calm environment in which the girls can begin to heal. Even small disturbances can disrupt the delicate recovery of girls who need so much care. It becomes a horrendous conundrum, then, for any community to try to care for victims of child sexual abuse if there is no agency that will hold the children in protective custody against their "will."

Although it is understandable that an aftercare provider would say it needs to release disruptive girls from its care, it is unacceptable if you believe in the value of *the one*. Jesus of Nazareth taught about the value of the one in the parable of the lost sheep, and he told how the good shepherd would leave the ninety-nine to go find the one lost sheep because the one mattered. Each of the four girls just rescued mattered to us and to God. Each desperately needed someone to do the right thing for her, even if she didn't agree that it was what she needed.

Eventually, Sharon spoke to the Cambodian minister of women's affairs, who got a judge's order to require an aftercare facility to keep them. The judge's decision underscores the truth of this thorny issue—that these child victims must be kept in a secure facility regardless of their wanting to "go home." They need mature, caring adults to step up and make decisions for them that they are not capable of making. This decision-making ability is impeded not only because of their youth and immaturity, but also because of the eroding of their psyches by repeated abuse. Think about these kids' warped view of reality—to be bought and sold for sex, some by their own parents, and some when they are as young as three, four, and five. There's just no way they are going to be equipped to make informed decisions about what's best for them after spending a few hours or days in a new place with rules they aren't used to. Brave adults have to take the responsibility for these kids' well-being, and they, in turn, must be supported by law in doing what is best for the kids in the long run.

"Go home," indeed! What informed kid would ever want to "go home" to the life these kids had experienced? Even in their worst moments of temper, anger, or frustration, my kids—and any kid I've ever known—would never say they wanted to "go home" to repeated sexual molestation.

Will finished the affidavit, stopped by the hotel to pick up his gear, then headed straight for the airport. When he started through security, the officers pulled him aside, double-checked his I.D., and made him empty all his bags out on the floor. All his personal belongings, along with the undercover camera gear, was spread out on the floor of the airport. Then they wrapped all his camera batteries together in tape so sticky and gooey that it rendered them nearly useless for the future. Though none of his videotapes were confiscated, all he had with him at that time were some family vacation tapes he carried as a cover. He made it on the same flight as Sharon, and they returned home to the States safely.

That was May 2002. We had no idea how long it would be until we could come back for the other girls of Svay Pak. But we certainly had a clear idea of what we were up against.

CHAPTER 14

HERE WE GO

As soon as Will Henry and Sharon returned from their trip to Svay Pak, Will went into Mosier's office with a video camera in his hand. "I have to show you something from the undercover footage in Svay Pak," he said. "You're not going to believe this."

Mosier adjusted the small screen so he could see the display. He watched the unspeakable revealed before his eyes. "Unbelievable," Mosier said, understating the obvious. He got up, camera in hand, and came straight to my office.

"I've got something for you, Gary," Mosier said soberly. He walked around to my side of the desk and stood behind my chair so we could see the images together.

"This is what Will and Sharon found in Svay Pak."

He turned on the tape, and I watched as the scene unfolded. Obviously shot with an undercover camera inside a brothel, the images were amazingly clear. As many as a dozen young girls, some appearing to be eight or nine, paraded before the camera, smiling for their prospective customer, gathering around him like a group of excited little Girl Scouts trying to get a customer to buy cookies.

It made me think of comments I've heard over the years from some who don't understand the brutality and complexity of the sex-trafficking business. They say, "Look, it can't be that bad, or they wouldn't seem so happy to be there. Look at their smiles."

In response, I sometimes tell them about Simla, the girl who was beaten severely because a customer—a police officer—had complained about the service he'd received; she hadn't smiled when he finished raping her. I tell

56

them what rescued girls have told me—about the angry slaps, the cigarette burns, and the beatings they received if the brothel keeper didn't think the girls had smiled and giggled enough while the customers inspected them.

Other times I tell them about customer quotas that must be met. If a girl doesn't serve a certain number of customers each day, she is punished, sometimes with a beating, other times by withholding food. It's all part of the very sick fantasy world that the brothel keepers viciously enforce for their customers. And for children who see no way out, it doesn't take much for them to learn what they need to do to avoid another beating.

So I saw past the sick display of young girls brutalized into smiling for a chance to be sodomized. I had seen too much of this before. But I had never seen girls so young, eleven, ten, maybe eight. And then as the footage rolled forward I saw a tiny girl—no more than five years of age—held on the hip of another girl and pushed forward for sale. It was a horrible moment, captured in clear black and white and repeated in slo-mo.

In fact, in the months to follow, it was a taped moment Sharon and I would play over and over again for anyone who was willing to watch the reality of modern sex slavery. It was always the point in my presentation when men would finally turn away in revulsion and women would quietly gasp and involuntarily lift a hand to cover their mouths.

Over the coming months, after watching these visceral reactions to the video, it seemed that this particular little girl shown in this black-and-white video would help senators, ambassadors, network producers, and thousands of others finally to see the unspeakable evil of child forced prostitution. Eventually she would also end up teaching us all about miracles and hope. But in that moment when she first came clear in the undercover footage for me, there was precious little hope. There was, frankly, only an ocean of despair.

I know people generally see me as a tremendously hopeful and optimistic person. What fewer people understand, however, is the professional perspective that actually makes that optimism hard to come by. If I have a professional expertise, it's sizing up these situations for what they are, not for what we would like them to be. With clinical clarity I could see six reasons, which I could number on a white board, why it was ill advised and, practically speaking, impossible to do anything about this little girl and the other brutalized victims of Svay Pak. This is what I knew:

1. It was not a reasonably safe place to conduct undercover investigative operations. The odds of an investigator being caught were small. But, if caught, the reasonable expectation was not a broken nose but a bullet in the back of the head. In some environments there are just too many guns and the bullets too cheap.

2. Even if we did get in and out with the video evidence (which would have to be refreshed just prior to presentation to authorities to avoid the predicable response of, "Well, that was months ago"), there were no authorities to go to. No one had acted on the video evidence we'd presented three previous times, and Svay Pak clearly had very high-level police protection.

3. Even if we did have a high-level authority willing to act, that official would have to mobilize the foot soldiers to actually execute the raid, and that window of opportunity would last for precisely as long as it takes for a subordinate police officer to get on a cell phone and alert his benefactors in Svay Pak so they can scatter the kids.

4. And even if we could get a secure unit to conduct the raid without a tip-off, we knew how such raids were conducted; the children were all just slipped out the back as the police wrestled with the padlocks on the front door. If the raid was to be effective, it would require IJM staff and the police working together. Moreover, given the sheer number of victims spread throughout the numerous brothels, as soon as we hit one, all the others would scatter their victims through a well-developed system of alarms and escape passages.

5. But even if we could overcome all these obstacles and get a significant number of these young kids out, there was nowhere to take them. There was a very limited number of aftercare agencies, and they were at full capacity and felt unequipped to take the toughest cases—that is, very young victims of severe sexual trauma who were likely to be pursued by the pimps, family members, and police who had sold them, and who would experience moments when they would "want to go back home." Another complication: Almost all of these girls were Vietnamese, and complicated cultural distinctions and prejudices presented unique challenges, particularly if they were cared for alongside Cambodian children. What's more, we couldn't prematurely discuss

989

999999999999

our intentions with a broad range of agencies, because we were repeatedly advised that word would inevitably make its way to Svay Pak. And finally, we couldn't tell agencies how many children to expect because, depending on how an operation went, the number could range from one to one hundred.

6. Even if you could get girls out and in secure, quality aftercare, the simple fact was that the Svay Pak brothel keepers would simply go shopping for more kids to replace them, unless the operators were brought to justice—not just arrested or prosecuted but actually convicted and sent to jail. The problem with that was not only the corrupt police but an even more corrupt court system where most judges had no formal legal training and cases went to the highest bidder. We had example after example of cases in which the vilest offenders were set free in the face of overwhelming eyewitness testimony of brutal sex crimes against children. As our in-country experts and contacts assured us, the courts were incapable of sending such powerful and well-heeled operators to jail.

To be frank, there were another twenty smaller reasons why trying to rescue the girls in Svay Pak and bringing the perpetrators to justice was simply not possible.

In such moments, it's stunning to step back and realize that there is a place on the globe where hundreds of children can be openly sold for rape in broad daylight, and governmental leaders all over the world can know about it, and there can even be several Web sites telling sex tourists how to get to it and get the most out of it—and there is, it would appear, nothing you can do about it.

Given the list of Six Impossibilities, it seemed as if we would have to take a pass on this one. After all, the world is full of brutal injustice, and IJM can't do everything everywhere. Certainly no one would blame us for being realistic about what can and cannot be done. Why even take the risks? Something was bound to go wrong, and then IJM would have exposed itself to all manner of criticism. Why not move on to other worthy needs where we wouldn't run such risks? Certainly the humanitarian agencies and Christian ministries in Phnom Penh that already knew about Svay Pak and felt helpless to be able to intervene for the girls would affirm the wisdom of such a decision.

But frankly we were stuck—stuck because of what we knew. We weren't stuck because of what we knew about the impossibilities but because of what we knew about the girls. We had simply gotten inside and too close. There they were on our video. There was the little five-year-old forced to be sodomized every day by pedophiles. There were the scores of other girls being serially raped. We knew their names. We knew by name who was abusing them. We knew exactly where the rape and molestation were taking place. And quite simply, in the moral universe engineered by a holy God, knowledge carries responsibility. For followers of Jesus Christ, it carries the responsibility of love. Knowledge simply forces the question: What would it mean to love these girls, these specific girls whom we know about? If you or your own daughter were in that hell, what would you want done? Put that way, the way Jesus specifically put it, I hadn't yet met a human being who didn't say, "I would want someone to get me out."

Funny though. Many times it is our knowledge that allows us to *escape* responsibility rather than *take* responsibility. Like the characters in the story of the Good Samaritan, our abused neighbors were lying on the road before our eyes. What would we choose to do? There were very good reasons to cross over to the other side of the road and walk on. In fact, I imagine if we asked them, the priest and the Levite in the Good Samaritan story probably had very distinct reasons why it was imprudent to help the abused man who lay before them. But Jesus' teaching was pretty clear, just as it was clear what was being done to the little girls in Svay Pak.

So we were stuck. I thanked Bob for the update, got up from my desk, and turned to the window as Bob left the room. From my twelfth-floor office I stared out into the gray of the day. There was a lot of gray. But then some light began to break through.

Gradually, as I turned it all over in my mind, it seemed less and less that *we* were stuck, and more and more that *God* was stuck. *He* was the one who called himself the God of justice. *He* was the one who was supposed to love these girls so much. *He* was the one who said we should treat these girls the way we would want to be treated. *He* was the one who told us to "seek justice, rescue the oppressed, defend the orphan, and plead for the widow." And *he* was the one who promised to go with us, to give us power, and to answer our prayers if we obeyed him.

If I, as a parent, ask my little kids to carry all the luggage into the house from the car, they will protest that some of the bags are too heavy for them to manage, because they are. But if I say, "Fine, I'll help you with the big ones; you carry the ones you can," then it is I, not they, who am on the hook if they've lugged all their little bags inside and only the big ones are still sitting out in the car. The children have done their part, but the dad hasn't done his. Likewise with Svay Pak. If I really believed there was a God, and I believed what Jesus taught about him, then he was on the hook for all of this a whole lot more than we were.

But then again, what if he didn't show up? What if we chose to believe all this stuff, acted as if it were true, and then he didn't show up? Maybe it would be better to *believe* it was all true (because it would be nice if it was) without actually testing it in real life in a way that might be proved to be false. Tempting. But pathetic.

No, let's keep God on the hook, I thought. Let's do our best to do exactly what Jesus said we should do, and leave the God-parts to God. Of course one can never be precisely sure what God wants done (at least I can't), but the situation for these girls in Svay Pak was about as clear as it gets, as far as I could tell. I was happy to have people tell me otherwise, but whenever I put it in terms of the girls in the video—pausing the picture, pointing to the specific child, and asking, "What are we supposed to do about her?"—what we should do was always crystal clear: Get her out and bring her abuser to justice.

So we would just have to go do this—or at least do everything we could to carry in all the luggage that we could manage and let God pick up the rest. There was a mountain of luggage to bring in, and we would just have to start at the beginning and take the mountain apart piece by piece. Anytime the Father wanted to call us off the task, or carry it all by himself, that would be just fine. And we would certainly carry the big ones as far as we could, and then ask for his help when we just couldn't budge them another inch. Along the way, I figured, we would also claim one of the most extraordinary and wonderful promises of Scripture. The first chapter of James's epistle promises that if we don't have enough wisdom to proceed, and we admit that fact and ask God for wisdom with faith, God has to grant it. He doesn't actually have an option.

Well, perfect. We were going to lack sufficient wisdom every day for this journey. So all we needed to do was to admit that, ask God for it, and we would get the wisdom we needed.

I turned away from the window, opened my door, and headed down to see Sharon and Bob. "I think we just have to go do this," I told them. "The girls are right there, and we've been looking at them for almost two years. It's time to just do whatever it takes. We are just going to have to take each problem as it comes along. Break it down and solve it. Take it step by step. This is why we exist.

"What do you think?" I asked.

"I don't know how this is going to work, Gary; I have to be honest," Sharon said. "But we have to do it. To not do it is to say, in effect, to the kids in the brothel, 'We're sorry. There was nothing we could do. This is the best the body of Christ has to offer you.' We have to throw everything we have at it."

"Bob, do you agree?"

"Gary, I think it's just going to happen," he said. "I've got a peace about it. It's just going to happen."

I think Bob and Sharon both had God on the hook for this already and were even more sure than I about what kind of God this was they trusted.

"Okay, Sharon, you need to figure out a way to make it work. How are we going to get the government to act? What do we need from Bob's investigative team? Where will the girls go when we get them out? How will we encourage the government to prosecute?"

With that, I was placing Sharon in charge of the entire operation. She now had responsibility for the whole project; she was accountable for the outcomes: release of victims, proper aftercare, and prosecution of the perpetrators.

"Bob, we need a tactical plan for getting in there and getting fresh, definitive video evidence of specific transactions involving lots of specific girls and specific perps. Then we need a plan for how to go in and rescue a large number of these girls and grab a significant number of perps without everybody scattering. In other words, even if we can swing the political part and the Cambodians say, 'Fine, what do you want us to do?' what will we say we want them to do?"

We chatted a bit about the possibilities, and then I headed back down the hallway to my office. In those strides, it felt right. All the impossibilities were still there, but it felt right to commit the ship to its course. Inside I felt a simple conviction: This is why we are here. If we are not going to go after this, who is?

Okay, God, here we go.

CHAPTER 15

POWER TO DO GOOD

In one of the great misquotes of history, Lord Acton is said to have concluded that "power corrupts and absolute power corrupts absolutely." In fact, what the great English historian actually said was that "power *tends to* corrupt and absolute power corrupts absolutely." This difference is subtle, but it represents a tragic misunderstanding that costs lives in the world today.

The Acton misquote is frequently used to support the vague notion that the exercise of power is itself an evil. And although there are, indeed, dangers associated with power and grave dangers in absolute power, the truth is, the *failure* to exercise power can be just as evil, especially when one possesses the power to rescue those in deepest peril. This comes to mind in these days, of course, as we remember the tenth anniversary of the Rwandan genocide, perhaps the most exquisitely preventable disaster in the history of man. The retrospectives have all reached the same verdict: Evil triumphed in Rwanda simply because good men and good women did nothing.

Indeed, the teachings of Jesus Christ put much more emphasis on the sins of omission than on the sins of commission. Jesus talked more of the joyous good we get to do than about the grim evil we must avoid.

Nearly every day at IJM, I see God handing us amazing power to do good. Sometimes it comes dressed in the extravagant robes of power: White House ceremonies, United Nations commissions, network television. But more often it comes in the simple but beautiful robes of faith and courage that move with transforming power in the darkest places. The question is: Whom does such power serve, and whom does it glorify?

Late afternoon one day in January, an overseas office of IJM received a frantic call from a bonded slave who had heard about our work from someone we had previously rescued. In a voice filled with both bravery and fear, Shaibya explained that her owner had sexually assaulted her and that she had fled the rice mill where she was forced to live and work. That night IJM staff members met with Shaibya as she represented her fellow slaves and detailed the horrors of their lives. Over the next week, Shaibya and her husband, at great risk to themselves, worked with IJM in a coordinated plan to sneak small groups of slaves out of the rice mill at night to be interviewed by IJM staff. We learned about the physical abuse, sexual assaults, and fear-filled days endured by these families. During these conversations we learned about Bharat, a man who had died as a slave in the rice mill and whose family still worked to pay off the same debt for which he was bonded. After the secret interviews the victims snuck back to the mill before their owner knew they were gone.

In the next week, IJM staff operating under a ruse entered the rice mill and met the arrogant slave owner, a man who laughed at the victims and their inability to pay their debts. He gloated, boasted, and shamelessly explained how these slaves helped enlarge his profit margin. Less than two weeks after we received Shaibya's call, we were able to work cooperatively with officials in the local government to raid the facility. While victims gave courageous testimony to the police, their owner hurled threatening insults at them. But at the end of the day, eighty-three people were emancipated. It took the victims all of ten minutes to pack their belongings and board a truck, not sure where they were going but knowing it had to be better than the place they were leaving. They were free, because Shaibya knew whom to call. Because Shaibya desperately hoped people who possessed the power and influence she lacked would also be people of goodwill and courage.

I'm reminded of other courageous, oppressed people of ancient times who knew where to go for help. Mordecai was in grave danger. In fact, his entire race was in danger of extermination. But Mordecai had an ally in a young woman named Esther, his cousin, who was queen. Queen Esther bravely appealed to the king on behalf of Mordecai and his people—her people. She knew her appeal could cost her very life. But she understood the importance of using her influence and power to help those who had none. Esther's bravery resulted in the salvation of the Jews living in a whole empire.

Through the examples of Shaibya and Queen Esther, we can see how the boldness and courage of victims increase when they know there is someone with power whom they can trust.

CHAPTER 16

CATCH-22

One reason we sent Will Henry and Sharon Cohn to Svay Pak in May 2002—to conduct an investigation and implement a rescue if the opportunity presented itself—was to "wake up" the Cambodian government. We had already forwarded documentation to them several times, but we wanted to keep the pressure on by putting real girls' faces before the appropriate officials. *Something needs to be done about this. Lots of young girls like these are being sold in brothels, and they want to get out.* We needed these officials to use their power and influence to make something happen quickly.

This time it appeared to make a difference. The week after Will and Sharon returned home, our sources in Cambodia informed us that the government had conducted a raid on the three brothels that Will had investigated. In the raid, police had rescued fourteen underage girls and taken them to an aftercare facility. That was the good news.

The bad news? The police later went back to the aftercare house and arrested all seventeen victims for being illegal immigrants in Cambodia. (This number included the fourteen they rescued plus three of the four girls we had taken to the aftercare facility. Sadly, one of those girls had run away, leaving a total of seventeen.) After the arrest, the three we had rescued were released back to the aftercare facility. We heard through our contacts that of the fourteen remaining in custody, six were convicted, sentenced to thirty days in jail, and prepared for deportation to Vietnam.

This was yet another example of what we were up against in trying to bring relief to the child victims in Svay Pak. Most of the girls were Vietnamese. Governmental officials usually treated Vietnamese as aliens and illegals and refused to treat these girls as victims rather than criminals. Thus these children were caught in a "Catch-22" of being forced into a place by brutal adults and then being arrested by other adults for being there. In fact, that's why many people had given up and simply said, "Let them be," an idea that seemed to make sense until you actually stopped to think about where you were leaving them. No, these children deserved better. They deserved to be rescued, *and* they deserved to be treated as victims, not criminals, with compassionate and caring aftercare. That simply meant we had to address *both* problems, the government's corruption and apathy that left them in the brothels to be abused *and* the government's callous incompetence that abused them as criminals.

The arrest of the seventeen victims was an inexcusable outrage. We worked with our governmental contacts and nongovernmental allies to make sure the Cambodian authorities knew it. We isolated this example with the Cambodian authorities so they clearly understood the perfect illustration they had provided to the world of how *not* to treat trafficking victims. They needed to know that the world was watching, and that this kind of conduct would affect diplomatic relationships that they deemed important. Fortunately a vast chorus of outrage from inside and outside Cambodia was targeted upon the incident; we had reason to believe that the authorities had gotten the point.

CHAPTER 17

COVER BURNED

In the summer of 2002, just a couple of months after Will and Sharon had returned from Cambodia, Bob Mosier sent Will back to gather additional evidence of the sex-trafficking epidemic. This time, he would stay out of Svay Pak but would concentrate on the commercial sexual exploitation in Phnom Penh proper, eleven kilometers away.

Soon after he arrived, Will was talking with some sex tourists in a bar named Barracuda's, a notorious hangout of those looking for sex with minors. Out of the corner of his eye, he noticed someone approaching him. He turned to look straight into the face of Mao, the brothel keeper from Svay Pak.

Both froze for an instant. Then Mao stuck out her tongue at Will, stomped her foot on the floor, spun, and walked to the back of the barroom. Will stood and walked out the door quickly, realizing that Mao's money and high-level influence on his earlier trip had prompted the threat on his life.

That mission for Will was quickly aborted, and Mosier realized that Will was burned, meaning he could no longer be a front person for our operations in Cambodia. It was too dangerous, and the sex-trafficking community was just too tightly connected. Will could provide a great deal of intelligence and assistance on future operations, but now he would have to stay in the background.

CHAPTER 18

CONFRONTATION IN THE STREET

Several months later, in September 2002, we geared up for a comprehensive investigation in Svay Pak. We sent Will Henry back to Cambodia with Pete, an investigative associate with twenty years of U.S. law enforcement experience. Will would direct this phase of the investigation from behind the scenes in this all-out, two-week effort to gather as much evidence as we possibly could on every brothel in Svay Pak and on the children who worked there. We knew that after we had garnered this information, we would be set to conduct a large-scale raid-and-rescue operation, as long as we could get the cooperation of the local police.

There was some basis for encouragement because the police had actually acted after we'd filed our last intervention report and had conducted the raid on the three targeted brothels. We might have crossed an important hump in being able to mobilize the police, but we were still a long way from being able to mobilize them to act properly, professionally, and effectively. Clearly if we were going to mobilize an effective raid of any significant size, we would need to provide them with all the intelligence necessary to justify the rescue of a large number of girls and a very clear tactical plan for how to do it right. And the police authorities would have to commit to following the plan, including the proper treatment of the child victims. But this time, things would turn south in a hurry.

Will Henry had arranged for two of his operatives to go into Svay Pak with Pete, while he hung back on the outside of the village on the main road, listening to the radio conversation, prepared to provide additional security if needed. One of the operatives went into the village alone and took up a position at a roadside café where he could see most of the street. The other stayed near his motorcycle in case Pete called for immediate evacuation.

When Pete had been in the village for only twenty or thirty minutes, he ran into trouble. Walking down the dirt main street of the village, he met a Western sex tourist and tried to strike up a conversation. Almost immediately the man asked, "Is that a camera?"

"No, it's not," Pete answered, giving him a preplanned explanation.

The guy didn't buy the story. He reached out and grabbed the camera, wrestled the equipment loose from its cables, and tried to take off with it. Pete reacted quickly to neutralize the threat and retrieve the equipment from the man. But then the sex tourist tried to alert his cronies and perhaps incite a mob against Pete. Running through the village, the man shouted, "Western policeman! Western policeman!"

The Svay Pak brothels are equipped with an integrated system of alarms. At the sound of "Western policeman!" doors slammed shut, gates closed and locked. Dangerous attention focused on Pete as the locals rushed out to see who was causing the alarm. Pete called in the operative on the motorcycle, and within a minute he was spirited out of the village. Though everyone made it out safely, we knew it might take some time before we could go back in and complete our investigation.

There was another reason why we chose to put our operation on ice for a while. We learned that a British journalist had recently conducted his own undercover operation in Svay Pak using equipment very much like ours to put together a story for television. With all the attention the village was getting, and with the attention sex traffickers would be paying to anything that looked like an undercover camera lens, we decided to wait a few months for tensions to cool in Svay Pak before going back again.

CHAPTER 19

GOOD GUYS OR BAD GUYS?

Moviemakers know how to ratchet up the tension in their suspense dramas to an exquisite climax of anxiety, and the formula is pretty simple: Have the good guys turn out to be the bad guys. Few things are scarier than to find out that the one you have been relying upon for protection, the one you expect to turn to for help, turns out to be the most ruthless and wicked character of all. In particular, few things are more deeply disturbing than to find out that the police, the ones in charge of protecting the innocent, are actually the bad guys abusing the innocent. Few things give you the sense of "no way out" like the realization that the ones in charge of enforcing the law are the ones breaking the law.

For most Americans, this profoundly frightening sense of an upside-down and unsafe world is experienced in a movie theater. But for most poor people in the developing world, this is the daily reality experienced in their streets. And this was surely the case in Svay Pak, where the police were not simply ignoring the children being abused, they were actively protecting the abusers and frequently engaging in abuse themselves.

Of course it doesn't happen only in Cambodia. In fact, a young girl named Achara who escaped from a horrific brothel in another Asian country told Sharon what it was like to have to clean the blood off the floor after two girls were murdered by the brothel keeper for trying to run away. When the girls had escaped out a window and run off, whom did the brothel keeper call for help? According to Achara, the brothel keeper called his police friends to hunt the girls down, and she saw the police drag the girls back to the brothel, where they were beaten, bound with a rope, and shot in front of the scores of terrified girls locked away on the fifth floor. Achara was told that the girls' bodies had been thrown into the rubbish bin out back.

Imagine the overwhelming sense of hopelessness for those forced to dwell in the unique nightmare where police terror dominates the streets. This, of course, was part of the reason so many had given up on the children in Svay Pak—the police were not only on the wrong side, often they *were* the wrong side. But we knew from experience that, as hopeless as it may seem, there are ways to address even the most vicious police abuses. In fact, many of us at IJM *are* police professionals, and experience has taught us that abuse doesn't have to be tolerated, even in the poorest communities around the world.

David is twenty-three years old and runs a little video-lending business in Nyahururu, Kenya. His story of police abuse is about as gruesome as they get, but as I sat with him and listened to the way he and my IJM colleagues in Nairobi had seen justice prevail, it reaffirmed the testimony of hope that we could take into Svay Pak.

David is much loved by his neighbors, and it's easy to see why. He is jovial and kind, an active volunteer in his local church and in the community's HIV-AIDS program, a stellar citizen by all accounts.

One Sunday David gathered up the neighborhood children to take them to church. He had specific responsibilities this week: reading the appointed psalm and the Scripture selection, then helping with the youth committee.

After church David ran an errand for neighbors who wanted to borrow a video when some police officers came into the shop where David was conducting business. As he walked by the police, an officer said, "You are one of them, too!" The policemen grabbed David and threw him, along with two other men, into the police vehicle with no explanation. The officer who rode in the backseat of the squad car demanded money from David, so he gave the officer all he had, less than one dollar.

Having completed their business, the police pulled up to their station and let David go. But as he walked away, one of the officers drew his weapon and shot David in the arm and side. David crumpled to the ground. No one came to his assistance, but he managed to collect his strength, get to his feet, and, soaked with his own blood, stumble to the hospital, which happened to be just across the street. He made it, but had it been much farther away, I doubt he would have lived to tell me his story.

Five minutes later, police officers entered the hospital and demanded that hospital staff withhold treatment from David. They courageously ignored the police order and cared for David's injuries. Unfortunately the gunshot wound to his arm was so severe that his hand couldn't be saved. His right arm had to be amputated below the elbow.

The corrupt officers went so far as to take out their inexplicable wrath on David's godfather when the elderly gentleman came to the hospital to inquire about David's condition. They arrested the old man on the spot and threw him in jail without any charge or explanation. The scenario repeated itself the following day when David's brother went to the police station to ask about David. He was also arrested and locked in a cell, but both men were released within a day or two.

The evening after the shooting, police officers came to David's hospital room again. This time they chained him to the bed, again without explanation. He had become a prisoner, an amputee, a victim of oppression in just a few short hours.

Eventually the police charged David with a robbery that had been committed in the neighborhood, but David clearly was innocent. The victim stated that he had reported the robbery to police *after* the time David had been shot, and he never implicated David in the case in any way.

IJM lawyers in Nairobi heard about the case and mobilized an immediate investigation into David's shooting. And though they worked to keep David from being put in jail, the police had other plans. When David was barely well enough to leave the hospital, not fully recovered from his wounds, the police took him to prison—a disease-ridden and overcrowded hellhole where he had to fight for his life against infection and wake up daily to the staggering trauma that his right hand was gone.

IJM lawyers aggressively pursued justice for David, conducting interviews with more than fifty witnesses in less than forty-eight hours and using the overwhelming evidence they gathered to convince senior authorities to drop the charges against David. To ensure that the police officers were held accountable for their crimes, our lawyers also levied charges against the offenders for the shooting and the subsequent cover-up.

In a great victory for David and the citizens of Kenya, the police officers involved in his shooting and cover-up were arrested and held for trial. During preparations for the trial, IJM staff members befriended David. In fact, Victor Kamau, an IJM attorney, has become a role model for David—a role model for all of us. Victor is brilliant, compassionate, one of the most respected lawyers in Nairobi. Victor is also blind. David says, "If Victor can accomplish all he has with the challenges he has faced, then I can try to do the same." David is studying to be a lawyer and says he wants to "help other people the way IJM helped me."

CHAPTER 20

REFUSING TO GIVE UP

Though he may be innocent of criminal activity, the incompetent police officer can be just as troublesome to our rescue efforts as the crooked cop. In developing or rebuilding countries like Cambodia, it is sometimes just as hard to find well-trained, competent officers as honest ones. Most officers simply don't have the training, the understanding of common police practices, or the resources to conduct rescue operations with any degree of efficiency.

Four-year-old Martha lives in Kenya, but her story could just as easily have occurred in Phnom Penh.

She was playing outside with her good friend, Fae, also four. As the girls played, a neighbor approached to talk to the girls. The man, who had moved into the house directly opposite Martha's two months earlier, asked Martha to come into his house. He said he wanted to send her to a kiosk to buy him cigarettes. The man pulled Martha by the hand into his house and closed the door. He threw her on a mattress on the floor, removed her underclothes, and sexually violated her. Outside the house, little Fae heard Martha crying and calling her name, but the door was locked and she couldn't get in. I can't imagine the helplessness this little friend must have felt. Her playmate needed her, but she didn't have the power to do anything for her. A grownup, someone much more powerful than she, was hurting Martha. Before he let Martha go, the neighbor threatened to beat Martha if she told anyone what happened.

Martha went back outside to play with Fae, but in a few minutes she began to cry, telling Fae that the man had "done her bad manners," the term Kenyan children use for sexual intercourse. When Martha's mother and a neighbor woman examined the girl a short time later, they both found evidence that Martha had been sexually assaulted recently.

That evening, a group of young men went to Martha's house and promised the parents they would pay medical expenses, with the understanding that the family would keep the assault quiet. Later, in the middle of the night, the same group of men came back and threatened to kill Martha's father if he reported the matter to police; they also told him that he was not to take her for a medical examination.

The following day Martha's mother decided to take her to the hospital anyway. On the way they ran into the young men, who again threatened to kill the victim's father if Martha was taken to the hospital for an examination. Overcome with fear for her family's safety, Martha's mother returned home with her daughter and did not take Martha for a medical exam that day.

Several days later Martha's parents took her to the police station to file a complaint. They were pleasantly surprised when it appeared that justice might be served rather quickly. They were even more optimistic when the perpetrator was arrested the next day and placed in jail. However, the suspect was soon released on a free bond, because witnesses had failed to appear to file statements, and because a victim's medical document (called a P3 form) had not been submitted. Martha's parents had been too frightened by the threats of the suspect's friends to get the proper medical evaluations.

The same day he was released, the perpetrator went to Martha's house and spoke with her father, threatening to kill him if he pursued the defilement case any further. The next day, tired of being held hostage by threats, Martha's father reported the death threat to the police. At the same time, chief vigilantes, who were weeding out drug dealers in the area, had taken the suspect to a holding cell, from which he was handed over to police. These vigilantes have no arresting power, but they knew this perpetrator was a drug dealer, so they took him into custody without any knowledge of the death threat. It seems the perpetrator had been paying police for protection but had not been giving money to the vigilantes because they had no arresting power.

IJM staff members first heard of the case after the perpetrator was released from jail. They immediately conducted interviews with the victim and her parents and began to uncover the web of deceit, threats, and corruption that complicated this case. Our investigators then located the suspect in the holding cell and went to police to ask that he be detained based on Martha's sexual assault.

In the meantime, Martha had finally received a medical examination and had obtained the forms necessary to file a complaint with the police—twenty-two days after the crime was committed against her. But when Martha's mother went to the police station two days later to record a statement about the crime against her daughter, officers told her she would have to pay for yet another medical examination of both her daughter and the accused at Nairobi Hospital. Because she did not have the required money, Martha's mother returned home, discouraged and frustrated. At this point, nearly three and a half weeks had elapsed since Martha's assault.

After getting a basic understanding of the situation, IJM investigators conducted interviews with the other major players in the case, including the next-door neighbor and Martha's young friend who had witnessed her being pulled into the suspect's house and had heard her cries for help. IJM made trips to the police station to gain information about why documents had not been filed and helped Martha's parents understand what they needed to do to help prosecute the case effectively. They talked with arresting officers and with a friend who had examined and treated little Martha but who actually had no training or license to practice medicine.

IJM went to the police station with Martha and her mother to request the required police medical form and to secure an appointment with the police doctor. (This was the P3 form that Martha's mother was told earlier she would have to pay for if she wanted to proceed with the case.) When they arrived, the officer in charge tried to dissuade our staff from pursuing the case further, because of the lengthy time that had elapsed since the alleged crime. He said he wanted to release Martha's abuser, because the man had been held so long already without being charged. When IJM asked to talk with his supervisor to explain that the delay was because of police handling of the case, the officer acquiesced and authorized a female police officer to accompany a female IJM staff member to the police doctor. Martha and her parents received the necessary P3 form.

After concluding its investigations, IJM staff believed that some police officers had been compromised by bribes. Supporting evidence? For example, even after IJM became involved in the case, and maybe because of our involvement, two police officers, a male and a female, came to Martha's home in the middle of the afternoon. They threatened to arrest Martha's mother if she did not withdraw the case against her neighbor. This poor, brave woman had been through so much already. Just when she thought she might finally see justice served, this new bombshell dropped. I look with deep respect upon parents like Martha's who continue to persevere through fear, danger, frustration, and uncertainty until they see the powerful, well-connected oppressors run out of tactics.

At preliminary hearings, IJM staff stayed involved, lending their presence in the courtroom and their support to the family. There were some complications with the charges and the medical reports, so IJM met with the police commander to insist upon a change in the official charge, to bring greater likelihood of a conviction. The evidence would not have supported the earlier charge listed by police, and the accused probably would have gone free, unpunished.

When the judge heard the case, two four-year-olds brought the most compelling testimony against Martha's abuser: The victim herself and her playmate on the day she was "done bad manners" bravely recounted a consistent, compelling story, corroborated by the adults who had also witnessed the results of the suspect's actions. Several court dates later, the accused was found guilty of indecent assault against Martha and sentenced to four years in prison with hard labor. IJM's lead lawyer in Kenya wrote to us: "In the future, when Martha is old enough to ask what anybody did to protect her, I have no doubt her parents will tell her that there's a friend for little children who watches over their every step. We praise God today, as we feel honored to participate in such an act of love."

Though this case got off to an extremely slow start because of threats, confusion, and police incompetence, it was concluded remarkably quickly. Less than five and a half months after an evil man attacked an innocent, helpless girl playing in her yard, justice was done. My only regret is that Kenyan law doesn't permit harsher sentences as a deterrent for this predator and all others like him.

The criminals and their friends understand something very clearly. Deep in their guts they know they cannot defeat the forces of good in a fight to the finish, so they have learned to prevail in the only way they can—by making the good guys quit. They believe if they just keep chipping away at the good guys' resolve, the good guys will simply give up.

My colleagues spend thousands of hours each year infiltrating the world of aggressive evil. We covertly break into the dark company of those who intentionally and methodically prey upon the weak and the vulnerable—the bullies who enslave, torture, rape, rob, humiliate, and even kill the poor. And it is both fascinating and profoundly instructive to see what they understand so clearly about human nature. What they have learned is this: You and I tend to lose heart long before we actually lose the battle. The strategy of evil is, therefore, simple and focused: Make the forces of goodness quit the struggle. The bullies begin their work with the victims by crushing the force of goodness that lies in their will to resist.

You see, the bad guys, like Martha's rapist and his cronies, wake up every morning thinking about how they can keep themselves out of trouble. They are incredibly committed, because they're looking at going to jail and staying there for a very long time. Somebody has to be equally committed to making sure the perpetrators get in trouble and stay in trouble, including prison, every single day. That's what Martha deserves, and it's what the children in the Cambodian brothels deserve. That's the kind of protection all children deserve, regardless of how poor or marginalized or voiceless they may be.

CHAPTER 21

A SAFE PLACE

Rescuing children from the rape-for-profit vendors doesn't fulfill our complete obligation to those victims. If we believe God calls us to take them *out of* something unspeakably horrendous, we also believe he requires us to help transition them *into* something good, healthy, and stable. They need to be delivered to a place where they will be cared for in body, mind, and spirit, as every child deserves. They also need someone to help them begin the healing process required for the deep scars inflicted upon them over the weeks, months, and years in the brothels.

The girls who have been in the brothels are not just victims of rape or even serial rape; they have been sold and purchased for this purpose like animals or other property. It doesn't take long in that situation, our young friends tell us, to lose their whole sense of self. They simply begin to see themselves as merchandise.

These girls have been traumatized in the most intimate form of torture, and they have been subjected to it day after day in a community that finds such treatment perfectly acceptable. The wide-ranging needs that must be met by an aftercare facility, then, start with an assurance of safety, attention to serious medical needs, particularly after being subjected to sexual abuse repeatedly over time, and psychosocial needs for trauma recovery.

Without good aftercare, it is nearly impossible for the girls to find a life outside the brothel. The exception would be in a case where a girl is put into a brothel but then gets out in a number of days. For a few girls, the best form of care may be at home with a loving family. Dacie was in aftercare only a couple of months, and most of that time was required to get her processed out of the country, not because she needed to be away from her family that long.

Aftercare providers tell us that most young victims of commercial sexual exploitation require a minimum of two years of aftercare. A fundamental look at their young lives explains why. Say a girl of six or eight, like several we met in Svay Pak, lived in a community that endorsed her being sold to be brutalized by foreigners, and her parents make money from her exploitation—one can see how that level of trauma and the needs attendant to girls like this are something a lot of aftercare providers don't fully understand yet. Some have told us that quite frankly.

One aftercare provider, a psychologist who specializes in treating girls after sexual exploitation, said that without the powerful intervention of the hand of God these exceptionally young girls' cases look for best results in terms of "coping" more than "recovery."

In a real sense there is no rescue without aftercare. We must realize that a D-rated aftercare facility is better than an A+ brothel. That would imply that you don't need to find A+ aftercare before you rescue the kids. To truly rescue a kid means to place her in a situation that is better than the one she was taken from. If all that happens is that the child is taken out of a brothel and then three days later she's sent back in, you may have saved her from two nights of rape, but not a lot more than that.

Aftercare is so important that we have included it as one of the four pillars upon which our rescue work stands. Once victims are liberated from any form of bondage, someone must take care to help them into that "better situation," and nowhere is that needed more than in cases of child sexual exploitation.

One of the most frustrating challenges to our aftercare preparations for the Svay Pak operation was the extremely guarded way we had to handle the information about our intentions. All it would take to blow our cover would be a simple rumor about a nongovernmental agency preparing some kind of rescue in Svay Pak, and all the kids could be scattered for weeks. This made broad, open conversations with the aftercare providers very difficult. So we were very conservative about what we would say, even to the aftercare providers, because we couldn't guarantee where that information would end up. One incautious word from a low-level staffer to a relative who had a friend or connection in Svay Pak could put the entire village on alert. We had put such a tight gag on our own mouths that we wouldn't even tell reputable, Christian aftercare providers any more than absolutely necessary before the rescue was completed.

It made for some awkward conversations with people we were just getting to know at the aftercare facilities. Sharon would tell them, "Sometime in the near future we may have some kids—we can't tell you from where or how old—whom we'll need you to take care of for an indefinite period of time. Are you open to that? Oh, and by the way, there may be as many as forty or more." I know I would have wanted more information if I had been in their shoes.

In general, I think they could appreciate our position because these people were familiar with the corruption that abounds in many segments of Cambodian society. But aftercare providers also felt some trepidation as a result of the May 2002 episode, when the police brought fourteen girls to an aftercare house and then came back and arrested them. Because of the resulting international outcry, we believed we probably wouldn't have to worry about that this time around. We also felt we had the high-level support needed to protect these girls from any immigration concerns.

The second challenge was that most of these girls were Vietnamese. Several aftercare providers would not take Vietnamese girls, and none provided a separate facility just for Vietnamese girls. We weren't talking about adding one or two Vietnamese girls but about completely changing the balance of the cultural mix in an aftercare home. If you're helping girls to recover from trauma, asking them to also cross the cultural and ethnic divides that are generations old can seriously complicate and lengthen the road to recovery.

Probably our biggest challenge involved the lack of existing aftercare facilities prepared to take the very young victims, especially when the girl's own family was directly involved or complicit in the abuses. Such children inevitably pass through moments when they say they "want to go back home" or don't want to stay at the aftercare center. Unfortunately most existing aftercare providers in Cambodia indicated they just weren't equipped to handle such cases.

Professionals who have spent decades working with children of sexual trauma expect moments of confusion and sadness when the children say they want to "go home" or "back to Auntie." But such comments aren't taken as an indicator that the abused child should be surrendered back to the abuser. In fact, child protection officers in America would be swiftly terminated for malpractice if they were aware of a child being sold for sexual services by their relatives but failed to rescue the child because the child "wanted to stay." Likewise, any aftercare provider for sexually abused children in America who got confused by a child who wanted to go "back home" to the abuse would be quickly judged unqualified to serve such a child.

These definitely are the hardest cases, and in Svay Pak we had the hardest cases both because they were very young and because families had been involved in the abuses in many cases. Such children would be most confused by being taken out of their environment. But we couldn't have aftercare providers who didn't understand the fundamentals of how to care for such children. Paradoxically, the neediest children, the youngest and most brutally and intimately betrayed by family relationships, are the hardest to place and care for. We found agencies equipped to take children *vulnerable* to abuse but not yet abused; they provided services to reduce their economic and social vulnerability. A few providers would take children who had already been abused, but they did not feel equipped to serve the hardest cases, those who inevitably want to "go back" precisely because they are the ones abused most traumatically (i.e., when they are very young, abused by family, or abused for a very long time).

Some aftercare providers expressed anxiety about their legal exposure; Cambodian law seemed to lack clear provision for standard protective custody of a minor who has been severely sexually abused by a family member. We had heard of nongovernmental organizations that had been threatened with charges of illegal detention by parents who didn't want their daughters kept in those facilities. Naturally those in charge are hesitant to put themselves at risk legally in these kinds of situations.

One extremely difficult case in this regard—a case that almost prompted Sharon to make a special trip to Cambodia—involved two girls from different families but in the same predicament. A pastor friend told us about these girls and asked for our help. One was a fourteen-year-old who had grown up in his church and attended the church's school. She had come to faith in Jesus Christ at the school, even though her family was animistic. The girl lived with her grandmother because her mother was a prostitute. She was known to boldly proclaim the gospel to her friends, even though her grandmother made fun of her or refused to feed her as a punishment for worshiping God.

The girl approached her teacher one day, crying because she had heard her grandmother and her uncle bargaining over the price of her first sexual encounter. The grandmother had placed her granddaughter's virginity on the open market to be sold to the highest bidder. Our pastor friend was extremely troubled over the situation. He couldn't bear to see this bright little flower of his church being sold, and yet he felt he really couldn't get involved in the case because it could jeopardize his entire ministry.

So he came to us and asked if there was anything we could do for this girl, who had actually been taken out of class one day to meet the customer who had offered four hundred dollars for her virginity. At the last moment, he backed out of the deal, saying the price was too high, and she was returned to class. Imagine the thoughts and emotions she must have been experiencing. Imagine the pastor's concern; each morning watching her desk, desperately hoping she would show up to do her schoolwork, praying for another day of childhood innocence.

We quickly contacted people we knew in the area. An aftercare provider went to the grandmother and said, "We'll be happy to take care of the girl from now on. We will take her into our school and teach her, provide for her needs. We know she is costing you money, and we'll take that responsibility off your shoulders."

The grandmother said no.

"Imagine the 'no,'" Sharon said. "No to losing four hundred dollars. No to protecting her granddaughter from rape. For this woman, greed had won out over love and protection.

"Make no mistake about it," Sharon continued. "The grandmother was not 'forced to sell' her granddaughter because she was poor. There are millions and millions of people in the world who are desperately poor and who do not sell their children. She was selling her granddaughter because she wanted four hundred dollars and because she believed she could."

The aftercare facility believed there were no legal provisions by which it could take custody of the girl. Ultimately the pastor went to someone from the governmental office of Social Affairs, who then went to the grandmother and impressed upon her what would happen to her if, in fact, this girl ended up being exploited. But Sharon could not persuade anyone to take the girl out of the grandmother's home based on her being in imminent danger.

That's the kind of legal boundary the aftercare facilities face. If a facility takes custody of such a girl and the grandmother comes to get her back, the facility administrators feel they have no legal right to retain custody of her. And even though there are protective laws on the books, the tough issue is persuading the court to do what the law clearly permits it to do. It's the kind of discussion Sharon has had with governmental officials in Cambodia. And the talks will go on.

In the end the grandmother pulled the girl out of the church school because of the trouble the pastor had caused for her, and had her selling fruit at a roadside stand. So, although she wasn't in school any longer, those who knew her could check on her periodically. At last report she was doing well.

CHAPTER 22

INCREASING THE RISK TO DO EVIL

Many developing countries face tremendous challenges as they try to establish a sound legal system that actually works, especially one that works for the poor. I've mentioned the shortage of legal advocates in countries such as Cambodia, and I've detailed police corruption of several varieties. As these problems add up, they present a complex obstacle course for those who strive to establish the rule of law through effective prosecution. Often, even if perpetrators are arrested, cases never go to trial, and if they do occur, trials rarely reach a conviction. In fact, in the poorest neighborhoods, police don't even make arrests for the purpose of successfully prosecuting the suspect, but rather view the case as a way to extort money from the detainee or as a way to maintain a credible extortion threat that keeps the bribes coming.

As in the case of four-year-old Martha, prosecution of the perpetrator may be stopped in its tracks because parents receive threats on all sides. From the abuser's friends to the corrupt police officers, Martha's family was surrounded by reasons to *not* push the case further. So many victims and their families simply acknowledge that the cost of justice may come too high for them. Sadly, they are forced to decide between paying a price of fear, injury, or death, and persevering through those threats to seek an uncertain justice. And when the police are on the side of the bad guys, it is understandable why so many turn and walk away.

In our work in Cambodia, we were committed to participating at the highest level to gather information from victims to prosecute any perpetrator we discovered profiting from the sexual abuse of children. It wasn't enough for us to rescue the girls. If we merely rescued the girls, the brothel operators would simply go buy more. If we got the perpetrators arrested, even prosecuted, *but not convicted,* we would not have done anything to help the Cambodian authorities establish the necessary deterrent against such abuses.

On the other hand, if we could get them convicted and sent to jail, we would prevent the abuse of hundreds of girls who would have fallen victim to these particular offenders during their jail terms; and we could prevent the victimization of many more by making it too risky for other child brothel keepers to run their businesses. We wanted the punishment to be so great, the risk so high, that the problem would be addressed at the demand level.

We have been eager to do that even with the pedophile customers; IJM has been involved in a number of cases against foreign sex tourists. But from the sex traffickers themselves—those who acquire victims, either by coercion or kidnapping, and then offer them for sale to brothel keepers—we had learned that the most strategic generator of demand is the brothels. However, unlike the traffickers, who are highly mobile, the brothels are sitting ducks for enforcement. The brothels have to open themselves to the public for business and have to hold their victims out openly to their customers if they hope to make money from their trade. But if the customers can find the brothel, then the police can as well; if they want to, the police can catch the perpetrators whenever they want. That's why sex trafficking flourishes only where the police are actively protecting it, because whenever the police want to switch sides and stop it, they can. And that's precisely what we were trying to do, to move the police and the courts from being the protectors of the perpetrators to being the protectors of the children.

CHAPTER 23

IT DOESN'T MAKE SENSE

While we were making preparations for these enforcement operations in Cambodia, in another part of the world we were also trying to ratchet up the costs on a massive business of abuse: the business of human slavery. We tend to associate slavery—the selling of human beings into forced labor—as a phenomenon of a bygone era. But as *National Geographic* made plain in a special feature in September 2003, about twenty-seven million people are held in slavery today. Not in metaphorical slavery, but literal slavery.

The editor in chief pointed out, "There are more slaves in the world today than were extracted from Africa during four hundred years of the transatlantic slave trade." Millions of these victims are held as bonded slaves in South Asia. And, like child sex slavery in Cambodia, it's completely against the law. But there is huge money to be made in the slave business, and the poorest of the poor frequently do not get the benefit of law enforcement. With massive profits to be made and no criminal cost to be paid, the brutality of bonded slavery runs rampant.

Nowhere in the world is the plague of bonded slavery more overwhelming than in India. This massive subcontinent has more computer programmers than any other nation on earth, but it also has hundreds of millions of people who subsist on less than a dollar a day and live as virtual serfs in an ancient system of caste feudalism. By the millions they endure grinding poverty, illiteracy, and oppression that is largely indistinguishable from circumstances of the poor a thousand years ago. Reports by journalists, academics, and human rights researchers have abounded on the brutalities of bonded slavery in India, and over the years IJM has developed operations in India to assist local authorities to respond in a hands-on way to the crimes of bonded slavery, to bring rescue to the victims and justice to the perpetrators.

And of all the areas of the world where IJM is working, I personally have found India the most overwhelming. The sheer scale and relentless intensity of human suffering are, at times, almost suffocating. And yet, the beauty and brilliance of my beloved Indian friends are even more powerful, and we have found unrivaled opportunities to bring transforming help to people and to experience the joy of God. In India my colleagues found the drama of justice on a grand scale: dramatic confrontations with sensational evil coupled with mind-numbing routines of relentless frustration; thrilling moments of liberation and crushing discouragements of wasted effort; courageous acts of loyalty and love and maddening episodes of human weakness.

As you might imagine, it takes an extraordinary sturdiness of heart to provide leadership through both the rapids and doldrums of such a journey, and I don't think they come any sturdier than John Richmond, the director of our bonded slavery work in India. In fact, John's journey to serve with IJM is one of our most inspiring stories of courage and love.

John had just completed his fourth year of practicing law at a firm in Roanoke, Virginia. One of the firm's rising young attorneys, he lived comfortably in his historic neighborhood with his wife, Linda, and their daughter when he heard about the work of IJM and felt an undeniable tug on his heart.

"Are you serious?" his friends and family asked. "Come on now, John. This doesn't make any sense. Linda is seven months pregnant. What do you know about medical care in South Asia?" Even some of his friends at church expressed reservations about his accepting the position with IJM in India. Still, John and Linda decided to go.

"It was not a universally popular decision, even among our church family. Most people thought I was committing career suicide. My wife had never been overseas before, and I certainly had never lived there," John said. "There were plenty of reasons to not go: church, career, budding ministry in our neighborhood, involvement on boards in the community, Linda's pregnancy, and her master's program . . . the list went on and on."

The decision for John and Linda to go to India was based simply on their answering the quiet, persistent call of God on their lives.

"It was not in a dream. I did not hear the voice of God audibly," John explained. "It didn't make sense, and it still doesn't. It's completely foolish. But

God doesn't always make a lot of sense in our human minds. He asked Noah to build a big boat in the desert where it never rained. It didn't make any sense that the Israelites walked around Jericho for seven days singing "Kum Bah Yah" while everyone on the walls laughed at them.

"It didn't make sense for Moses to charge toward the Red Sea with Pharaoh's attacking army bearing down on them. It didn't make sense to leave Ur for Canaan when you're already a pretty wealthy guy like Abram was. It didn't make any sense to be willing to kill Isaac before he could grow up and have kids himself so that Abraham could be the father of a nation, with descendants as diverse as the stars.

"Not everything foolish is of God, but God certainly is a God of foolishness, at least when viewed from our limited perspective. It's a wild thing to leave a great community, great ministry, good job, and take a position that has no vertical or long-term opportunities. In fact, one of my responsibilities is to build a support base for IJM work among the people of South Asia so that I work myself out of a position. Now that's great security for the future! It just doesn't make sense. So we simply tried to get people to understand that, yes, we knew it sounded foolish, but we felt it was what God had called us to do."

I have seen so many times the way God provides blessings for his children when they answer his call, even in extremely trying circumstances such as the Richmonds faced shortly after arriving in India.

When Linda went into labor, they called friends they had just met to take care of their daughter. The friends didn't really know the Richmonds, but they were willing to step in at a moment's notice to come and care for their daughter while Linda went through labor. But labor and delivery were far from routine.

Linda had serious complications during and after delivery and needed a lot of blood in a short period of time. But medicine in India is not readily available as in the United States, where they just order up more blood from downstairs if they need it. John quickly learned that he would have to provide the blood Linda needed to survive—five units.

John immediately gave one unit of his own blood, and wanted to give more, but they wouldn't take any more from him. Linda needed another four units of blood and she needed them in the next few hours. The Richmonds knew only a couple of people in India, and they had only just met them recently, but John called them right away. He also called the church they had visited twice and told them about the danger Linda was in. People started showing up right away, but there was another complication in dealing with the healthcare system in India.

The doctors in the blood bank were all going home; it was the end of their shift. They said, "Sorry, we must go home. It is time for us to go." They had put in their hours and were closing up shop. They seemed to not care, at first, that a life was in jeopardy if they refused to stay and help.

"You can't leave," John said forcefully to the last staff member remaining. "You have to stay here so my wife can live. She needs this blood and there are people coming to give it now."

Reluctantly, the man agreed to stay. But even then the process wasn't an immediate one. First, the blood had to be drawn, then screened, then cross-checked before it could go to Linda. Meanwhile, John was meeting people, introducing himself as they drove in to give blood for a woman they did not know, thanking them for this incredible gift.

"I realized right then that God, in that moment, was wrapping his arms around us, saying, 'I love you all so much that I'm going to take care of you, and I'm going to do that through people you don't even know,'" John said.

They weren't out of the woods yet, though. Not by a long shot. Linda was still in grave danger.

Though they had finally gotten the units of blood started, it wasn't clear if it had happened in time. Linda was in a great deal of pain and she looked close to death. Even the doctors thought she wasn't going to make it.

John walked out of Linda's room and down the hospital hallway, far away from friends and family, far away from Virginia and the life he knew and loved. He began to pray.

"What are you doing, God? If anybody deserves your blessing, and an easy pregnancy and delivery, it's Linda. She's here, she's following you, but she's also following me. You have given me this cool, superhero, exciting job. She's got the same job she had before, the one she loves, which is to raise our kids right now. She could do that job just as easily in Virginia as she could in India. I can't do mine anywhere else. I think she deserves your mercy."

John felt like God spoke to him in that moment that: "No. You don't deserve anything. You haven't earned my favor or my blessing by coming to this country. I'm your Father; I'm the sovereign God, and I give out of the wealth of my blessing. You've got to trust me that I love Linda and I love your baby more than you do. I want what's best for them more than you do. You've got to trust me."

Miraculously, Linda pulled through. She and the baby would be fine.

"I didn't want to trust God in those moments," John said. "I wanted to use my wit, wisdom, ingenuity, creativity, education, and experience to go in and fix the problem.

"It was a great lesson for me to learn as I look at this huge problem of slavery in South Asia. My wit, wisdom, ingenuity, creativity, education, and experience are not going to budge that system. It is going to be because God is there, and God cares for those people.

"Linda's struggle to survive after the delivery of our baby reminded me that this has nothing to do with me, but that God invites us to participate with him, remembering that it's about him and his love for the people. It's about the fact that God wants to rescue them, that God wants someone to come and intervene on their behalf because he created them. Their value doesn't come from their caste. It doesn't come in their ability to make us Westerners feel good that we're putting a band-aid on a major problem. We do not do this so that we can feel better about the plight of the developing world as we live in luxury. It really is only about God. He makes their rescue a reality."

CHAPTER 24

CHAINS OF SLAVERY BROKEN

Representatives from a well-known nongovernmental organization contacted our field office headed by John Richmond about a sponsored child who had gone missing.

"His name is Muni Raj," they told us. "He is thirteen, and he has been attending school and receiving care from our facility. He's seemed distracted, distant lately, and he mentioned that he might not be able to come to school anymore."

"Did he say why?" asked John.

"No. But we believe he lives in one of the villages near the school. He's a really sweet kid, and we're very concerned about him. Do you think you can help?"

John and his team tracked Muni Raj down in a nearby village, where Muni Raj's father was a bonded slave on a huge agricultural plantation. His father, wanting more for his young son than he had experienced, had been sending Muni Raj to the school, but now the plantation owners thought the boy was old enough to perform a man's work in the fields.

The first beating his father received because Muni Raj was not working on the plantation wasn't enough to keep Muni Raj home from school. Though he was willing to drop out to save his father from future beatings, both his parents urged him to return to school the next day. Soon the owners' men were back again, this time delivering a more severe beating.

It was too much for the boy to bear, and he pleaded with his parents to let him work in the fields instead of going to school. Reluctantly, they agreed and Muni Raj gave up his education, along with his hope for the future. Instead of spending his days in a classroom, Muni Raj was performing backbreaking labor in the fields, forced to witness the harsh treatment of his fellow slaves, and in the process losing his playful demeanor, his boyish wonder about the world, and the optimism that had characterized him until now.

Early in John's investigation of Muni Raj's case he met Ashok, a bright, determined seventeen-year-old. Ashok stood out because he was unusually large, a tall, strapping young man with broad shoulders. If he had attended an American high school, there's no doubt he would have caught the attention of the football coach.

"How did you come to be here, Ashok?"

"My father, grandfather, aunts, and uncles have always been here."

"Are you free to go?"

"No, but I would love to get out of here."

John told Ashok he had some ideas about how he could gain his freedom.

"Can we meet your father?"

"My father is an old man," Ashok answered. "He is frail, but he still works eighteen hours a day as a guard, a watchman. Yes, I'll take you to meet him."

So our investigators met Narakalappa, indeed, a very old man. He was so thin, just skin and bones, standing about five foot eight and weighing maybe a hundred pounds, with wild gray hair and a scraggly beard. He had a sweet, crooked-toothed smile and dark, leathery skin baked hard by decades of labor in the hot sun. He had remarkably deep eyes that had no doubt witnessed a great deal of India's history, from partition to Gandhi's walk across the nation—eyes that had witnessed the promise of hope and change but never saw any of the hope and change applied to his own life or family.

Narakalappa willingly told us his story. He thought he was born around 1933, but we have found that the older generation in India often underestimates its age. Though he said he was seventy, he looked more like eighty to our team.

When he was born, his parents had already sold themselves into slavery to pay off a debt of about twenty dollars in medical expenses for Narakalappa's grandparents. They simply signed themselves over and began to work on this plantation because, at the time, they had no other options. And this is where the great deception occurs, where the real evil of the system is evident. Narakalappa's parents may have thought, *We'll both work here at the plantation, and we should knock out this twenty-dollar debt pretty quickly, then get back to our normal lives.* That was back in the 1920s, and now, eighty years later, several generations of this family were bonded slaves on the same plantation, for the same, original debt.

Even back in 1920, twenty dollars, now equivalent to about nine hundred rupees, was not an exorbitant sum. Under normal circumstances it could be earned in a few months, especially by two people working together. But these slaveholders do not work under normal circumstances.

Instead, the plantation owner never paid them any wages. They never received a single rupee for their labor, not in the first year, not in the second year, never. They still owed the original debt *and* accrued interest. Because they weren't receiving any money, there was no way they could save or pay down the debt. They were spending their lives' energies and all their waking hours working for their owner.

While living and working on the plantation, they had a son, Narakalappa, who became a second-generation slave, property of the plantation owner. As soon as he was able to do any work, around early elementary-school age, Narakalappa was forced to labor for the owner as well. By the time he was a teenager, he was performing a grown man's job, with no opportunity to go to school, though he was able to gain some education from groups that ventured into the village from time to time. He viewed labor on the plantation as his lot in life and believed it was all he would ever know.

Narakalappa later married a woman in the village, where hundreds of other plantation slaves lived, and they had children together. His first wife passed away from an illness, and he married again, this time to Ashok's mother.

Over the decades people simply forget about paying off a debt and accept slavery as their purpose in life. They are born into slavery and will always be slaves. There is no sense that things can change. And the caste system in India feeds upon this mind-set. Those of the higher caste need those of the lower caste; otherwise, there is no one beneath them to stand upon. Many, not just the slave owners, benefit from the existence of a class of slaves.

Like his parents, Narakalappa was paid just a small amount for his labor, never enough to satisfy his debt. From time to time, if a family member had a medical expense, or if a daughter needed a modest dowry, the plantation owner would give a worker more money and add it to his debt. If Narakalappa had normal needs, such as money for sandals or clothing for his children, his owner would provide it, then add the amount to the rising total of his debt.

Most victims just don't understand that there's any another option until after they are freed. At this plantation the circumstances had become so bad that many, including Ashok, were ready to find a way out of the situation. He was further motivated to speak out when the owners' men harshly punished a slave who had left the plantation to visit relatives in a neighboring city. The slave had stayed with the relatives and found a job where he actually began to earn real money, until the plantation owners hunted him down and brought him back to the plantation. They beat him severely to provide a deterrent to the rest of the slaves. In actuality the act stirred up the restless hearts of the younger generation. *This is all we've ever experienced, and we don't know what the other alternatives are, but they can't be worse than this. There must be something better.*

The owners continued to perpetuate the abuse of the younger generation. When children tried going to school instead of working in the fields, the owners beat up the parents until the kids felt guilty enough to quit school. That's what happened with Muni Raj.

IJM staff members completed the investigation, gathering evidence, recording the names of bonded slaves at this plantation. They put all the information in an intervention report and submitted it to governmental officials. As part of the report, they calculated that even if Narakalappa and his family had worked only seasonally for the plantation owners, and if they had made minimum wage, they would have paid off the original debt hundreds of times over. And yet they hadn't received any wages at all.

The debt itself really becomes an insignificant piece of their stories. They are simply owned by another human being. That's how they see themselves; that's how they are viewed by others. In fact, the people of this village even used the taboo word *slave* to refer to themselves. In most parts of India, even when people are owned by others, they refuse to call themselves slaves. In contrast, this community used the term freely.

Narakalappa agreed to speak up during the governmental inquiry of the case, which IJM staff participated in for all ten hours of the process. It actually turned into a race with the plantation owners, who were rushing around the fields trying to round up their slaves and secret them away to a place they wouldn't be found by the government. IJM staff also scurried about the property trying to round up workers to get them to testify. As in so many situations we're involved with, if we can't get victims to testify, we don't have a case against the perpetrators because there are no grounds for prosecution. In this case, if we couldn't locate victims who would testify, these bonded slaves would not be released. It was an intense few hours spent just trying to find people, for their sake and for the sake of our legal efforts. John and the other team members did locate many but not all of the slave families.

Narakalappa testified well. But the real, gripping testimony came from his son, Ashok.

Naturally the slave owner denied any wrongdoing on his plantation. "All these people work for me, but they are free to go at anytime they wish."

Seventeen-year-old Ashok stood right next to his family's owner. "No, that's not true. We are not free to leave. We can't just go anywhere, anytime we want."

The slave owner turned to Ashok and tried to shout him down. "No! You're a liar!" he screamed. "That's not true!"

Ashok looked the man in the eye. "You'll say that in front of these men, but it's not the truth. We are threatened with beatings if we ever try to leave this place and go do something different with our lives."

Ashok showed incredible courage for someone who has been completely powerless to this point in his life. He was risking everything at that moment. If the prosecution was not successful, he would be a young man without refuge, without a place to go, without hope. He was betting his future, possibly his life, on the fact that IJM was going to help break the grip that slavery had held on his family for generations.

"It is such a moving experience to see people who are willing to put it all on the line for their freedom," John reported after Ashok's testimony.

In a fairly quick decision, the government ruled that Narakalappa and his family, along with several other families of slaves, must be freed from the bonds of slavery held by that plantation owner.

Muni Raj, the thirteen-year-old who had been forced to labor in the fields alongside his father, also was released and allowed to go back to school.

After the release, John Richmond brought together all the people who were freed to discuss what had just happened. "Your problems haven't ended," John told the group of freed slaves. "They have changed, from being in bondage to managing freedom. In many ways, it may be even harder for you in the next few weeks than it was before, but no good will ever come for you or your family unless this change occurs."

We have learned that it is important at these times to give freed victims a fairly sober view of what is to come.

"It is extremely important for you to support, care for, and look out for each other," John said. "The slave owners are going to come and say to you, 'It doesn't matter what the government and these lawyers just did, you still owe us; you still work for us. We own you.'

"You need to be ready for that, and you need to stand up for your freedom. Your former owners are going to harass, and they're going to compel; they're not going to go quietly. But if we all stand up to them consistently, we can achieve the desired result, lasting freedom."

Unfortunately all those things happened in this case. We visited the victims many times over the following weeks, offering support and financial assistance from time to time to help them make it through a really hard time. One of the owners actually came and stole one of the freed victim's clothes, so he had nothing to wear. The plan was that the former slave would be desperate enough that he would go back to the owner for help. Instead IJM staff bought him a set of clothes.

Every time our people visited they talked about the importance of not selling themselves back into slavery, which would just continue the cycle for their children and grandchildren.

For Narakalappa, his seventy-plus years of slavery were over. He didn't need to work any longer. He needed rest. He needed to be free to retire. IJM staff took him on a trip to the capital city, Chennai. He was amazed at the huge number of cars, the speed with which they traveled, the pace of life in the city. I was privileged to join him on a trip to the Bay of Bengal, where he saw the ocean for the first time in his life. He stood there as wide-eyed as a child, smiling at the vast expanse of sea. What a dramatic picture that made: the striking contrast of a life that had been bound to a single plot of land for decades, now standing before the boundless ocean at the start of his life as a free man.

Ashok wants to be a professional driver, so we researched the requirements and the resources that would make possible his dream to support his family.

The day of the police raid of the plantation, John said to Narakalappa, "Tonight you're going to bed for the first time as a free man. How do you feel about that?"

The old man smiled and said, "That's right. No one owns me. . . ." And he smiled some more.

John told him, "We didn't really rescue you. It wasn't IJM or the people you see around you. You were rescued by a loving God who created you from the beginning, who cared enough to hear your plight and to come to your rescue. He wants you to be free and to know him."

The next morning Narakalappa woke up free.

CHAPTER 25

A YOUNG WOMAN'S VOICE ECHOES ON CAPITOL HILL

It had been nearly four months since our investigators' last trip into Svay Pak. Bob Mosier and his investigators believed enough time had passed to release much of the pressure in the brothel village since our investigative associate had fought with a sex tourist in the street. Mosier appointed Robert Earle, a former police detective from New Zealand, as the new lead investigator in the case.

In a series of strategic planning sessions, Bob Mosier, Sharon Cohn, and I had gathered at our Washington, D.C., headquarters with the investigators and other critical staff members now on our Cambodia project team. The puzzle broke down into three large pieces: (1) a law enforcement challenge to rescue the kids, (2) a legal challenge to bring the perpetrators to justice, and (3) a social services challenge to provide long-term aftercare for the children. We have developed a systematic methodology for analyzing cases, and this is where the relentless process of strategic problem solving goes to work. The initial puzzle was to figure out how we were going to bring rescue to a large number of the victimized girls in Svay Pak. This was largely a political and tactical challenge. How would we get the most senior political authorities in Cambodia to direct their police resources to cooperate fully with us? What would we ask the Cambodian police to actually do? In other words, what tactical plan of operations could we provide that would *actually work*?

First, we examined the political challenge. Given the failure of the Cambodians to respond to the Svay Pak problem over the past two years and the high-level police protection of the Svay Pak brothels, how would we get the Cambodian authorities to make this a priority now? Fundamentally these child victims of horrific sexual abuse carried no political weight in Cambodia at all, especially Vietnamese children. They had no voice of influence to mobilize the

Cambodian authorities to come to their rescue. No Cambodian authority feared the political consequences of failing to address child rape in Svay Pak. In such situations, we have simply learned to ask: If the political authorities are not interested in the children, what are they interested in? There can be a great variety of answers to this question depending upon the country and the context, but many times the answer is that they are interested in their relationship with the U.S. government. Accordingly, if the U.S. government brings its influence to bear on behalf of these child victims, it can frequently provide the necessary incentive for the authorities to act.

But that simply raises another question: What is going to motivate the U.S. government to make this issue of child sex trafficking a priority in its relationship with a foreign government? After all, the U.S. government will already have a host of diplomatic, economic, and security priorities it is trying to emphasize: trade issues, terrorism issues, counternarcotics issues, geopolitical issues. What will move the plight of powerless sex-trafficking victims up the list of priorities of the U.S. government?

The answer, which might surprise many Americans, is quite straightforward. It turns out that it is the American people who can effectively make this issue a priority for the U.S. government. Before the year 2000, issues of sex trafficking and forced prostitution were simply not a significant priority in the U.S. government's relationships with foreign governments. All of that changed, however, with the passage of the Trafficking Victims Protection Act of 2000. A diverse coalition of advocacy groups and grass-roots Americans fought for and secured passage of a law that would require the U.S. Department of State annually to rank countries on whether they were meeting minimum standards in combating sex trafficking (and other forms of human trafficking). Moreover, if specific countries were found to be failing to make even "significant efforts" to try to meet minimum standards, they could be placed on Tier 3—the lowest tier of the rankings—and some of the goodies they received from the U.S. government might be jeopardized through sanctions.

IJM worked very hard with a number of friends on Capitol Hill and advocacy groups in helping draft the bill and in seeking its passage. I was able to testify before Congress on several occasions to explain what IJM had learned about the global epidemic of sex trafficking and the need for the U.S. government to use its influence to make the protection of sex-trafficking victims a priority with foreign governments. I think our experience in the field, particularly the thousands of hours we had spent infiltrating the commercial sex industry, allowed us to contribute a number of important insights in the debate. But I think our most important contribution was in bringing the stories of victims before the Congress, victims who provided a human face of urgency to an issue that could otherwise be lost in the fog of abstraction, euphemisms, and sterile statistics. And by far the most powerful moment in that effort occurred when we brought one of these victims to testify personally before the U.S. House of Representatives committee on international relations.

———

It took an enormous effort to get Anita from her home in Nepal and all the way to Washington. Perhaps even greater for Anita was the cultural and psychological distance she had traveled from growing up in rural Nepal. In fact, she had never even seen a train until she was twenty-six years old. And now here she was, less than five feet tall, escorted by two large IJM security personnel into the dark-wood-paneled chamber of a congressional hearing room with its deep carpet, massive chandeliers, imposing portraits, and row upon row of microphones. The truth is, few victims of forced prostitution can articulate their stories to strangers, even in the most comfortable, intimate, and familiar settings, let alone before glaring lights and amid the intimidating chambers of the U.S. Congress. Such an experience would traumatize most trafficking victims. But Anita was extraordinary. A young woman of great intelligence and dignity, she was eager to tell her story to the world; and, as it would turn out, none of the trappings of power and authority in that chamber could possibly compete with the simple majesty and moral power of her story.

When I had completed my brief remarks before the House committee, I adjusted the microphone for Anita and sat back and watched as her simple words proceeded to roll back the sea of confusion, apathy, and ignorance that beset the sanitized discourse around sex trafficking.

My name is Anita. I am twenty-eight years old. I am from Nepal. Last year, my husband took another wife. Soon after, he began to beat me, torment me, and disregard my children. I decided it would be best if I and my children moved out of our home in order to support myself and my children.

I made money by buying vegetables from farmers and selling them in the village market. On November 22, last year, I boarded the bus in order to go pay for my vegetables. I sat next to a Nepali man and woman. They offered me a banana to eat and I took it. Soon after I ate the banana, while I was still on the bus, I got a very bad headache. I told the man and woman that I had a headache, and they offered me a pill and a bottle of mineral water to help me swallow the medicine. Immediately I felt myself becoming groggy, and then I fell unconscious.

The next thing that I remember is waking up in the train station in Gorakhpur, India. I am from a mountain village. I did not know what a train was, and of course I had never been to India. I asked the man where I was. I was confused by the long cars that I was riding in and the strange surroundings.

The man told me not to cry out. He informed me that there were drugs (hashish) tied around my waist and that I had just smuggled them across an international border. He told me that if I brought the attention of the police, I would be in trouble for smuggling the drugs. I did not remember the drugs being tied around my waist, but I could feel plastic bags on my stomach under my dress.

The man also told me that if I stayed with him, I would receive twenty thousand rupees from the sale of the drugs when we arrived in Bombay. I did not know how to get back to Nepal, I do not speak any of the Indian languages, and I believed that I was already in trouble for carrying drugs. The man told me that he was my friend and that I could refer to him as my brother. I decided to stay with him. It was a five-day journey to Bombay by train.

When we got to Bombay, he told me to wait at the train station while he went to sell the drugs. When he returned, he told me that the police had confiscated his drugs and that he did not have any money. He said that I would have to go to his friend's house and wait while he got some money. He called his friend on the phone from the train station, and she came to meet us there. She was a Nepali woman. She said her name was Renu Lama.

I left the train station with Renu Lama. My "brother" told me that he would meet me at her house at four o'clock that afternoon.

As I walked with Renu Lama, she told me not to look at people because she lived in a very dangerous neighborhood and there were some bad people that I should not make eye contact with. When we arrived at her house, Renu Lama told me that I should take a bath. I told her that I would wait until four o'clock when my "brother" came because he was carrying my clothes. She told me my "brother" was not coming. I waited until evening, but he never came. Finally I took a bath, and Renu Lama gave me some of her old clothes to wear.

Renu Lama then asked me if I could write a letter for her. I did. She dictated what she wanted to say to her family, and I wrote the letter. When I had finished writing the letter, Renu Lama took away the ink pen. She went to my room and took away all of the pens, pencils, and paper that I could possibly write with. I realized that the writing of the letter had been a test. Now that they knew I was literate, they were keen to keep me from communicating with anyone outside.

I felt very scared that evening, and I refused to eat anything. I soon noticed that many men were coming in and out of the house, and I realized that it was a brothel. I began howling and shouting. I said that I wanted to leave.

Renu Lama told me that I was ignorant. She said that I did not just come easily, and I could not go easily. She said that I had been bought, and I would have to work as a prostitute in order to pay them back. I was never told how much they had paid for me. Renu Lama and two of her associates told me that all the women in the house were "sisters" and that we had to support each other. I cried a lot, but they comforted me and brought me a fine dinner, complete with chutney and a pickle.

The next day, though, I insisted that I wanted to leave. The women began to slap me on the face. They cut off my hair. It was shoulder length in the back with short bangs in the front. Now that I had short hair, I knew that I could not leave the brothel without everyone identifying me as a prostitute. In my culture, short hair is the sign of a wild woman.

Then I was told that all of the women in the brothel had to bathe three or four times each day. The women all bathe nude, and they bathed together, four or five girls at a time. I had never bathed nude before, and I had never bathed with other naked women. When I expressed my shyness, the other women mocked me. They grabbed me and stripped off my clothes. They forced me to bathe with them.

For the next couple of days the women beat me often. They slapped me on the face and head with their hands and hit me about the waist and thighs with metal rods. I begged to be let go. I said that I wanted to return to my children in time for the biggest holiday of our culture. The women mocked me. They told me that if I worked with them for a couple of days, they would send me home with three bricks of gold and thirty to forty thousand rupees for the festival.

I was also forced to learn Hindi, the language of most of the customers. At times I couldn't speak enough Hindi, I was beaten about the waist and thighs with the iron rods.

When I was alone with one of the other women, I offered her my gold earring if she would let me go. She said no. Later I learned that three of the women were in the brothel voluntarily, and they were in charge. There were six other women in the brothel, and, I learned, they had all been tricked and forced like me. Renu Lama and the woman to whom I had offered my earring were in the brothel voluntarily.

All of the women in the brothel were from Nepal. The six who were forced had all been brought from Nepal but under different pretenses. One girl married a man who said he was taking her to Bombay to buy gold. He then left her in a brothel.

None of the other girls could read or write. I am literate, because I am Brahmin and the women in my community are educated.

The women tried to reassure me that being a prostitute was not that bad. All of my food, housing, and clothes were provided. All I would have to do, they said, was sell my body.

On the fourth day that I was in the brothel, my first client came to me. I refused to have sex with him. He had already paid for me, so he grabbed me and tried to rape me. I fought him off. He had managed to get my clothes off, but he was very frustrated because I was resisting him so much. He stormed out and asked for his money back. A couple of the brothel owners (voluntary prostitutes) came in and beat me. When they were done, the same man came back in. I then said that I would have sex with him only if he wore a condom. I knew about the need for condoms, since I had learned that some of the other victims had very bad diseases. At first he refused, but after another fight he finally agreed to wear a condom. By the time he left, he had used three condoms.

I only had one client my first day. But the next day, and every day after, I had three or four clients each day. I managed to get an ink pen. I would write messages to the police on the inside of cigarette boxes and send them out with my clients. Many clients promised to help, but none did.

Each client paid 220 rupees to be with me for an hour. I had to give the entire sum to the brothel owners. Often the men would give me 5 or 10 rupees extra. I used the money to buy condoms, since the brothel owners would not provide them for me.

Still I was not able to go out to buy the condoms myself. In fact, for the entire month and a half that I was in the brothel, I was never allowed to go out into the sun. Some of the other girls got to go to the hospital when they fell ill. But I never got sick, so I could never leave.

I lived on the second floor of the brothel. The six of us who had been brought there against our will were kept on the second floor. There were no windows on our floor. The three who ran the brothel lived downstairs.

Downstairs there was a door that led outside. Several iron rods used for beatings leaned against the wall beside the door. One of the owners always guarded the door. Outside the door was a metal gate. When customers were not coming in and out, the gate was closed. The gate was held by a heavy chain that was locked by a large padlock.

One night I tried to run away with one of my associates. We were caught by the brothel owners before we even made it to the gate. My friend was sold to another brothel in Sarat where the brothels are said to be even more torturous than the ones in Colaba, Bombay, where I was held.

After serving clients for about eight days, an elderly man came to me as a client. When I was alone with him in the room, I told him that he was old enough to be my father. I told him, "I am like your daughter." I told him my story. He said that he had plenty of money and a Nepali friend. He promised to help me escape. He spent the entire night with me. That was the first time I had been with a client for more than an hour. I cried on him all night long.

The next morning he left with a promise that he would send his Nepali friend to help me. He said that I would know his friend had come when a Nepali man came to the brothel, asking to be with Anita, and carrying a gift of candies.

A few days later, a young Nepali man came to see me. He brought a gift of candy. I told him my story. He promised to help me escape. I told him that I did not trust anyone. In order for me to trust him, he would have to go to Nepal, report about me to my father and brother, and bring back some of my personal photographs as a result. The elderly client paid for him to go to Nepal. Before he left, the boy gave me his address in Bombay.

Some of my associates overheard the owners saying that they were also planning to sell me to a brothel in Sarat, because I was too much trouble. I decided that I could not wait until the boy returned from Nepal. I had to try again to run away. I asked some of the other girls to run with me, but they were too afraid. We had been told that we would be killed if we tried to run away. But I determined that I would rather die than stay in the brothel. The other girls pooled their money together and came up with two hundred rupees. In exchange for the two hundred rupees, I promised that if I made it out alive, I would get help for them.

A couple of days later, I had a perfect opportunity. Renu Lama was out of town again. The owner who was watching the gate was drunk. A new maid had just been hired to clean and cook in the brothel. The new maid was doing chores and had left the gate open just a little bit. In the middle of the night, I would guess about 4:00 A.M., I ran out of the brothel. I was wearing only my nightgown and carrying a slip in my hand. I just ran down the street as fast as I could.

As I was running I saw two police officers. They were in civilian clothes, but I knew they were police officers by the belts that they were wearing. I ran to them, told them my story, and handed them the address of the Nepali boy. They took one hundred rupees from me in order to pay for a taxi. They put me in a taxi that took me to the Nepali boy's house.

When I arrived at the house, the Nepali boy was not there. But another Nepali man and his wife were there. They were friends of the Nepali boy and they agreed to take me in. The police left me with that family.

I did not know it at that time, but that same day, the Nepali boy had met Bob [Mosier], Director of Investigations, International Justice Mission. He told Bob my story. Soon after I ran away from the brothel, Bob and the police raided the brothel where I had been. After searching through the brothel, the police with Bob learned that I had run away ear-

lier that night. They came with Bob and met me at the house where I was staying.

Bob told me that I could go back to the brothel to get my things. I was too scared to go back, because I thought I might be forced to be a prostitute again. But Bob assured me that I was safe. I went back to the brothel with Bob. I showed him all of the hiding places where they found the other girls. All of the girls who were forced were released from the brothel and a way was provided for them to go back home. The two owners who were there that night are now in jail. Bob also arranged for me to return home to my family in Nepal.

First I went home to my family, but it was very uncomfortable. The people in the village laughed at me. In my culture a woman is scorned if she is missing for just one night. I had been missing for two months. It was very hard for my family, especially since we are members of the Brahmin caste. So today I live in Katmandu. I work as a domestic servant in the city. I am still without my children since they went to live with their father when I was taken away. I am told that my husband's new wife is very cruel to my children. But my husband does not want my children to be with me, because of where I have been.

I know that my story will help other women who are forced into prostitution. I am proud that I already was able to help Bob free the other girls in the brothel where I worked. Though I am grateful to be here to share my story, I am sad that I am not with my children—that my children cannot be here with me.

Thank you.

With that, Anita slowly withdrew from the microphone. She sat back in her chair, with the same simple dignity she'd exhibited while speaking. A stunned silence filled the chamber. Everything and everyone in the room had suddenly become very small compared to this tiny woman in a sari from Nepal. For a moment, it seemed as if the last meaningful word in the universe had been used up, and there just was nothing left to say. Then the committee chairman thanked Anita and expressed earnest commitment to "the issue."

Over the next year, things would not simply return to normal in the world. Anita's testimony brought to light the blinding truth of what was happening to millions of sex-trafficking victims all over the world. Americans and their elected representatives were finding their voice and demanding that sex trafficking be made a priority in American foreign policy. On October 28, 2000, the voice and values of the American people were placed on the side of Anita and the millions of women and girls being tortured and raped in the global business of rape for profit—the Trafficking Victims Protection Act became law.

After her testimony Anita graciously joined my family for dinner in our home. It was an extraordinary event in the life of our family. I'll always remember the way she lingered so gently and affectionately over my small children, aching in her heart for her own little ones, whom she had not been permitted to see or embrace or hold for more than a year. I remember her reciting the bittersweet poem she had composed about her losses. There was an unmistakably sacred beauty to the evening. Yet no one then could have anticipated the way Anita and the Trafficking Victims Protection Act she helped pass would be the critical tool for seeking justice for young girls abused in a remote village on the other side of the world.

CHAPTER 26

PREPARING TO INFLUENCE

When Will and Sharon returned from that first operation in Svay Pak in the spring of 2002, we knew we had fresh, appalling evidence in living color of the abuses taking place there. We wanted to prepare the political climate in Washington, D.C., to bring maximum pressure upon the Cambodian authorities to clean up the cesspool of abuse in Svay Pak and to use the leverage of the new Trafficking Victims Protection Act to make the children a priority they would never otherwise be.

As the U.S. Department of State prepared to issue its report ranking countries on their performance in combating sex trafficking, Sharon took on an important task: ensuring that they and their watchdogs on Capitol Hill and in the media saw what we had seen in Svay Pak. Appropriately, Cambodia was placed on Tier 3 of the report and faced sanctions if it did not demonstrate decisive action in responding to the open and notorious epidemic of child sexual exploitation in their country. Moreover, as the new U.S. ambassador to Cambodia was being prepared for his confirmation hearing before the Senate, friends in the human rights community taught us how to prepare formal questions from friendly senators to the new ambassador that requested his response, on the record, about what he was going to do about sex trafficking in Cambodia and Svay Pak in particular.

So when we gathered the Cambodia project team at IJM headquarters to consider how to motivate the Cambodian authorities to direct their police to cooperate with IJM in a large-scale Svay Pak action, a consensus emerged. After hours of intense discussions in the executive conference room, the walls were covered with large sheets of paper, filled with multicolored lists, arrows, diagrams, and flow charts.

"So," I summarized, "the objective of the next investigative deployment is to develop fresh, compelling evidence so overwhelming that we can take it to the ambassador and ask him to meet with the highest Cambodian authority and request, on our behalf, the full police cooperation that we need to run a large-scale rescue and arrest operation in Svay Pak."

Mosier, searching for the bottom line, turned to Sharon. "Sharon, what do you need from the investigative team to build the strongest case possible?"

"Well, first of all we need a large number of videotaped transactions involving very young girls and specific perpetrators who are not just towel-boys but significant entrepreneurs," Sharon answered. "There's no use getting the petty pimps on video if the actual entrepreneurs who bring business energy to Svay Pak just walk away and then hire their next towel-boy. So we have to videotape specific transactions with specific victims and perps that include all the elements of the crimes taking place, not only for purposes of convincing the ambassador, but also for eventual prosecution. We need the actual location where each transaction took place, so we need a detailed mapping of Svay Pak. We also need lots of victims, to justify large-scale law enforcement action, and we need lots of young victims so the perps face serious jail time."

"What's the law on that, Sharon?" I asked. "How is a 'minor' defined in Cambodia for purposes of these offenses in order for serious jail time to kick in?"

"It's under fifteen," Sharon answered, "so we need victims fourteen and under."

"How many do we need?" Bob asked.

"To really capture the scope of the crimes being committed, we'll need to document a large number of victims. If we got two cases from each brothel, that would provide a significant amount of evidence," Sharon said.

"I agree. I think we need at least thirty to give the case overwhelming weight and to justify a large enforcement action," I said. "Do you think that's a realistic goal, Will?"

"Yes, sir," Will Henry replied.

There were still huge, unanswered questions about what investigative tactics to use, how we would make the presentation to the ambassador if the investigation was successful, what we would ask the Cambodians to do in Svay Pak, and what we would do with the kids and the perpetrators after a rescue operation. But at least we had our investigative target defined and a clear idea of whom the investigative material would have to convince. So now it was time to deploy members of the investigative team and take the next big step forward.

CHAPTER 27

IT'S WHO YOU KNOW

"Robert, you'll need to pick up the investigation where Will and Sharon left off," Mosier told Robert Earle. "I want you to complete a comprehensive documentation of the brothels in Svay Pak that are using minors for sexual exploitation. You'll need to set up an operative network if you're going to succeed; there's just no way to do this all on your own."

"I have a law enforcement friend in the States who offered to connect me with a couple of guys who are doing freelance investigative work in Asia if I ever needed it," Robert said. "I'll start with him and see what I can find."

So much of good police work depends upon your contacts, whom you know, and Robert's relationship with this contact really paid off. He referred Robert to two operatives: American nationals who operate in Southeast Asia on a covert level, doing various work for private, corporate, and governmental organizations. As a favor, Robert's friend approached these two operatives, told them about Robert and the work of IJM to rescue kids from forced prostitution, and asked if they would be able to assist IJM in the operation. Both men agreed.

One of the operatives, Mark, was a highly trained and skilled former U.S. special forces member who now works independently as a security consultant and investigator. Mark was willing to fly from his base in Southeast Asia to Cambodia to work with our team for a week at no charge. Because of his skills and reputation, Mark has earned the right to charge very high rates for his services, but he graciously donated his time and efforts to IJM because of the kind of work we were doing and the vulnerability of the victims he would be helping. IJM simply covered his travel expenses, food, and lodging. Mark is just one more example of the way God continues to provide the very best in this work of rescuing the oppressed, work that I believe is so very close to his heart.

The other operative, already working in Cambodia, also agreed to help, making himself available for one or two nights' investigations.

When Robert found out he would now be the primary undercover investigator in Svay Pak, he began conducting preliminary research on Cambodia, including the language, culture, climate, currency, and political situation. Much of this information had been pulled together by Will Henry, and Robert began studying it aggressively. He also researched the political and organizational allies in and around the area. He went over escape and evasion plans in case the operation turned imminently dangerous and our staff had to leave the country in a hurry. The last piece of in-office research was to review case information from earlier investigations, including our investigators' trips into Svay Pak in 2000, 2001, and 2002.

The importance of thoroughness and preparedness cannot be overstated when lives are on the line—ours and the victims' we're working to rescue. You never know which detail may come back to you at just the right time to help you set someone free or save a life, including your own.

CHAPTER 28

BUILDING A NETWORK

At the end of January 2003, Robert Earle flew to Cambodia for the first time with Will Henry, who was making his third trip to the country. They met up with Mark, the former special forces member, and described to him the nature of our operation in Svay Pak, our previous investigative findings, and all that we hoped to accomplish there. Early on, Mark reviewed and agreed with our team members' existing plan for how to get out of the country in case the information they gathered caused their lives to become endangered.

To accomplish one of our major objectives for this phase of the operation, Mark then instructed them on how to run an informants' network in Cambodia, a critical task because on previous trips they had met only a few people they could trust. This was one of Mosier's main objectives of this trip, to build a network of people who would serve us each time we returned to Phnom Penh. We knew it could take quite some time to do the intervention, so we also needed someone who could go check on the girls and send reliable information back to us in the United States.

Mark then introduced Will and Robert to a couple of his own informants who turned out to be instrumental in our operation. These informants were people our team members could call upon to give us information, but they never had the full picture themselves. They didn't know who we really were or what we were really doing there; of course they may have surmised or guessed about our purpose, but they were not operatives.

Operatives are trusted individuals who have moved to the next level of involvement in an operation. At some point we have conveyed to them some pieces of information on a need-to-know basis, so they can serve our purposes most effectively. We have trusted them with more information, resources, and funds. And we pay them generously for their help.

Mark helped map the target area, Svay Pak, and talked with our team about various options for bringing about some sort of intervention in the village.

"At times, it was almost humorous for us to hear his perspective, coming from the military," Robert said. "Will and I come from a law enforcement background where we want to cordon and contain the place, execute a search warrant, apprehend the bad guys, and extricate ourselves safely. Mark wanted to go in there, get the victims out, and blow the place up."

Mark had heard about Svay Pak and was aware of the problem of forced child prostitution throughout Asia, but he had never been there. It was good to have Will Henry along because he had been in the area twice before. Will helped Robert and Mark understand the village layout and gave them a good idea of what to expect when they arrived.

On their first trip into the village, Mark and Robert went together, while Will provided backup security, waiting on the main road a few hundred meters outside the village.

Here's how Robert described the experience:

We located a couple of informants who drove us into Svay Pak at night. It was an isolated rabbit warren of shacks. To get there, you drive off the main road and go into a little valley and around a couple of bends. Then, as soon as we entered the village, even on motorcycles, young pimps identified us as Westerners and ran toward us, alongside our motorcycles shouting, "You want young girl? You want young girl?"

We wanted to play it very cool and not give away the fact that that's what we were there for, so we brushed them off and proceeded into the village. But they were very persistent, a whole lot of young guys, running next to us: "You want young girl?"

Svay Pak is a very dark shanty settlement—many of the buildings pieced together with whatever materials were available at the time. It was a surreal scene, driving into this dark village where you know there is horrendous crime being committed against children on a daily basis.

We went putt-putting past these little gatherings of Western men who were there for only one reason. They eyed us suspiciously as we rode past, because they have their own little society of pedophiles, and we weren't members of their group. They are always fearful of their identities being discovered.

So as the teenage boys ran alongside us, asking the persistent question, "You want young girl?" we continued to drive the 150-meter length of the village, noticing dark alleyways that branched off the main street, as well as the shady-looking pimps and customers lurking in the shadows. Along both sides of the street, brothels were interspersed with little cafés or bars where the Western men would sit together and talk between their visits back inside the buildings.

The mood was made even tenser for our investigators because of the International Tourism Conference that was under way in Cambodia at the time. Just two days earlier, the government had announced that it was shutting down Svay Pak, so it wouldn't be a blemish on the face of Cambodia while the world was watching. But when you seek to shut something down, you have to do two things: First, you have to actually shut it down operationally so it can't work anymore. Second, you have to bring those responsible for its operation to justice. The premise is that if someone is doing something illegal and bad, then someone needs to be properly prosecuted for doing it. That did not happen, but the brothel keepers seemed wary, watchful, looking out for any potential threat to their very lucrative business.

In this setting, just four days after the authorities had announced that Svay Pak was shut down, our investigators began a systematic sweep through the brothels of the village, which were still open for business. Within two and a half weeks, they were able to identify forty underage victims by name, location, and obtain an undercover photo of each.

Things had changed quite noticeably, though, from earlier visits. In the past, when investigators had entered Svay Pak, young girls had stood outside the shanties, dressed provocatively, enticing customers to come inside. This time, no little girls were in sight. We would soon discover that they were still being forced to sell their bodies to sex tourists, but now they were hidden inside the walls of these shacks. There were a few older girls out front, but the younger ones now were hidden behind the scenes.

Robert Earle continued his firsthand account:

We got off our motorbikes in front of one of the cafés, sat down at a table, and ordered a drink. While we became acclimated to all that was going on around us, we kept pushing away the young pimps who continued to pester us with the question: "You want young girl?"

After ten or fifteen minutes of talking and being checked out by these suspicious pedophiles, we accepted the offer of one of the boys to take us to see young girls. Then came the greatest sense of apprehension as we left the main street, which was at least partly lit, enough to see all the other foreigners who had come to the village. We followed the boy away from the café down a dark alleyway, away from the brothels that were known to use "older" girls, those who were fifteen, sixteen, eighteen years old. We had told him, "Yes, we want young girl," so he led us down one dark alleyway, then turned down another dark alleyway, then another dark alleyway, until we had soon lost our sense of direction— our sense of how to get back to the main street.

As we followed our pimp-guide, we were having this discussion: "Okay, if this turns bad, here's what we're going to do. . . ."

We hoped we wouldn't have to call in Will Henry, our lone backup out on the main road. And even if we did call him, at that point, chances were very slim that he'd be able to find us so far back in the recesses of the village.

So we're following this teenage kid to who-knows-where, thinking, Could we be getting set up for a robbery? Perhaps worse? *But then you start to realize that Western men are their lifeblood. To have Western men come into Svay Pak and get robbed or killed, that's going to be really bad for business. Although we're vulnerable and this is risky, it's still in their best interest to protect us and get our money, as well as the money of people we'll tell about Svay Pak in the future.*

We walked through this dark, stinking maze, on high alert for four or five minutes, stepping through putrid water and passing piles of garbage through which rats ran freely.

The courage of our people in these settings is often remarkable to those who hear our stories, but our investigators don't have time to pause for a fear break or to think of their families back home or to watch while their life passes before their eyes. That's not to say they don't experience fear or think of their families before and after these intense moments, because they certainly do.

But during the heat of these pressure-packed moments, they operate with a sometimes mind-boggling sense of purpose—of calling—that is undeniable, as if there is no way they could turn back from the mission at hand, even if they wanted to.

Will Henry describes the phenomenon well: "If someone said he was not afraid in these situations, he is either crazy or a liar. You do what you do and face the fear, control the emotions, because God gives you the grace to do it and the promise that, if you are called home, you will be with him. We see it in each other's eyes when we are about to go into the darkness, and we feel it every second between check-in times."

Neither are the victims we meet allowed to pause for a fear break. They can't call 911 for someone to come and save them; they have no weapons, no recourse, no defense. Our investigators march into these dark, ominous settings because they believe they are called by God to be that defense. As Sharon Cohn often says, "We can't expect the children to be more courageous than we are."

Some Christians are uncomfortable with the idea that God has been in a dark, repulsive brothel, that he could possibly be a witness to all the evil acts that take place there. Our investigators are not only comfortable with the idea—it's a truth they count on.

Robert Earle explained his emotional state during this first journey into Svay Pak. "I don't mean to discount the feeling of apprehension or vulnerability that comes from being in the dark, completely disoriented in an entirely unfamiliar setting," he said. "But I also don't want to discount the fact that prior to going into this village we had prayed. I know that sounds very simple, but it makes all the difference in the world, certainly on an emotional and mental level but, more important, on a spiritual level—to draw upon the resources of a God who is already in that place and is familiar with it. He's already aware, sadly, of every horrible thing that happens in there. So you call upon his promises that he'll be with you. You're not going in there alone, someplace that he can't lead. He's been in there for years, and he'll be there long after I'm gone. You're simply not going in there alone.

"I believe I'm there only because he has orchestrated it. It's completely his operation. I remember his promises to be present, to be faithful, and his words that I should be full of courage because of that."

Although their faith in an all-powerful God is a great source of courage, sometimes rescuers also get a boost from one another. When he was a young police officer, Robert was standing next to a veteran cop during a tense situation in which an angry group was threatening to riot. As the officers faced the menacing crowd and refused to budge, Robert glanced at the older officer and took courage from his colleague's bravery, steadfastness, and resolve.

After the crowd finally dispersed and they were leaving the scene, Robert asked the experienced veteran, "Could you hear my knees knocking back there?"

"No, I couldn't hear them. Mine were knocking too loudly for me to hear anything."

A large quantity of adrenaline pumps through the body when confronted with danger, but God's presence and the desire to not let down their colleagues helps our courageous warriors stay focused on the task at hand, rescuing innocent victims.

As we were walking, Mark and I carried on a quiet conversation: "If this goes bad, I'll take the first threat, you take the second. . . ." We were both primed, both ready, both a little uneasy about this. . . .

Then, boom, we arrived at the place and were taken inside the building. The first person we met was Mr. Kha, the papasan, who deferred to his younger pimps so they could take us from there. One of them, Victor, whom I would get to know very well in the weeks ahead, led us farther into the dark house. A couple of bare light bulbs were burning in the small, dark, dirty, hot little room with what was supposed to be a double bed, but it was a piece of wood with an old, dirty mattress and a blanket thrown on top.

One of the other considerations I had during this time was that I had my camera running, collecting evidence as I went. From the time of riding into the village, sitting at the café, then walking back into this place, it had been recording. The camera complicates matters because if one is robbed in a normal setting, he loses his wallet, and that's too bad. But if we were robbed and found to have camera gear on us that had been collecting evidence against them or their family, friends, or colleagues, the stakes suddenly would become much higher.

When you're wearing camera gear, you also have to be very conscious of where you're standing and where it's pointing. There are a whole lot of things going on in your head at once. You're thinking about safety, but you're also thinking about gathering evidence. So you might choose to stand next to someone in a way that you normally wouldn't because of safety considerations, but you need to get a good shot of his face.

Always alert, Robert and Mark knew the importance of appearing calm, even while assessing the physical threat posed by the four young men and the papasan in his forties. They remained always aware of the route to the exit while gathering the evidence needed to make a case against the perpetrators. "I have to act cool and nonchalant, as though this is something I do all the time; as casually as going to a convenience store for a soft drink, I rent kids to have sex with them," Robert said.

CHAPTER 29

"YOUNGER? NO PROBLEM"

Almost immediately after Robert and Mark were taken into the tiny bedroom of that first Svay Pak brothel, lit by one bulb in the corner, two girls came in, both age fourteen.

Mark, the former U.S. special forces guy, took the lead in asking the questions at first, because he had been in Cambodia before and had worked with the people, whereas this was Robert's first time. Mark asked all the normal questions, such as, "What can this one do? Who do we pay? How long can we have her? Can we take them back to our hotel?"

After he had gathered all the evidence he thought was needed, he stopped and looked at Robert, who turned to the pimp, Victor, and asked, "Do you have any younger girls?"

Mark threw Robert a perplexed look, because the girls in the room looked extremely young and small to him.

"What do you mean?" he asked Robert. "You want younger than this?"

"Yeah," Robert answered, because he had heard there were extremely young girls in Svay Pak.

Victor didn't miss a beat. "Oh, yes, yes. You want younger? Sure, no problem."

Then he spoke a few words to one of the younger pimps, who quickly left the room.

Within a minute or so, three children between the ages of eight and ten walked in.

From that moment on, Mark was silent. Though he had been conducting the interview up to this point, now he was speechless.

"I have profound respect for Mark," Robert said. "He is an amazing professional, and he taught me a lot in the week he was with us in Phnom Penh. He has been a lot of places and seen a lot of things, including the worst that special forces military personnel are forced to see, but I don't think he had ever seen anything like this."

Because Robert was the one who had requested younger children, he took over the conversation. "What's your name?" he asked one, then another.

Then he asked Victor what sex acts the kids could perform. He would point to one and ask, "She do yum-yum?" referring to oral sex. "You good?" he asked her directly.

"Yes," she answered, expressionless and professional, with the quick nod of her head.

"They do boom-boom?" Robert asked the pimp, using the term for regular intercourse.

Robert knows most civilized people find this type of interaction deplorable, sickening. But he knows it's essential to gain the evidence necessary to prosecute the ones who victimize the kids day after day. At that moment he was thinking only about gathering evidence and getting out of the place safely. "Your survival is dependent upon your ability to be convincing, so you have to completely enroll in the charade," he said. "Actually, in one way I'm excited that he has shown us the evidence, just as I would be if a drug dealer brought out his stash of cocaine. Now I've got the pimp on tape, and there's no way he can say he didn't know they're minors, because they're six or eight years old, and he's just told me that. He's caught. From an investigative point of view, there's a real sense of satisfaction at the moment that I've got what I came here for, and with it justice will be served. I'm looking at evidence that can put someone in jail for a long time. I don't think of the children as kids right then; I can't afford to."

Afterward, though, back in his hotel room when he checked the videotape of the investigation he had just completed, he noticed their eyes for the first time. "That's when I see them as children, as innocent victims. That's when I shed tears for them and pray for them because I see how young, how innocent, how vulnerable they really are."

On one undercover tape, Robert's whisper can be heard as he leaves a brothel: "May God keep you safe. May God keep you until we come back to get you out of here."

The look on that little girl's face would make a soldier's knees buckle—fear and vulnerability mixed with indescribable dignity. We see it all too often in places like this. And we know the girls' stories. Not all of them; not specific details. But our investigations have taken us down all-too-familiar paths that lead these innocents to dark pits of inhumane treatment at the hands of greedy abusers.

Many of them come to these places through circumstances like Jyoti's.

CHAPTER 30

RESCUED BECOMES RESCUER

When she was fourteen, Jyoti left home in Hydrabad, India, to work as a domestic servant in the village of Guntur. (Years later we would learn the reason Jyoti had left home at such a young age.) She had recently completed two months of work and was returning home with her saved money to visit her family. As she sat in the railway station alone, she was approached and befriended by four women she had never met before. As they spoke, the women secretly purchased another ticket for Jyoti, headed not for her hometown, but to Mumbai, which is in the opposite direction.

When it came time to board the train, the women convinced Jyoti that the train routes had been changed because of some construction on the rail lines, and that she should join them on their train. She trusted them and boarded their train.

Jyoti became suspicious when the train did not arrive at her stop within the normally scheduled time. She grew angry and began to yell at the women, who tried to assure her the train was just traveling slowly. They offered her some tea to calm her down. Unfortunately for Jyoti, the tea was drugged, and she did not awaken for three days.

When she came to, she found herself in a brothel in a major city far from her home village. Shortly after she awoke, a brothel keeper named Mrudula came to see her. She told Jyoti she was now part of the sex-for-sale market, and that she should get used to the idea that she was going to "do this business." A physician came in, examined Jyoti, and said she would be fine in a few days when the effects of the drug wore off.

For the next two months, Jyoti was beaten for her refusal to participate in the sex trade. The brothel keepers assaulted her repeatedly, more than fifty times, she said, with sticks, plastic water pipes, and electrical cords. She reported even being bitten on two occasions on her back and arms.

Finally the brothel keeper had had enough. Demanding a high price because she was a virgin, she sold Jyoti to an eager customer. Still resistant, Jyoti was beaten on her legs, then pushed violently into the room. Falling forward, her face struck a mirror, cutting the left side of her face and her chin. Even so, the customer demanded his pleasure. She struggled against him, but he held her hands above her head and sexually assaulted her, her bangle bracelets causing more cuts to her face in the fight. When he was finished with her, the customer paid the brothel keeper about two hundred dollars. Pleased that she had been a virgin, he gave her an additional twenty-two-dollar tip. Jyoti took the money and threw it in the face of the brothel keeper.

After that episode Jyoti became ill and was not forced to have sex with customers for about a month. But eventually, sensing there was no way out, she decided to give up the fight—outwardly. Day after day she looked for an opportunity to escape, but found none. Jyoti even asked her customers to help her escape, but none took pity on her.

Occasionally the police would raid the brothel. When they did, all the girls were quickly shepherded into a subterranean hiding place, a soundproof room or crawlspace that prevented any noise from getting through the walls. Even if the victims had shouted for help, no one could have heard their cries. Once inside the dark, cramped, dirt-floored room, the girls were guarded by an agent of the brothel owner to prevent their escape.

Jyoti's average workday started around noon and could go as late as 4:00 A.M., with no days off and no holidays. She was forced to have sex with an unbelievable average of twenty-five customers a day, often without the use of a condom. A conservative estimate? Jyoti could have been forced to have sex with more than fifteen thousand customers over the three years she endured this assault, each contact a potential death sentence if he was an HIV carrier.

The brothel keepers regularly injected Jyoti and the other girls with a drug to help "control them." We don't know what kind of drugs they used, nor what long-term effects it may have on the victims.

One day another young woman who was held captive in the brothel told Jyoti about Jesus. "You are worshiping gods that cannot relieve you," she said. "Jesus came into this world to save us from sin. Jesus can definitely relieve you from this place."

So Jyoti began to pray that God would rescue her from this place.

"I prayed for one week: 'God, give me this salvation.' I was praying all the time, everywhere, praying to Jesus," she said.

And soon relief came. A governmental official who had become a friend of IJM heard about Jyoti's situation. Interestingly, he was tipped off by one of her customers who claimed to have fallen in love with her. When she had begged for his help in getting out of the brothel, he couldn't refuse, and sought out the governmental official who was well known for his efforts to stop sex trafficking of children.

This friend came to us and suggested that we join forces with him to conduct a raid to rescue Jyoti. Her case was compelling because she was a minor and she desperately wanted out. So, on January 17, 1999, at one o'clock in the afternoon, the raid was conducted. It was so different from the way we conduct most raids nowadays. This official and his assigned body guards, along with IJM personnel, simply went to the door of the brothel and told the brothel keeper, the notorious Mrudula, that they wanted to see Jyoti.

After only a few moments, Mrudula, realizing she could be in seriously hot water, complied and yelled into the brothel for Jyoti to be sent out. Eventually Jyoti stepped cautiously out of the darkness of her dungeon and into the crowd that had now gathered outside the brothel door. Emerging into the bright midday sun, Jyoti squinted and even flinched when someone's hand moved quickly near her head. With her face held nervously in her hands, she walked out of her hell and toward the IJM vehicle awaiting her. Although she found no familiar faces around her and held on to no guarantees about what lay before her, Jyoti simply refused to stay where she knew she did not belong.

Jyoti had been tricked and betrayed many times before by people promising to help her, and so it would be hours before we finally saw Jyoti's smile emerge. As she sat with Bob Mosier at the police station and began to believe in the reality of her rescue, a dazzling smile dawned upon her face; light and life filled her brilliant eyes. This was the smile many of us at IJM would come to know so well over the years as we traveled with Jyoti on her journey of healing, restoration, and eventual rescue of others.

That journey began with the loving care extended to her by the Mar Thoma church community in Bombay, an indigenous Christian community that finds its origins in the missionary journey of the apostle Thomas to India two thousand years ago. These loving brothers and sisters provided a residential community where Jyoti could find healing love, faithful care, and spiritual nurture over the ensuing years.

When we met several years later, she extended that famous smile yet again. She was now married and showing off to me her new baby girl. She explained with confidence and joy her release from the darkness and humiliation of the nightmare she had been forced to live. "The old Jyoti is dead," she said. "I came to know Jesus; now I am like a newborn baby."

"I am released from my bondage," she added in a soft, direct, matter-of-fact voice. "Now I am free."

For me there are these extraordinary moments when trite and overused words find their rightful place in the universe and recover their deepest and truest resonance. And for a moment I lingered in the exquisite authenticity of Jyoti's simple words. In such moments I want to run home and find every exhausted friend who is paralyzed with despair and every friend who is hiding in the fears of sophisticated cynicism. I want them to come meet Jyoti, and I want to say, "See, there is such a thing as bondage, and there is such a thing as being free, and we can actually help someone move from one to the other."

Of course, there is nothing easy about Jyoti's journey, and it has had its ups and downs. But the brilliance and resilience of Jyoti's smile has been a powerful inspiration to me and to the thousands of people who have come to know that story and that smile. It is for me a picture of a glory that is worth fighting for.

Frequently the victims of brutality become so debased by their abusers that we bystanders misplace the urgent sense of what has been lost. We can put the victims of oppression in a separate category of human existence where people must somehow get used to being crushed, beaten, and despoiled. I think this is perhaps why the founders of the Holocaust Memorial Museum in Washington, D.C., chose to begin the grizzly tour not with pictures of emaciated and skeletal holocaust victims, but with bright photos of European Jews laughing at birthday parties, dressing for a night at the opera, and dancing cheek to cheek with romantic grace, lest we forget the great beauty, life, and goodness that were destroyed.

Likewise, Jyoti's brilliant smile, clever wit, and stubborn dignity remind me of what we are fighting for—and that I should not be fooled by the darkness, death, and resignation I see so commonly in the eyes of the most tragically abused. They didn't start that way, and they don't have to stay that way.

None have endured more ugliness than Jyoti; and surprisingly, few would also help bring release to so many.

After introducing me to her husband and baby in a hotel lobby in Bombay, I asked in a normal effort at small talk, "What's your little girl's name?"

"We haven't named her yet," Jyoti replied. "We wanted you to name her."

I was taken aback. *Name your child?* I suddenly felt uncomfortable as I considered how significant names can be in Jyoti's culture, to express family heritage and identity, hopes and aspirations. But it didn't seem like the time to argue with Jyoti about it. This wasn't, after all, about me. It was about Jyoti's wanting to express her gratefulness to IJM and wanting to connect her child to her experience of goodness with us.

"Perhaps, Jyoti," I said after a moment, "you may wish to call your little one Esther. Like Esther in the Bible, this baby girl comes out of a story of great courage that will give hope to many."

Jyoti and her husband seemed to like the name; in fact, it would not be long before hope would indeed be brought to many. That very night my colleagues and I were making plans for the next day, to raid several brothels where IJM operatives had located children being abused. When Jyoti learned of our plans, she asked, "Can you bring the police to Mrudula's brothel?" where she had been so brutally abused. "I will show you where they hide the girls underground."

The next morning Jyoti led me, IJM colleagues, and the police on a raid that rescued more than a half dozen other girls from a dark underground dungeon. Continuing the cycle of rescue, one of the girls freed that morning eventually led us on yet another raid that liberated about a dozen other children.

Amazingly, however, the legacy of Jyoti's extraordinary story of hope did not end even there. Years later IJM would learn that the brothel wasn't Jyoti's first experience of captivity. About a year before her abduction by the four women on the train, Jyoti had begun working in a brick kiln to pay off a loan her father had taken out to help pay for his family's daily sustenance. To secure the debt, the moneylender had taken Jyoti on as a laborer in the brick kiln. But, as with so many "loans" given by moneylenders, this one never diminished and instead increased with the additional expenses of eye treatment for Jyoti's mother. Her wages for working in the kiln were equivalent to about eighteen cents a day.

Realizing he would never be able to repay the debt, Jyoti's father had agreed to give her—just fourteen years old—in marriage to a man, probably in his late thirties, who had offered a large sum of money for her. Before the marriage occurred she had run away and found a temporary job as a domestic servant. Returning home with money from that job, she was drugged aboard the train and taken captive into the brothel.

Several years after she was set free from the brothel, Jyoti returned home to her village to see her family. While she was there, the brick kiln owner recognized and confronted her: She still owed him money, he said; she needed to come back and pay off her father's debt.

Jyoti contacted IJM, with whom she had remained in contact, and told us about the brick kiln situation. Our investigators found a compelling case of both bonded labor and child labor, and sought more information from the victims to build a case against the perpetrators. But the kiln owner was a wealthy, influential, and fearsome man. If laborers left and tried to find work elsewhere, he would send his men to beat them up and bring them back. Children, women, and men worked long hours in the heat of the kiln under pathetic conditions and a shroud of hopelessness and fear.

Because of the sizable intimidation factor, IJM could not find any witnesses willing to testify against the owner. Only one brave woman mustered the courage to talk with IJM about the pathetic conditions of work at the kiln, and she was willing to sign an affidavit detailing the crimes committed there.

After four attempts to secure governmental support for an intervention, our team had a breakthrough. IJM staff and governmental agents entered the brick kiln together to conduct an inquiry into the claims of Jyoti and the other woman. As the team entered the front of the kiln, the owner forced children to flee the rescue by rushing them out the back door. The kiln had been raided in the past for the illegal use of child labor, so the owner was most anxious to hide the live evidence of the same crime. As they exited the building, the kids ran into surrounding fields, but IJM team members conducting surveillance managed to round up the children and take them to the inquiry area.

In all, thirty-six workers were documented that day by the local officials, who also interviewed the kiln owner. Our staff on the scene got the impression that the officials were reluctant to complete the investigation, hesitant to build a case against such an influential man.

Naturally the victims had the same fear and trepidation about leaving the kiln. They had heard the horror stories and witnessed the beatings, perhaps even suffered the brutality themselves. How could they trust that we would take them far enough away, keep their destination secret from the owner, and keep them safe once they got there?

As the investigation was concluded the victims were told to pack their belongings and gather in the front to be transported to temporary housing. Although thirty-six individuals had been documented and received release certificates, only twenty-nine came forward. The others remained in the kiln. Those who came forward came cautiously, but as the trucks arrived, they slowly realized the gravity of the situation. It took them a while, but they began to understand that they no longer had an owner.

Their faces were a picture of the revelation within, transforming from looks of distrust to confusion to joy to excitement. Then they celebrated with childlike enthusiasm. They were free!

Those who remained in the kiln did so out of fear of retribution from their owner. They lied and said they were daily wage laborers, not bonded slaves. Then, as the trucks began to roll out of the compound, eight more victims ran out to join the group of freed slaves, making the last-minute decision to take a shot at freedom.

In addition to those who received official release documents, children and spouses of some documented slaves added to the number of those freed. In all, eighty-six people were released from slavery that day. And Jyoti's legacy of freedom lives on.

CHAPTER 31

PREPARING TO GO

Robert continued to gather evidence throughout Svay Pak over the next two and a half weeks, collecting names and ages of the victims to go with the undercover photo images of their faces. In an effort to not raise the suspicions of brothel keepers, Robert began telling the story that a large group of his rich Western friends were coming to Phnom Penh on a sex tour, and they wanted as many young girls from the brothels as they could get for a party at a private residence in Phnom Penh. At first the ruse appeared to meet with the approval of many brothel owners. Later it would become much more complicated.

Robert found it fairly easy to get to know a couple of the leaders in the Svay Pak sex trade: Kha, the self-appointed village chief whom Robert and Mark met on their first trip into the village, and Victor, the proud, high-ranking pimp who was also in the first brothel that night. Robert invited the pair out to dinner in Phmom Penh on a couple of occasions, brought them gifts, and found other ways to gain their trust. When Robert learned that Victor's soccer team couldn't afford new equipment, he bought several soccer balls as a gift for his new "friend." On subsequent visits into Svay Pak, Robert brought them other presents, and they gave him gifts as well. They were always happy to see him because they had grown to like him, and because he meant a large payout for them one day soon.

Back at headquarters, we were monitoring the progress of Robert's investigation, and were incredibly encouraged by his successes in documenting so many cases of very young girls—girls we hoped to rescue in a very short time. He had videotaped individual transactions of forty separate girls being sold for sex, all between the ages of five and fourteen. Each videotaped transaction featured a specific perpetrator and could be traced to a specific location, a numbered brothel, with a plot on the Svay Pak map and a global positioning satellite setting for good measure. Each videotaped transaction recorded the elements of the crime necessary for clear prosecution and conviction.

Now that our investigative goal had been miraculously—and safely—achieved with overwhelming results that vastly exceeded our expectations, we looked at three major questions: (1) Could we mobilize the U.S. ambassador to secure high-level cooperation from the Cambodian authorities to conduct a large-scale rescue and enforcement action with us? (2) Could we design an enforcement action that would actually be successful? (3) Could we secure quality aftercare for the victims?

Sharon gathered her staff and interns to prepare the intervention reports, which would prove to be the critical documents in the operation. Her instructions were clear:

"Remember, there are no points for poetry here. It is all-important to capture the truth of the crimes. If you get these facts right we may be able to get these girls out. You should take no liberty with the facts. An A+ paper here is one where all the facts are correct.

"Please feel no freedom to wax poetic, embellish, explain, or add. Our credibility lies in these reports. They have to be perfect.

"I don't want to read about the 'brutal rape.' I want to hear that on a certain date, a girl called by a specific name, age X, was offered *by* a specific person, *to* a specific person, to perform specific sexual acts for a specific price.

"Triple-check everything. It could mean the difference between conviction and acquittal."

Phase 1, the investigative phase of our Svay Pak project, was overwhelmingly successful. But miraculous success in completing one impossible phase of the operation always seemed simply to give us an opportunity to confront the next impossible phase. And before long, we would get used to that feeling.

Now that we had the investigative product, it was time to make the decision about whether we were going to launch the deployment of the entire project team to Cambodia, an investment of tremendous human and financial resources, and an organizational risk for IJM. At this point it was still possible to call the whole thing off with a minimal loss of investment. But once we made the decision to deploy the team to Cambodia, there was no turning back; only victory or tragedy would return home with us. To make that decision, I had to be sure of a number of things—first, that Sharon Cohn believed the political intervention through the embassy had a reasonable chance of success and that aftercare partners would be in place if the rescue operation succeeded.

Additionally, I had to know from Bob Mosier that he and his team had a reasonable plan for the tactical operation of victim rescue and perpetrator arrest. It was up to Cohn and Mosier to make the case that they were good to go, and then to look me in the eye and take responsibility for their piece. They explained their operations, subjected them to team scrutiny, and took responsibility for their recommendation. We had been relentlessly asking God for wisdom in navigating all we could not see; now the moral imperative to extend courageous love to the girls in Svay Pak, and the best analysis and wisdom we could muster led us to the conviction that it was time to go.

At that time in the planning process, Bob went to talk to Sharon. "I need to know if we are going to do this no matter what," he said. "I need to know whether I should deploy people now from other countries, or do we need to wait and see if we're going to get people to act?"

Sharon paused only momentarily, then looked Bob in the eye. "Yes, it will happen no matter what," she answered, a million details circulating through her mind, yet enveloped in the fact that this was God's timing, God's mission. There would be several other points throughout the mission that could make or break the effort, but this was Sharon's vote of confidence that if God wanted it done, the obstacles would fall.

Indeed, a firm deployment date was starting to take shape driven by two go factors: Sharon had secured an appointment with the ambassador to make our case, and Robert Earle had solidified the ruse among the Svay Pak perpetrators that he would be returning with friends to host the sex party, which must come together soon to remain credible. With determination, we made arrangements to travel to Svay Pak.

The team completed an enormous amount of work in a short time in order to launch the deployment. This included all the very technical, evidentiary work of documenting for all forty victims each one of the transactions caught on videotape. That meant picking out the videotape for each girl and selecting enough of the videotape to show all the elements of the crime taking place. We then had to package a narrative report noting the specific place and time that the crime occurred, along with a diagram of all the houses with global positioning satellite locations, because in this shanty village you don't have street addresses you can find on MapQuest.

All this evidence had to be prepared in an orderly fashion, because we anticipated its being passed along to the highest-ranking Cambodian authorities. As Sharon had told her team, "This might be our one shot, the girls' one shot at freedom." It's not an overstatement to say lives were hanging in the balance.

This is where an organizational commitment to rigorous standards of evidence preparation pays off, but it's a whole lot easier to say than to do. It requires relentless eighteen-hour days of unyielding attention to detail and tedious scrutiny of documents, words, diagrams, captions, and maps. On and on it goes. Sometimes the rescue work of IJM can look dramatic and even glamorous, but that notion feels like quite a farce when you are actually doing the work, most of it painstakingly tedious and exhaustingly exact. Preparing legal briefs and incontrovertible investigative packets on forty independent sex crimes in less than a week with a tiny staff is about as demanding a professional ordeal as there is. Law enforcement and public justice professionals could readily appreciate this, but it's an inside view that few people get. Perhaps that's why the occasional reference to IJM "cowboys" gets quite a good laugh at IJM, unless you picture cowboys obsessing over typos, redundant contingency plans, tedious mission memos, endless equipment checks, relentless checklists, and mind-numbing operational rehearsals. Like all precision performances, it's all about preparation, preparation, preparation. It's the stuff that gets a quick photo montage with inspirational music in the movies, but for the folks in the field, it's the stuff that delivers. And sometimes, such tedium can end up delivering life itself.

It's difficult to thoroughly diagram or describe the multilayered relationships that simply had to deliver for any chance of success in the Cambodian operation. At each stage there were multiple make-or-break contingencies, any one of which would send us packing for home and leave the Svay Pak children in their hell. For us, it was a walk of desperate faith, testing core principles of the trustworthiness of God. We presumed to believe that God was an indispensable actor in the unfolding drama, and we were willing to reserve very little dignity to ourselves in putting such a proposition to the test. We believed that it was the active God of creation, life, and human history who would have to grant us favor, open doors, and bind together an incredibly complicated chain of influence, link by link by link, to create the apparatus of power needed to attempt this rescue in Svay Pak. And along each link in the chain of influence, there was still so much that could go wrong.

We knew that, in Cambodia, the antihuman-trafficking police were the officials charged and empowered to raid, rescue, and arrest. We also knew some of those very officers had raided the brothels after Will rescued the four girls in May and then arrested them for being illegal immigrants. We knew we needed someone higher ranking than those officials to compel them to conduct themselves according to the law and to get the girls out of Svay Pak.

Numerous times following 2000 we had submitted evidence of sexual exploitation of children to the Cambodian police with no response. It was time for a different tactic. Perhaps our most critical ally in this effort would be the new U.S. ambassador to Cambodia, Charles Ray. In fact, after his confirmation, we had invited Ambassador Ray to meet with us in our office, and he had accepted the invitation. He had arrived with the desk officer for Cambodia to meet with Sharon, Bob Mosier, and me. We had briefed him on our activities in Cambodia, introduced him to some of the victims through the undercover footage, and described what our investigations were uncovering in the brothels of Svay Pak.

He had invited us to call on him if we were ever in Cambodia and needed assistance, but it still wasn't clear to us at that time whether sexual exploitation was something he felt the Cambodian administration could aggressively pursue. We knew we needed help at the highest levels. None of the other things we'd tried had worked. We really needed either the prime minister, Hun Sen, or the deputy prime minister, Sar Kheng, to work with us. With an order issued from one of them, the obstacles created by the local police would be removed. How do you get to the heads of state of Cambodia? You go through the ambassador.

So, a few months after meeting Ambassador Ray, while Robert Earle was completing his evidence gathering in Svay Pak, Sharon wrote to the ambassador's office, suggesting we meet to go over the alarming evidence we were discovering, and to seek his advice and assistance in taking our next steps toward rescuing these victims. The ambassador agreed to meet with us in Cambodia. With this detail in place, we made our travel plans. It was mid-March 2003.

CHAPTER 32

"HAPPY IS NOT AN OPERATIVE"

We didn't all fly together, nor did we stay in the same hotel when we got to Phnom Penh, but we all arrived on the ground in Cambodia within twenty-four hours of one another. Our tasks were many but focused, and each person played a role in accomplishing the mission. The investigative team was present in force, with a clear mandate to keep the ruse going, monitor intelligence flows, and make logistical preparations for the rescue operation and transitional security for the children.

We also needed to meet with Ambassador Ray to deliver our most compelling evidence on the crimes of Svay Pak, then prepare for follow-through, high-level meetings with police officials whose cooperation we hoped to secure. There was just no way to conduct a massive rescue effort like this without them.

We had to arrange aftercare for the girls we rescued, to ensure that they would have a safe, caring place to go once they were freed.

Then there were a myriad of other logistical arrangements to be made as part of the ruse and the raid, such as renting a gated home where we could hold the supposed sex party and lure the perpetrators out of their safe zone into the trap we were planning to spring on them.

We also were bringing along our intervention tool of last resort, the national news media. We had been approached by *Dateline NBC* about doing a story about sex trafficking in Southeast Asia, and ultimately we decided to embed them into our Svay Pak operation. Obviously we hoped they would help us tell the story of the sex-trafficking nightmare and help mobilize compassionate outrage among the American people and a conviction to do something about it. We had reasons to trust that the particular producer and correspondent from *Dateline* who wanted to cover the story would do so with integrity and professionalism.

Although telling the story about global sex trafficking and publicizing the work of IJM was nice, it was not a sufficient reason for taking on the risks and operational encumbrances of having a network TV crew in tow. We agreed to the partnership with *Dateline* because we believed that, given the overwhelming and grotesque video evidence we already had, if the Cambodian authorities failed to act effectively to address such a preventable atrocity, we would let the story be told on network television, with the hope that it might generate overwhelming pressure to clean up Svay Pak and rescue the children.

It was undeniable: the open and massive, sadistic, sexual abuse of children in a village in Cambodia. If we presented this information clearly to the U.S. and Cambodian authorities along with a tactical plan to do something about it, one of two things could happen: They could both do their jobs well and publicly get the credit for it, or they could fail to do their jobs and publicly get the blame for it. Either outcome seemed appropriate to publicize and would advance the fight against sex trafficking. Of course another possibility was that IJM could make a mistake on national television, but that seemed a risk worth taking for the sake of mobilizing the most powerful response possible for the victims in Svay Pak.

The presence of an internationally recognized media outlet certainly added tension to the whole operation. We had made a commitment to the folks at *Dateline NBC*, who were counting on our giving them virtually unhindered access throughout the mission. Now, whether we were successful or not, we were allowing the world to watch what we do and how we do it. Any blunders we made at this point would open us up immediately to national, even international, scrutiny.

So the team ready for action in Cambodia was . . .

Sharon Cohn: Interventions, ultimately responsible for the overall outcome of the operation, including securing support from governmental officials who could require the cooperation of the local police and ensuring proper aftercare for rescued victims.

Bob Mosier, Will Henry, Robert Earle, Mathew, and Jasper: Investigations, developing the operative-informant network, gathering evidence, setting up the ruse and all its logistical requirements.

Kayrn Withers: Director of program development, on this trip to gather firsthand information she could share with donors and governmental agencies for potential funding grants, but also to provide critical support to Sharon on the interventions team.

Ted Haddock: Communications manager, here to document the mission through still photography and video; joined the investigations team as needed.

Shannon Sedgwick Davis: Public affairs director, responsible for assisting the *Dateline NBC* crew during this mission.

Dateline NBC: A producer and a cameraman who captured on video nearly every aspect of the operation once they arrived.

———

Bob Mosier peered through binoculars from behind the sheer curtains covering the fourth-floor hotel window.

"See the guy over there in the blue shirt with the baseball cap?" Mosier asked the three team members who stood near him. "He's our informant. His name is Happy. Now, when I say 'informant' . . . he has no idea what we're doing here, but he will give us information. He'll sit across from the hotel waiting to take people where they want to go on his motorcycle.

"One of you will need to go down and hitch a ride from him, then when you're away from the other drivers, you'll ask him for information."

A few minutes later, when someone called Happy an "operative," Mosier quickly and firmly corrected the terminology.

"He is an informant, *not* an operative. An operative is a trusted individual. An informant has no knowledge of what we're doing. Happy is *not* an operative.

"It is absolutely critical to keep the players straight in an operation like this," Mosier explained. "If you don't have a clear understanding of who each person is, it can get someone killed."

Bob was right to make this distinction. If a team member in a hotel room uses an incorrect label to describe an informant, another team member may hear that, then assume it is safe to divulge information or discuss details in a more open manner with that person. You can see where that kind of mistake could be critical to our mission. It may seem petty to be so particular about labels, but we have to be careful or the whole mission could be jeopardized and people's lives could be at risk.

When we're new to a culture or a country, it's sometimes difficult to maneuver around without drawing too much attention to ourselves. So we rely on a multinational team of senior law-enforcement-trained staff to conduct our investigations. These are people with ten to fifteen years of experience in looking for, and finding, critical information that can make a case against a criminal and help bring him to justice. This is the type of investigator we brought to Cambodia with us because we had faith in his judgment and ability to help us complete the mission. In addition to our U.S. team, two other investigators showed up from their posts in other countries, Mathew and Jasper, from the Philippines and Ghana, respectively.

This operation would require investigators who have experience in undercover operations, planning, and logistics. They have to be able to operate with little backup. In the United States, there is a wealth of backup support one can call upon in a moment of crisis. In a developing country, an investigator is often on his own, using just his wits and experience to get out of a jam.

CHAPTER 33

SEEING SVAY PAK FIRSTHAND

Shortly after I arrived in Cambodia, I made preparations to visit Svay Pak to familiarize myself with the site and its atmosphere, the intangibles I couldn't get from all the briefings. The senior members of our team already had plenty of familiarity with the village and the brothels, and I had seen more than enough video footage of the children being victimized. But in trying to provide guidance to a tactical operation such as the one on which we were now embarking in Svay Pak, there is just no substitute for being on the ground and getting a physical and tactile sense of the field of operation.

One can analyze ideas from anywhere, but smart analysis of operations depends upon a hands-on familiarity with the terrain. I wanted to get a feel for the place, so I could picture exactly what my colleagues were talking about as they discussed the various steps of the operation. I also wanted to see if I could take a temperature reading on the brothel operators' level of suspicion and alertness to outsiders, and how relaxed or nervous the surrounding atmosphere was of pimps, sex tourists, prostitutes, café operators, and their neighbors.

Will, Ted, Mathew, and I drove the eleven kilometers by motorcycle on a two-lane road out of town. Will stayed positioned just outside the village as backup security, while Mathew, Ted, and I turned off the short dirt road that led into the main strip of Svay Pak. After parking our bikes, I was immediately approached by a teenage boy beckoning me to come get "young girls, young girls."

"You want young girls? Small girls? Small girls for yum-yum? Boom-boom? Everything?"

I dismissively ignored him, and we shuffled down the dirt road choked with motorcycles, carts, and café tables and chairs that spilled out from the storefronts to the edge of the road. We took up one of the outside café tables across the street from the main strip of brothels and sat in the plastic chairs. The pathetic groupings of Western customers seated nearby looked us over, and a weary young woman came to take our drink order while a young pimp seated himself patiently nearby, just waiting, like a dog watching for crumbs to fall from the table.

Svay Pak brothels were definitely open for business, but there were not the crowds of girls hanging outside the front of the brothels as I had seen in videos from years before. Nevertheless, those same brothels were clearly open for business with girls inside behind the grated doors, and there was clearly a thriving and unabashed market of "young girls," based on all the invitations from young entrepreneurs who immediately approached us.

Soon young women from the brothel across the street approached us at our table looking to meet their quota for the day, and we talked with a couple of them who spoke English. One who sat at our table was twenty years old and had been working in Svay Pak for six years. It was hard to imagine that at fourteen she had somehow been brought here and was still surviving the daily abuse of body, mind, and spirit.

She invited us to come into House 10, the brothel where she worked, to see what she could do. With my eyes I followed her glance to House 10, with its barred doors pulled shut and locked. They had cracked open that door when we first arrived, so the girls could look at us, and us them, young and dolled up in tight clothes.

"It doesn't look very inviting," I said. "Why is it all barred up like that? It doesn't look very friendly to a visitor."

The girl mumbled something about her mamasan, then moved on to another prospective customer. We sat for a good bit, taking it all in, when I noticed a chubby Westerner in his late forties wearing a loose shirt, shorts, and sandals as he duck-walked slowly down the dirt road. He looked past me to exchange grins with some of his apparent acquaintances seated at nearby tables. He seemed the picture of the pudgy, grinning Western customer in Svay Pak. But then he also looked like someone I had seen before. After he had passed by, the image of his face finally connected with the visual in my memory.

I think that was the guy in Will's video, I thought, rushing back to replay in my mind the face that had just passed me by. *I think that's Alton, the guy bragging on Will's undercover tape about how he likes to have sex with the young girls. I'll have to ask Will or Sharon if they have a clip of that video with them so I can double-check. But if that's him, he's in-country at the wrong time, and it won't be hard to find him again in the close little circle of bars and brothels that these guys circulate in.*

After lingering over our drinks and letting all air of eagerness dissipate, Mathew and I eventually took up our patient pimp's offer to go get some girls. Ted stayed at the table, while Mathew and I followed this thin young man as he eased unhurriedly down the road on his routine errand of delivering strangers to their pedophile haven. It was a two-minute walk behind the brothels to a narrow dirt alley that wound through shacks into a cramped little house made of wood scraps. I was escorted into a back room and immediately presented with no fewer than a dozen girls between the ages of five and ten who were available to sodomize, rape, or molest for a few dollars. It was certainly one of the most appalling scenes I had ever encountered, but it was also one of the most surreal.

The sight of elementary-school-age girls, like those who gather in giggling groups at my own kids' school, being assembled not to play a game or hear a lesson or watch a movie, but to be forced into sex acts, was one of the most disorienting moments of my life. Of course at the time I was not processing these emotions or any others, because I was very much on task. I was watching my manner and my words to stay in role, noting carefully faces and my physical surroundings, keeping an eye out for emerging threats or changing exits or a heads-up from Mathew, all the while feigning boredom and staying relaxed. Feelings are definitely not helpful in such settings; they are very much on hold.

I had never indicated I was interested in such young girls, and so I made it clear that they were not my thing and went back into the street. Mathew and I swung by the café where Ted still sat. "Time to go," I said. We got back on the motorcycles and drove to Phnom Penh. As disorienting and appalling as the whole scene had been, I now had a much clearer picture of the physicality of our target, the mood in the village, and the openness of the commerce. Deep in my spirit, everything confirmed that we were on target and should keep taking the next steps.

Even deeper in my spirit, however, I felt a low-grade nausea I couldn't shake. The twisted sickness and profound evil of what I had seen in that back room in Svay Pak were fundamentally jarring. It was actually possible for human reality to be completely upside down: for children to occupy a space where everything we associate with children—everything good and innocent and loving—would be diabolically wrenched backward into a world of sex and sadism and violence for children.

It was as if someone had reached inside to grab my deepest internal compass of reality and orientation and had sent the arrow spinning in violent circles with a massive flick of the finger.

Wow. I sighed to myself as I stared aimlessly past my colleagues' conversation at moments during dinner that evening. *Hell is just not many circles below the surface. And human beings can actually make it a routine abode. The darkness is very nearly total. And it's here. And that's where we've got to go.*

CHAPTER 34

IN SEARCH OF AFTERCARE

On Friday, March 21, Sharon, Kayrn, and Ted traveled into the Cambodian countryside to visit a potential aftercare provider. The several-hour drive was beautiful, past small villages, across open plains, through wetlands next to rivers. The ingenuity of the Cambodian people was evident in the construction of their homes in this area. The rustic dwellings were perched on stilts, like large tree houses, to accommodate the significant fluctuations in the water levels from dry to rainy seasons. Out in the pastureland, they saw haystacks wrapped around tall poles, probably to prevent the precious hay from being swept away by strong winds or flash floods.

When the team arrived, they found a comfortable aftercare house managed by compassionate people.

"You have a beautiful place here," Ted said as their hostess offered them seats on a concrete patio under a thatched-roof awning.

The fenced-in property exuded peace, a sense of refuge. A small yard included grass, trees, bushes, and open space. Small nameplates marked out plots of ground for the girls to work into gardens, either as a class project or for enjoyment.

Beyond its appearance and ambiance, though, Sharon needed to determine if this facility would be right for some of the girls of Svay Pak. It clearly was too small to house them all.

When the director of the facility stepped out onto the patio, they all introduced themselves and took seats around a table. Sharon immediately began gathering information she needed. "What is your capacity here?"

"We have room for twenty right now," the director answered. "Currently eleven girls live here, and two more are arriving today. We intentionally want to keep it small, so it stays more like a family. We sense that if we get much larger than twenty, we'll start to lose the emotional security and intimacy that our girls have in the family setting."

"How old are the girls you care for?"

"Most are between fifteen and twenty-two. The youngest we have now is fourteen. Girls much younger than that we refer to another nongovernmental organization."

"Are all your residents sexual exploitation victims?"

"No, not all of them. We meet our girls in a number of other ways, including our outreach in Phnom Penh to AIDS victims. We also go directly into the brothels to lead Bible studies; when the girls want to come, they're welcome."

She explained the staff's desire to work with and mobilize the local church, to educate them about how they can help girls with these specific needs.

The director continued, "We recently decided to take in victims of sex trafficking, but about three-quarters of our girls have volunteered for prostitution, as a way to make money. We don't currently have any girls who were tricked or sold into prostitution. We did have one case recently, but the girl was ready to leave. We decided it would not be good for her to go home to her parents, so we sent her to live with an aunt."

I doubt that there are many who enter the sex trade willingly, but those termed "volunteers" have been victimized in a different way. Perhaps their parents pressured them into prostitution to make money needed to pay debts or buy food. Or the culture in their village or extended family may shape the way the girls view themselves and their worth to such a degree that it's the only choice they feel they have. Coming or going, it's all just brutality upon the human soul, slowly or swiftly, gradually or suddenly. It's all simply evil having its way upon the soul, bashing relentlessly away at the fragile *imagio Deo* that evil cannot abide in the human breast.

"We offer a two-year program to help them get back on their feet emotionally, physically, and spiritually. When girls come here, their parents often make them feel guilty. There's this understanding in their culture that the children help take care of their parents and younger siblings. Here they receive three meals a day, so they have it pretty easy in the eyes of their parents. Plus, if they're not working, they aren't providing any support for their families."

"I don't know if you've ever had it happen here, but brothel keepers have come to aftercare houses with guns looking for girls," Sharon said. "Have you ever experienced that?"

"No, that's never happened here. I think our remote setting helps us that way; it's a benefit to be more isolated."

Sharon then told more about the work of IJM, about how we rescue victims of oppression all around the world. Very tactfully and in general terms, Sharon mentioned that we were currently in Cambodia preparing for an event that may secure the release of several dozen girls from forced prostitution.

The director appeared moved by the information.

"If you rescue girls and want to bring them here, that's fine. If they're a little bit younger, that's okay. If they are very young, we can help you find places for them at one of two very good facilities we're aware of.

"It's an issue to discuss with our staff, as it would mean a longer period of training than our typical two-year program," she continued. "We could provide a warm, loving environment with counseling and vocational training, specifically sewing, handicrafts, tailoring, counseling, agriculture, human rights along with spiritual training, HIV-AIDS counseling, and sports activities. It's all very structured, because that's the environment the girls thrive in."

"What kind of programs do you have after the two years are up?"

"Many of the girls continue to work here afterward, and we give them a small stipend for that. We also have a savings program, so if they save their money, we will double it when they leave. We have a two-year follow-up program to keep in touch with the girls, help them with problems, let them know they are not alone as they transition back into the real world. And we help them connect with a church community, for their benefit and for the church's—to help a group of believers get involved and build its awareness of the problem."

Sharon and the team asked several more questions and gained a good understanding of the vision and mission of this facility's managers. Then they thanked the director and left. When they had first arrived, they noticed a verse on a poster hanging on the wooden-plank wall at the top of the stairs. It was the first thing one noticed when turning into the quiet, covered patio where they had met. It contained this verse: "Commit your way to the Lord. Trust also in him and he will bring it to pass." So appropriate for what we were trying to accomplish.

Sharon, Kayrn, and Ted drove into a provincial town for lunch. They walked down a dusty, narrow side street, past a girl standing by a bicycle with a baby in the handlebar basket. They followed the sound of loud karaoke music—even in this remote town—to a café where they relaxed and ate. All three were exhausted, but there was still so much work to do.

CHAPTER 35

COOPERATION GRANTED

The pressure from the top had finally trickled down. Bob Mosier, Sharon Cohn, and I were granted a critical meeting with a police general on March 27. Our purpose was to gain support for our efforts to rescue the forty girls we had identified up to that point. What we really needed was for the general to assign someone to work with Bob on coordinating the operation. We didn't know the level of authority or commitment we would encounter when we got to the meeting.

So we were putting together information that we hoped would move another high-ranking official to action. As we planned for our appeal to her excellency, Un Sokunthea—the police general of the Ministry of the Interior's Anti-Human-Trafficking, Juvenile Protection Department—Bob, Sharon, Kayrn, and I gathered in my hotel room.

"Use your judgment on how hard to push," I told Bob. "If they seem to be going into the mode of stalling, claiming the need for a few more days to take action, you be the gauge on that and mention that we are prepared to present all this information to the public.

"If they seem to be putting this off into the future indefinitely, I will interject and say, 'Your Excellency, I would like to make it clear why I have come to Cambodia, and why International Justice Mission is here, and what it is the embassy has encouraged us to convey to you. That is, we have evidence of an ongoing crime that can be stopped by law enforcement immediately. We would like to work with you to bring rescue to these victims right now.'"

"I would not mention the media at all," Sharon said. "You can be certain that it has been passed down to her, because I know that the ambassador's office has talked to the deputy prime minister about the media, and I think it undermines the strength of our position even to mention it. We just need to leave it alone."

Sharon's point was this: We should go into our discussion communicating our role as advocates for the young victims of trafficking. That's who we are and what we do. Using the media as a threat would only detract from the power of our message and our evidence. I agreed with her. It turned out that we wouldn't need a nudge of any kind, because of the general's willingness to cooperate in any way she could.

We arrived early for our meeting with the general, so we sat quietly in the waiting area until the appointed time. When we were ushered into her office, I introduced myself and described our background, explaining that IJM had a great deal of experience working with sex-trafficking cases from a law enforcement perspective. I told her how much we appreciated the work that had been done recently in Cambodia to try to shut down the sex trade, particularly where young children were the victims.

The general and her staff were obviously very well prepped for the meeting, and they knew full well why we were there. I felt that we made good progress when I told them we weren't interested in leveling criticism at law enforcement, but in giving them a concrete opportunity to do something positive.

From the outset of the meeting, the general told us that she and her officers were "eager to cooperate" with us, and she repeated this sentiment many times during the conversation. Certainly she knew the government of Cambodia was under a great deal of scrutiny for its reputation of looking the other way when it came to sex trafficking. With the pressure applied recently on Cambodia, and as that pressure was passed along to local law enforcement, the general was probably quite happy to hear of an opportunity to do something positive about the situation.

Then we explained what we were asking for. It was important to make clear that we weren't asking for their help in prosecuting criminals for past crimes—for that we could go to a magistrate and request a warrant. "This is ongoing criminal activity, and we want to be able to assist you in stopping it, rescuing the victims, and making the arrests immediately," Sharon said.

After assuring us of her commitment to help, the general asked if Bob would meet with her and a police colonel the next afternoon to discuss our specific requests in terms of officers, timing, locations, and other resources. We were thrilled to get this kind of response after so many other attempts had failed to capture anyone's attention. We were ecstatic, then, when the general asked us for help of another kind.

"We are hopeful that your organization might provide training for our commanders and officers in the methods you use to conduct these types of investigations and make the arrests," the general said. "Would you be willing to establish a long-term relationship with our police force, so you can deliver this type of training?"

I believed they were very sincere about the request. The unit we were meeting with was fairly new, and the leaders wanted it to be effective for many reasons.

"Absolutely. Yes," I said. "We would be honored to partner with you in such an effort to help train your people in the methods we use to conduct investigations in sex-trafficking cases. We have done this type of training for other police forces around the world, and we would be happy to discuss ways we can assist you in your efforts.

"We're here to help take responsibility for what's difficult about the problem, and try to beat those problems with you."

I don't think that portion of the meeting could have gone any better, though some prodding was needed to take our collaboration to the next step. Bob set up the meeting with the colonel to explain the evidence we had gathered in this case, and to go over the concept of the operation as we had planned it.

After that meeting we would get a read from Bob about how well it went and how fast we would be able to move. Time was of the essence, but our greatest concern was about confidentiality. Would the information leak out, as we had seen so many times in our communication with local law enforcement officials around the world? We reiterated the importance of keeping the information carefully protected. It would be a challenge to do that in the coming hours and days until the operation was completed.

But we couldn't move ahead without their knowledge of our operation, at least in very basic terms at this point, nor could we accomplish the rescues and arrests we hoped for without significant help from the police force. We simply had to trust and pray that God would thwart any attempts to undermine our mission. It was our only hope for success now.

Bob Mosier (left) and an investigative associate devise a plan to get an informant, "Happy," away from the hotel where he was waiting in the street, thereby eliminating the risk that he would see other IJM team members and compromise the mission.

(From left) Kayrn Withers, Sharon Cohn, and Gary Haugen pause for an impromptu meeting on a Phnom Penh side street. A multitude of issues needed to be resolved if the rescue was to succeed.

Lead undercover investigator Robert Earle takes a phone call from a brothel keeper who is anxious to set a firm time for the supposed sex party. On the hotel bed are his disguise and maps detailing every known street and alley in Svay Pak.

Ted Haddock © International Justice Mission

Mosier debriefs Gary Haugen after a critical meeting with the Cambodian National Police (CNP). This was a pivotal moment in the operation, as the team awaited the go/no-go decision on the anticipated raid of Svay Pak. Fifteen minutes later the call came in giving the green light to proceed.

Ted Haddock © International Justice Mission

After the initial raid and rescue at House C in Svay Pak, the CNP scoured the village looking for victims and predators. Here, CNP officers use bolt cutters to remove a padlock from the front door of a brothel.

Ted Haddock © International Justice Mission

With the raid in progress, a crowd of onlookers gathers to see what will happen to their friends and business associates inside House C. Police in bullet-proof vests, carrying assault rifles, deter the observers—some the same ages as the victims—from getting any closer.

Ted Haddock © International Justice Mission

As the rescue was concluding, Haugen rode ahead with Ted Haddock to location Bravo to ensure the site was prepared for the victims' arrival. Here he pauses to check in with other team members by cell phone.

Ted Haddock © International Justice Mission

Some of the rescued girls laugh and enjoy soft drinks at the safe house, location Bravo. Sharon Cohn and Robert Earle carefully document each girl to minimize the risk that any would be sent back to the brothels, charged with a crime, or deported.

Rescued victims from Svay Pak soak in their first few hours of freedom in the safety of the courtyard outside Bravo.

Ted Haddock © International Justice Mission

Ted Haddock © International Justice Mission

Arrested perpetrators file into the Phnom Penh courthouse to be booked and jailed. Four of the suspects were eventually convicted. Later Mamasan Lang and her son would face trial as well.

SOUTH ASIA RAIDS

Ted Haddock © International Justice Mission

Girls rescued from a brothel in South Asia wait to be escorted out and into safety. The night, after this raid, IJM lost contact for hours with Rajul, a staff member who had gone looking for another victim inside a nearby brothel.

A South Asian street in the red-light district prepares for business mid-afternoon. Doors begin opening and women come out to the street to meet customers. Young victims are kept out of sight for fear that they will run away or attract police attention.

The night before he disappears, Rajul climbs out of an attic where he searched for girls who may have been hidden. To reach the attic opening, he had to climb onto a chair placed on a table. Once in the attic, investigators discovered two frightened girls huddled in a back corner.

SOUTH ASIA—BONDED SLAVERY

Freed from more than seven decades of slavery, Narakalappa poses for a photo with John Richmond, one of his rescuers.

Photo by John Richmond

In a brick kiln a young slave boy carries heavy bricks three at a time to be laid in the hot sun to dry.

Photo by John Richmond

Children released from slavery in a brick kiln honor IJM's John Richmond with a salute as he snaps a photograph of their newly won freedom.

Freed slave children share a cup of tea with Gary Haugen. Many of these children were forced to roll cigarettes for ten to twelve hours a day with only a short break for lunch.

Ted Haddock © International Justice Mission

Ted Haddock © International Justice Mission

KENYA—Martha (left), who was sexually assaulted by a neighbor when she was four, walks through a park with her mother and brother. IJM helped bring the perpetrator to justice, despite numerous death threats and other intimidation of Martha's family by the criminal's friends.

SOUTH ASIA—After escaping from bonded slavery at thirteen, Jyoti was abducted and sold to a brothel. This photo captures the moment she walked out of the brothel and into freedom. The woman in the sari is the notorious brothel keeper Mrudula. Later, Jyoti would return to lead another raid at this brothel to find girls who had been hidden underground during raids.

Photo by John Richmond

Ted Haddock © International Justice Mission

KENYA—Gary Haugen meets with David, a victim of random and brutal police violence. After he was shot without cause by police, David's right arm was amputated below the elbow. He pursues a career in law so he can help people as his IJM lawyer, Victor Kamau, helped him.

Ted Haddock © International Justice Mission

SOUTHEAST ASIA—Sharon Cohn watches a Polaroid photo develop with freed teenage victims of sexual exploitation at an aftercare home in Southeast Asia.

Ted Haddock © International Justice Mission

PRAYER GATHERING

During IJM's annual prayer gathering, staff and prayer partners meet at the Lincoln Memorial in Washington, D.C. to pray for victims of oppression, IJM staff, law enforcement officials, and even perpetrators around the world. This symbol of emancipation is a poignant backdrop for the group.

CHAPTER 36

IS IT RIGHT?

Dr. Martin Luther King Jr. once said:

> Cowardice asks the question—is it safe?
> Expediency asks the question—is it popular?
> But conscience asks the question—is it right?
> And there comes a time when one must take a position that is neither safe, nor politic, nor popular; but one must take it because it is right.

Not all in the world ask themselves, "What is right?" Many are more concerned for their own protection and advancement. Sometimes we must be willing to ask the question and help others find the answer. On the other side of the globe from Svay Pak we were conducting a type of police training different from the efforts going on in Cambodia. This time we were in Bolivia.

Thousands of homeless children live in the streets of major Bolivian cities such as La Paz and Santa Cruz. These kids, outcasts of society, often find themselves in scrapes with the law, but in recent years the police officers who enforce the law have grown tired of using the same time-consuming methods employed with more "respectable" citizens.

It had become common practice for police officers to handle justice among street kids in an entirely different way from the mainstream population without asking if it was "right." If a street kid was caught committing a petty crime such as shoplifting or even sniffing glue, officers would regularly take the kid out back and beat him up rather than booking him and putting him through the system. Some officers would take the kids' money after beating them, and a few would even compel kids to commit additional petty crimes on behalf of the police officers.

IJM first heard about the problem from a pastor in Bolivia who had worked with the street kids and witnessed the cruel treatment they received at the hands of law enforcement officers who were pledged to protect all citizens.

After meeting with police authorities in La Paz and building a rapport with them, our staff was eventually invited to deliver a course on appropriate police treatment of street kids to the entire La Paz Police Department, which totaled fourteen hundred officers. We prepared a training curriculum that stressed humane, compassionate treatment of kids who already had so many obstacles to overcome just to survive day to day. At the end of the training, each officer made a pledge to not mistreat or beat the kids and to report other officers who do.

Apparently the training was well received. After La Paz, we were asked to train another thousand officers each in Santa Cruz and Cochabamba. So we have now delivered police training in three departments out of seven in the entire country. Soon we would begin discussing how to bring the same type of instruction to officers in Cambodia.

CHAPTER 37

THE WEIGHT OF THE MISSION

The lead lawyer in these police training programs and other casework in Latin America has been our brilliant colleague from Puerto Rico, Jaime Farrant. He directs extensive IJM casework in Peru, Honduras, Mexico, and Bolivia in partnership with indigenous human rights organizations. Recently, case referrals from Latin America have forced Jaime to also enter the ugly world of sex trafficking that exploits young girls trying to see a better life for their families. While conducting investigations with Robert Earle along the Mexico-Guatemala border, Jaime had to join Robert in playing the part of a sexual predator, and as he shared with me back at HQ about the experience, the agony for Jaime of drawing near to such pain was palpable. It ran very rough over Jaime's huge and compassionate heart.

"Each night becomes more difficult . . . once again brothel hopping, once again to look for girls, once again to pretend I enjoy doing this, once again a pedophile," Jaime explained. "Once again, we go out until 3:00 A.M. What a disgusting life, entering daily these God-forsaken places.

"One week of doing this is just too long, but what about the victims? What do we do about those girls who cry daily while they put on their masks? How much harder for them when they're only teenagers? How much harder when they recall that they were deceived into coming to this crowded but lonely and heartless place?"

It's the struggle we all experience at IJM when we encounter the world of the victim. From the comfortable vantage point of our American lives, we look down into the cesspool of the lives of little girls forced to rent out their bodies to strange men who care nothing about them as people. It's a sick and dark evil that leads the men who engage in it into deeper and deeper circles of depravity, and even a bizarre and heartless loathing for the girls they abuse. Like the ancient biblical story of the rape of Tamar, the psychological brutality of sexual violence is profoundly manifest:

> Being stronger than she, he forced her and lay with her. Then Amnon was seized with a very great loathing for her; indeed, his loathing was even greater than the lust he had felt for her. (2 Samuel 13:14–15 NRSV)

"One of the hard parts of posing as a pedophile," Robert Earle said, "is actually asking the questions of the pimps, using language you don't normally use, talking about things you just don't talk about.

"I need to get the pimp on tape telling me what the girls will do, what sex acts they can perform, and I have to be explicit with him. Of course, that's very unnatural, but it has to appear natural in order to get the evidence we need."

I know from my experience in Svay Pak that those pictures don't quickly fade from one's memory. It is nauseatingly uncomfortable to play the role. But such are the sacrifices my colleagues make—hearts that cannot remain unbroken, minds that now store images that can't be easily erased. And they continue to place themselves voluntarily in these situations where the thick, heavy darkness is palpable. They do it because they know their temporary presence in that underworld may be the only hope innocent victims have of seeing the light of freedom and experiencing the joy of rescue.

CHAPTER 38

NO LITTLE FOXES IN THE GARDEN

The afternoon Bob met with police colonel Touchgim and General Un Sokunthea, I took a van ride around Phnom Penh with Shannon, Ted, and the *Dateline NBC* crew. We didn't have a particular destination, but the producer wanted to tape an interview with me using the backdrop of the bustling city flowing by.

We had a growing sense of confidence in the crew's professionalism and integrity. They seemed to pass every test we gave them, the ones they knew about and the ones they didn't. They were pushing to do their story and to make good TV, no doubt. But they also kept their word to us on matters big and small, and they seemed genuinely committed to doing the right things for the right reasons. It was a careful dance for both parties. We both had to maintain our professional independence, but I think we also simply came to understand and respect what the other was trying to do.

Increasingly we believed that when the critical, unscripted moment was upon us, with no time for discussion, they would do the right thing, with integrity and good judgment. A baseline of unspoken trust had emerged.

Hour by hour we drew closer to D-day, but operationally a mountain of preparations remained. Mosier had to work out all the details with those in charge of the police resources, including timing, staffing, and locations. Mosier was in his element, and he was shifting into overdrive.

I recalled the words from Bob's earlier discussion with a TV producer: "If you think about law enforcement in the States and all the different planning options you would go through to conduct an operation like this, you can multiply that times ten in a developing country. Here, you have to be concerned with whether the tires are going to blow out on the vehicle you rent, or whether it's even going to start; you have to arrange for water for your folks, because they can't just stop and drink from a tap in a developing country, and you don't know when they are going to be near a place where you can purchase bottled water. Dehydration can be a serious problem in warm climates. If a telephone network goes down, you suddenly lose your only means of communicating with your colleagues. You need to have two network sim cards for your mobile phone so, at the very least, you have two networks you can use to get in touch with someone to communicate critical information or call for help. . . ."

And this was on top of negotiating with some of the top law enforcement officials in Cambodia about how we should command some of their troops during the raid. Mosier was carrying the weight of a very intense undertaking. The Cambodian police officials were also working on their own timeline, not ours. Each hour we waited for the final go-ahead seemed like an eternity. As the clock ticked, the risk grew greater that information could be leaked that would close down the entire operation.

"There's really no way to complain about the inaction of the police force, because they are just doing everything you would want to do if you were in charge of the police department," Sharon said to Bob as they sat in comfortable chairs in the hotel lobby.

"I have to tell you, I don't have a problem with what they're doing, but it's just not as expedient as it could be," Bob replied.

"It's not just about expediency," Sharon answered. "We're much less likely to get everything we want if they do it another way."

Rapidly changing the subject, Sharon said, "I want to be in a position where we have to buy teddy bears. I like them, first of all. Second of all, it means good news. So if you could just call me up and say, 'Start making that teddy bear run,' I'll be ecstatic."

Sharon was referring to the plan to provide each girl with a basket of essentials as she transitioned from life in the brothel to life in the aftercare home. Team members would rush to purchase quantities of personal items for each girl, simple things really. A toothbrush, soap, a washcloth, some clothing. And a teddy bear. "After all," Sharon explained, "doesn't every little girl deserve a teddy bear? A symbol of innocence and trust restored."

So "Operation Teddy Bear" became a dual reference for the latter stage of the mission, separate from the official code name for the whole operation: Hotel California. It was a reference to a 1970s rock song that contained the line: "You can check out anytime you like, but you can never leave." The team was trusting that this would be the fate of those who had kept these girls under lock and key with no hope of rescue—until now.

———

Every morning during the Cambodian mission, our team gathered to pray, usually in my hotel room. As the make-or-break time approached, just a couple of days before the raid would happen, many of us sensed the mounting pressure. More than ever, we knew we needed God's help in bringing all the details together to make the mission successful, to get the girls out.

"We are greatly in need of your sovereign intervention today, Father, Creator of these children who are being discussed in high places," Sharon Cohn prayed. "Break the hold of evil here. Allow no little foxes in the garden, Lord, no snares. Help us to be patient as we wait for your good news, but we pray that it would come quickly."

Mosier added his own plea: "In all these things, keep us mindful that your hand is upon us, the Maker of the universe. We are very small, yet the smallest is precious to you. You own the cattle on a thousand hills. Of all the billions on earth, you know all about us, our names, our hearts. Grant us here joy, peace, mercy, kindness, understanding . . ."

I closed our prayer time that day: "God in heaven, the apostle Paul urged us to be anxious for nothing, so that peace surpassing understanding will guard our hearts and minds in Christ Jesus. And we need this, looking at a day that seems so long. The fate of this mission is in others' hands. So the day looks long, Lord. In my own understanding it would be a day of anxiety and worry and fatigue that comes from anxiety, and waste of mind and heart that comes from worry. So much of worry comes from our concern, passion; we've given our best for these children. From the passion of our hearts we call out to you. Be in the midst of us in power. Help us to go through with peace and confidence in you and your love for these children—supernatural peace and confidence in each other. Thanks that we would be so much better together than we would be on our own, and for not leaving us to our own weakness of the flesh. We ask again today that we would be of one spirit, striving together shoulder to shoulder . . . in no way intimidated by our opponents. All this we ask in the name of Jesus. Amen."

CHAPTER 39

THUNDER FROM HEAVEN

Though Svay Pak was consuming so much of our time and attention, our staff members and friends in other corners of the world grappled with different challenges that burdened defenseless victims in need.

Around the time of Will and Sharon's first trip to Cambodia, a group of attorneys from Minnesota volunteered to take a trip to Uganda to document cases of oppression that IJM would follow up on. One victim they met was a widow named Christine. Her story could have belonged to thousands of women, especially in a country with so many husbands and fathers dying of AIDS.

After the death of her husband, Christine, like many other women in her predicament, was left alone with her only real asset being the home and land they had owned together. Now that her husband was gone, Christine lost what little social power she had and became vulnerable to oppression. Christine's late husband's brother and his family began slowly but surely to push Christine out of her home. First they took her land. Then they rented out rooms in her home until she was relegated to one room in the home she'd shared with her husband for years. Defenseless, she didn't know where to turn. But now, with the volunteer attorneys documenting her case and passing it along to IJM, Christine had a thread of hope that maybe her situation would end positively, unlike so many others. Maybe she could get back the land and home that were rightfully hers.

About the time the Svay Pak case was really heating up, we deployed a new director in our Uganda office, a Ugandan national named Jane Adong. Though small in stature, Jane is a woman of power and substance. After Jane visited our Washington, D.C., headquarters for training, one staff member said that listening to Jane pray was like hearing the thunder from heaven moving on behalf of the oppressed.

After five weeks of orientation and training in our headquarters, one of the first things Jane did when she landed in Uganda ready to begin her work was visit Christine. And whom should she run into but Christine's brother-in-law. I would love to have been sitting inside Christine's small home listening to the conversation. I can imagine Jane approaching the man and in a very low, controlled voice saying, "You will make this right. You will take care of Christine, or I will be back." And indeed that's exactly what she said. The amazing thing is that this man knew she meant business, and he promised he would do the right thing.

It wasn't long before rumors began to circulate among others attempting to prey upon vulnerable widows and threatening to take their land. They had heard about her conversations with Christine's brother-in-law and were now pleading with the widows, their victims: "Please give me a little more time. I've heard IJM is in the country. Please don't tell them about your problem. I promise I'll help."

Oh, the joy of power placed in the right hands. Hands like those of my sister Jane Adong.

CHAPTER 40

"IF YOU COME BACK, YOU DIE"

As we made preparations for the approaching Svay Pak intervention, our investigators had to continue operations in the village—to refresh intelligence, chase down leads on the perpetrator web, and sustain the ruse of the impending sex party for the Western tourists. Of course every day risked exposure and complications, and every passing day increased tensions and suspicions in Svay Pak about when all the rich Westerners were coming. One night about a week after the whole team arrived in Cambodia, events in one corner of Svay Pak turned sour.

Robert Earle, wired with undercover camera and microphone, approached a brothel asking for young girls. The brothel manager at the door appeared willing to do business with Robert and led him inside to a small room at the rear of the building.

After confirming that he did have young girls, the manager sent someone out to locate one for Robert. Moments later, a very small girl walked in.

"Here is young girl for you. Take her now," the manager offered.

"How old is she?" Robert asked.

"Five," replied the manager. "You can have sex with her now."

"I don't really like them that young for myself. I'm just setting up some girls for a party for some friends," Robert told him.

"How come you say you want young girl then don't do nothing?" the brothel manager fumed. He then told Robert that he would do business with him only if he had sex with the girl then and there.

Robert's refusal caused the pimp to grow angrier, and he was getting suspicious, too.

"Do you have camera?" he asked.

"Why do you think I have a camera?" Robert answered. "I have a cell phone—"

"And I think you have a camera, too," the manager said, pointing at Robert. "I don't care for you," he continued matter-of-factly. "And also, if you come back, you die."

Such words tend to ring in your ears and invade your sleep at night. They make you think of your spouse and kids back at home, and you pray again that God will protect you as you try to rescue those who otherwise have no hope.

"Okay, okay, we're out of here," Robert said and left immediately.

In the brothels of Svay Pak, the child sellers sometimes fraternize with one another, much like car dealers along a metropolitan auto row. Though competitors, they may try to build alliances or at least bearable relationships that would be mutually beneficial. We received information that one of the brothel keepers had begun talking to others about Westerners who were up to something that could cause trouble. They convinced a couple of our contacts—not all of them— to rescind their offers to allow girls to come out of the brothels for our party.

A few more days passed and the time it was taking to get support from governmental and law enforcement authorities was starting to make brothel owners and pimps nervous. Our team was feeling the mounting pressure as well.

Back in the hotel, Robert Earle talked with Ted Haddock, our communications manager. "I told them all that the party is happening tonight. It's four o'clock now, and they haven't heard from me."

Still, many were willing to support our plan to take the young girls out by bus to the supposed sex party, and we wanted to get as many victims out in this way as we could. We continued to wait for all the pieces to fall into place, but the mounting tension was sending light tremors through the terrain, and there was now a very narrow window of time remaining before the tension would resolve itself in our faces one way or the other, ready or not.

CHAPTER 41

THE SEARCH FOR RAJUL

Svay Pak certainly wasn't the only place our people experienced danger. In late 2002 IJM investigators led a raid on a brothel in South Asia that secured the release of six victims of forced prostitution. But one girl we knew about, Madeeha, wasn't found that night.

The next night our most experienced investigator there, Rajul, was giving Ted Haddock a briefing tour of the red-light district so Ted could photographically chronicle the areas where IJM worked. During the tour Rajul decided to check out a different brothel where Madeeha had been seen previously.

Located at the dead end of a narrow lane, the brothel had two entrances: one up a steep, tight outside staircase, the other from a stairway inside the building. The monsoon season was in full swing so the whole area was drenched and muddy. Because of the intermittent downpours, the dimly lit streets were mostly deserted, except for an occasional stray dog, cat, or rat scurrying for cover. An infrequent car or taxi moved slowly through the narrow lanes, its headlights on high beam to pierce the darkness.

An informant helped Rajul get inside the brothel, even though it was closed up (as a result of the IJM raid) and the lights were turned off. He found only two girls inside with the brothel manager, but one of them was Madeeha.

When he knew he'd found her, Rajul left the brothel and called Chris Livingstone, the IJM director in that country. Chris quickly called two other staff members, Peter and Jesher, who were in the same area as Rajul, conducting business at the local police station. The pair went to the police inspector right away and secured his help in trying to rescue Madeeha that night.

Rajul and Peter then devised a plan in which Rajul would go back into the brothel posing as a customer ready to purchase the services of this girl. Once inside, after he again identified the girl they were looking for, he would call Peter on his cell phone. They agreed that he would dial Peter's number and hang up after it rang, giving the "missed call" signal that it was time for the police to raid the brothel.

Not long after Rajul reentered the building, Peter got the call from Rajul. Immediately he and the police contingent left for the brothel, just minutes away from the police station. When they arrived, Peter and Jesher climbed the steep outdoor stairs with police officers, only to find that the brothel was locked with the lights off. When they knocked, no one answered the door.

Peter called Rajul's cell phone. When he answered, Peter asked, "Where are you? Are you in the brothel?"

"Yes, I'm inside," he answered in English so the brothel manager couldn't understand. "I can hear you knocking."

Then the brothel manager took Rajul's phone, turned it off and handed it back to him, telling him not to use it anymore.

Outside, Jesher explained to the police, "Our man is inside; we just spoke to him. They are just pretending the brothel is closed."

So after repeated knocking, hollering, and waiting, Jesher took action. He went out to the car, grabbed the tire iron, and ran back up the stairs. He used the iron to loosen a grate that covered a small window in the brothel door, from which the brothel keeper could identify people from the inside. When the grate was loosened, he reached inside and unlocked the brothel door. After a frantic search, Peter, Jesher, and the police discovered that Rajul, Madeeha, the brothel keeper, and any other girls kept there had disappeared.

Our staff people continued to try to call Rajul, but his phone had been turned off and attempts to reach him were in vain. Jesher called Chris Livingstone at home to report that Rajul had not been found and that some of the police were getting impatient and ready to return to the station.

Chris told Jesher, "Stay in the brothel at all costs. Do not leave, even if some of the police go back to the station."

After he received the update call, Chris left immediately for the police station, while his wife, Mala, notified us at headquarters that Rajul was missing. Deeply concerned that Rajul had been injured or abducted, Chris wanted us to pray that Rajul would be found quickly. We sent out immediate prayer requests to staff and prayer partners around the world for Rajul's safe return.

On his way to the police station, Chris picked up two other IJM staffers, arriving at the station at midnight. It had been three hours since they'd had any contact with Rajul, and they still did not know where he was.

Chris persisted in getting the necessary help from the police. "Please come with us to conduct a more thorough search for our staff member. The last we heard from him, he was still inside, and we believe he may still be there."

The police agreed and sent a search team along with the six IJM staff members. They again searched the brothel thoroughly, but found nothing. Concerned that Rajul may have been forced into the interior stairwell, Chris advised knocking on all the doors in the building.

At one door an irate resident protested. "What do you think you're doing, making all this noise and disturbing me this time of night?"

"My friend is missing after finding a minor girl in the brothel below. We are part of a police search party and would appreciate it if you would allow us to search your premises."

Realizing the seriousness of the situation, he allowed them to search his residence, and he also produced a set of keys to another door that turned out to be a closed-down brothel full of dusty furniture and cobwebs.

Back in the original brothel, Chris heard Jesher call to him from somewhere in the back. "Hey, Chris! Come and take a look at this."

Chris walked into the back room to find Jesher pointing at a large mirror that covered the entire wall. When Jesher leaned against it, it moved slightly. He then pushed on it, and it gave a little but then returned to its original position as if there was pressure on the other side of the glass.

Chris also pushed on the mirror, which gave about a quarter of an inch.

"Step back," he told Jesher.

He leaned back and gave the mirror a forceful kick. It immediately opened like a door as the internal lock broke off, revealing a small hiding space. There, huddled in the darkness behind the mirrors, were two girls, the brothel manager, and Rajul in a very narrow compartment, equipped with only an exhaust fan so people could stay for long periods of time without suffocating.

All were taken into police custody, including Rajul, who didn't want to blow his cover and suffered some mock verbal abuse for the sake of the brothel keeper. Rajul had patiently spent the past four hours gathering additional information—facts that could later be used in the brothel keeper's prosecution. Thankfully, all our prayers were answered and no one was hurt—this time.

CHAPTER 42

WAITING

I sat in a wicker chair on the rooftop terrace of our hotel and waited. The warm afternoon was turning toward a clear and mild evening, and this was a good place to sit quietly for a bit, out of my room and above the noise and commotion of the street. Phnom Penh stretched out below me to the horizon with its low-rise structures and rust-colored tiled roofs. Cambodians headed home on the noisy streets. The man far below in the open field had been working since morning chopping a downed tree into firewood. Now he doused and washed himself with water from a yellow plastic bucket, wrapped a sarong around his waist, and padded down the road. The workday was wrapping up, and I was waiting.

Mosier was having the go or no-go meeting with the police colonel who held control of the officers we would need to complete the complex raid operation we had prepared for Svay Pak the following day and the demanding set of tactical requirements the mission entailed. Generally you can't waltz into a police station and get commanders to direct scores of their officers to do what you want them to do when you want them to do it, in operations they've never done before, and in a partnership that's never been tested. But that's exactly what Mosier was trying to do over at police headquarters, and that's precisely what had to happen for this whole effort to work. They could very easily and reasonably say: "Well, let's think about this for a few days." Or, "Let's do this next week." Or, "Let's do this the way we usually do this." Or, "We just can't commit so many officers." Or, "Thank you for the information; we will take care of this. We'll call you when we're done."

All of these reactions by the police were a lot more reasonable than, "Okay, Bob, whatever you say, and let's do it tomorrow." And yet that's precisely what we needed them to say. It was clear that the ruse in Svay Pak would not last another day. That not only meant we would lose the driving operational momentum that we had built for months; even more dangerously, it meant Robert would be burned as an operative in Svay Pak and become vulnerable to an ugly reaction from suspicious and ticked-off operators. Moreover, the operation had a very easy botch factor threatening at all times and needed precise execution from the entire police contingent—and a very large contingent at that.

So I sat in my wicker chair and waited. Waited again for yet another impossible event that absolutely had to happen. Anything less and we would be packing it home and the girls would be left behind in their endless nightmare.

I lit my pipe again and waited. I took up once again the same idle questions about my pipe that I had been failing to answer for nearly ten years, ever since I first took it up in Rwanda as a strategy for coping with the faint but mildly sickening stench of mass graves that lingered inescapably with me and my UN investigative colleagues after a day in the field. I wondered if I put too much tobacco in the bowl. I wondered if I didn't pack in enough. I wondered if I should empty it and start another bowl. I wondered if my tobacco was stale. I wondered why it tasted hotter this time. I wondered what Bob was doing right now.

I put the smelly pipe away as Sharon and Kayrn arrived and joined me on the roof. They had continued to conduct meetings with aftercare facilities to secure commitments to take care of all the girls we hoped to rescue.

"Anything from Bob yet?" Sharon asked.

I glanced down again at the cell phone in my hand. "No, but I'm thinking we're in good shape. We're past the fifty-minute mark." Tongue in cheek, I went on to explain my intricate and overdeveloped time-probability calculations. Yet another indicator of the excessive time I had on my hands to think.

"You see," I said, "it would take them only about twenty minutes to say no. Then they would listen to Bob trying to convince them for another thirty minutes. But by fifty minutes, Bob would be getting the message, if it was no, and packing it in. It's been an hour and seven minutes, so I'm thinking they must be talking about how to get it done."

I asked how their aftercare discussions were going, and they reported on some encouraging progress, but also on the incredible difficulty they were having lining up the necessary social workers and counselors to be standing by for the immediate post-raid hours and days of transitional care. The fact that the kids were all Vietnamese rather than Khmer certainly made everything ten times more difficult. We began kidding one another again that we were desperately hoping God was doing a miracle with Bob and the police, while at the same time realizing that Bob's success would only mean that we would have to figure out solutions to the next hundred problems. It was a series of treadmills that if you sprinted hard enough would get you from precisely one exhausting treadmill to the other.

"At least if Bob and his team are ready to roll on the enforcement action, aftercare should not be an impediment to that," Sharon told me.

We talked through more details and extracted funny stories from the day. And we waited. More than two hours after Bob's meeting started, my cell phone buzzed. "It's Bob," I said as I glanced down at the I.D. on the screen. "What do you have, Bob?"

"Yeah, Gary. Just to let you know that we have gone over the full operational plan, and we have full cooperation to go tomorrow, with a full briefing of the officers at 8:00 A.M."

"Awesome, Bob," I said. "Just amazing. Way to get it done, brother. God is good to us."

Bob said he had some stuff to wrap up with the colonel and would meet us back at the hotel. It was night now. Phnom Penh beyond our rooftop terrace was bathed in soft darkness, haze from the traffic wafting up to the street lamps, and a surreal sense of having arrived at the appointed hour dawning somewhat uncomfortably in our minds and in our chests.

We made our way down from the roof and alerted the rest of the team that tomorrow was indeed the day. Police cooperation had, in theory, been secured. But we also knew that there was a great canyon to be crossed between cooperation and successful execution. Many children find themselves cast off from that very precipice, just when rescue seems so very close at hand.

———

Sometimes we just can't secure even the good-faith cooperation of police authorities, and the frustration can turn to aggravation, which can lead to discouragement if something doesn't break loose. Just recently some of my colleagues in Asia identified several brothels where they knew minors were being held. They diligently documented the cases and presented them to the authorities, and local police committed to conducting raids. But then night after long night IJM operatives showed up at the brothels with police, only to find the brothel owners had been tipped off, presumably by a mole in the police department who was probably benefiting financially by providing warnings to the brothel owners.

I remember getting e-mails from staff: "Please pray. We're going in for a raid with police and know of several minors who want to get out." Then within hours I would get another e-mail: "The raid attempt failed. We arrived to find the brothel empty." This went on for a couple of weeks, and I could tell my staff was getting discouraged. Then we had a breakthrough day. Perhaps it was just that the police mole finally took a day off. Or maybe he just realized he couldn't be everywhere at once. Whatever the reason, the tip-offs didn't happen that day.

IJM staff members had built a good relationship with a senior-level member of the police force who had expressed a keen interest in helping conduct a raid. Late one evening he made the call that he would assign five teams of officers to join five IJM teams of operatives and staff members to simultaneously raid five different brothels. Two were tipped off. But three were not. In one location our operative located hidden entrances, got through securely locked doors, and rummaged through the building to find the younger girls who had been secreted away in mysterious places. At the end of the night, eighteen females, both minors and adults who really wanted out, were rescued from their lives of abuse in the brothels. Finally, after so many frustrating delays, our staff got to experience the victory of rescue, as greed and corruption gave way to faith and perseverance.

CHAPTER 43

GO

"Okay, you tell Kha we'll be there at one o'clock tomorrow. Okay?" Robert Earle said into his cell phone. "Yes, we'll come to pick up the girls at one o'clock. See you then." He hung up and placed the phone back on the desk in his hotel room.

———

"You've got your vest on tonight," noted Will Henry as he watched Robert lay out his undercover gear for a final time. "Is there something I don't know about?"

Will was hinting that perhaps Robert was planning a last-minute evidence-gathering trip into Svay Pak, and that was the reason he now wore his bulletproof vest under his shirt. Will was in charge of security, and he needed to know everything that was happening, down to the minutest detail, in the tactical operation. If Mosier asked where Robert was, it was Will's job to know the answer without hesitation.

"I've never really worn it before, and I want to be used to it by tomorrow," Robert answered. "Can you tell I'm wearing it?"

"*I* can."

"How?"

"I know your body shape, and this changes it; plus, I can see a little bit of the vest above your top button."

"Well, they don't know my body shape, so they won't notice the difference. And I may have strapped it up too high so it's visible right now. I'll tape it up lower tomorrow."

"What are you going to do if they start patting you on the back?"

Robert paused for a moment. "What am I going to do if they start shooting me?" he answered with a sly smile.

The death threats he had received from pimps had prompted Robert to wear the bulletproof Kevlar vest for the Svay Pak raid. And Robert wore the vest the next morning when the entire team gathered at 6:00 A.M. in a hotel conference room.

With the rescue operation set to begin in just a few hours, the last briefing session got under way. Our whole team was packed into the small meeting room, along with the crew from NBC, most of us seated at long tables as Bob Mosier stood at the white board in front of us.

"This operational plan in front of you is meant for the investigators primarily, stating their mission objective," Mosier spoke loudly and clearly. "Your name is on your copy. Keep this close to you. It allows you to see what the investigators are doing at different points during the day.

"We will be operational starting at approximately 11:00 A.M. . . . Now, the first instance where we have the Cambodian National Police and IJM working together, bus number 1 coming back to Bravo with the suspects and the victims on board, should be about 1:30 in the afternoon. If you on the interventions team need assistance from interpreters, you should have interpreters on location at about ten o'clock. There should also be interpreters here at the hotel with you this morning, assigned to assist you with your different preparatory tasks."

Mosier also covered the small but very important issues that a field chief must cover.

"This handout contains a checklist to help you prepare for today's events. Our biggest potential hindrance will be communications, so we ask that you make sure all your cell-phone batteries are charged. We've also purchased phone cards to recharge your phones. I'll hand those out in a moment.

"If you're going to be in the village today, do not wear open-toed shoes or sandals. You need to have closed-toed boots if you're going in with us."

Mosier handed out another stack of papers.

"Attached to this map is your personal evacuation plan, outlining who is responsible for your personal security.

"In general, we are working in conjunction with the Cambodian police, and in most cases we should be able to rely on them for our security. But as a contingency, in a scenario where they are not able to provide the security we need, we need to take responsibility for our own. So if you skip down to 'The role of IJM Members,' you'll see that every IJM officer has a role to play in the execution of the contingency plan. Anyone working inside the village should be vigilant in reporting any sort of mob activity by cell phone or radio to Will Henry. He will then, in turn, notify Jasper, who will be assigned a detail of police officers, who would then come into the village and take us out. Three of us will also have transmitters on us, so you'll be able to locate us if you need to."

"Who has the receivers for the transmitters?" I asked.

"I do," Will Henry answered.

"Again, make sure your phone is fully charged, and make sure it is on," Bob continued.

"Take an evacuation bag with you. I don't know what kind of prescription medication you may be taking, but make sure you have a supply. If you wear contact lenses, take a pair of glasses too. If you lose a contact lens at ten in the morning, you could be taken out of commission for some time until you can get your glasses. Make sure you are prepared to deal with things like that.

"In case of an evacuation, follow the instructions you'll be given by the officers mentioned on the sheet. A forced evacuation will take place if I have received information and made an assessment that we need to conduct an evasive evacuation immediately. When you hear that command, our initial rallying point will be Bravo, the scene of the supposed sex party."

The team had given several code names to vital locations in the operation: "Alpha" represented all of Svay Pak village; "Bravo" was the facility we had rented back in Phnom Penh—a gated compound with a large house that would serve as the arrest point for the perpetrators and safe house for the victims for a day or two until they were placed in aftercare; "House C" belonged to the mother of one of our primary pimp-contacts, Victor, and was our rendezvous point to meet and pick up the girls for the party. Another location, "Whiskey," belonged to notorious brothel keeper Mamasan Lang in Phnom Penh. We had conducted several investigations there and planned to send a raid team to location Whiskey after we arrested the perps and rescued the girls from Alpha.

Mosier continued clicking through the items on his mental screen just as he'd done many times before while working as a cop. He felt the weight of responsibility for the team to be prepared, knowing that to some degree he was responsible for the safety of his colleagues as well as the success of the operation.

Steely faced, he described the scenario that had probably played out in each of our imaginations: "If problems persist at Bravo, and a secondary evacuation is needed because, for example, an angry mob is coming down the street chasing us, our second rallying point is the Intercontinental Hotel on the eleventh floor, close to some of our good friends, who will take care of us.

"If things really get bad, and we need a safe haven, we should go to the U.S. Embassy."

"Bob, if you're indisposed in the village, who's in charge of the operation?" I asked.

"If I am indisposed in the village, responsibility falls immediately to Will Henry according to the plan," Bob answered, taking another drink of coffee, which was flowing in large quantities around the table at this point.

Everyone knew what I was getting at. This mission could turn out to be extremely dangerous, and if Bob was injured or incapacitated in some way and unable to direct the operation, everyone would need to know whose orders to follow. As we reviewed the plan, we saw that first Will, then Robert Earle would take leadership if something happened to the acting field leader.

"The contingency escape route from Bravo, our first rallying point, to our second rallying point is on the attached map. There will be a bus on standby at Bravo. We have a separate bus set aside, dedicated for this purpose, and for other things that may be needed as the rescue progresses.

"If for some reason you cannot find anyone on the team, and you can't reach us by cell phone or radio, the attached map will help you get from point A to point B."

"Again," Bob continued, "please keep this evacuation order close to you. Do not allow anyone else to see it or gain access to it. Please fold it up and tuck it away so you know where it is in the event that you need it."

Mosier then handed out the phone cards so no one would run out of airtime at the most critical point of the mission. "If you would like to take a moment and load your phone, we would most appreciate it if you would do it now," he said, smiling.

There was laughter around the table, everyone scrambling to complete the assigned task. Even these moments were important breaks—"team-building exercises," as somebody said—in an otherwise very tense and serious meeting. We joked about racing to see who could complete the phone loading first and win a special prize.

When all our phones were loaded, Mosier turned to the white board and drew an operational map. "Here's what's going to happen today," he said. "Bus 1 will be picked up down in Phnom Penh. I will be on that bus, along with Robert Earle and a couple of other members of IJM and the Cambodian National Police. We will proceed to location Alpha, which is the village of Svay Pak. When we approach Alpha, we will park along the main road outside the village, so we have quicker, more efficient escape if we need it.

"We will then go into the prearranged location within the village, House C, and start to summon the children we've arranged to take out of town for this supposed sexual activity with these Westerners. The children and the pimps will be taken by moto driver to the bus; that is, there will actually be a short transport from the village to the awaiting bus.

"Once we get as many children and suspects on the bus as we can, the bus will depart for Bravo."

"Who's going to be on the bus at that time, Bob?" I asked. I wondered if he or Robert Earle or any other members of the team would be staying behind at Alpha.

"The plan calls for Mathew, Ted Haddock, and maybe one other Westerner to be on the bus at that time. Robert Earle and I will stay behind in the village awaiting the arrival of Bus 2.

"Bus 1 will arrive at Bravo, and once it pulls into the compound, it will be overwhelmed by the Cambodian National Police and the victims and suspects taken off the bus."

Location Bravo, the compound we had rented for this operation, would be ideal for keeping the pimps from running away once the bus pulled in and the gate was closed. We also didn't want a group of small girls panicking and bolting into the streets, where they could get hurt or lost in the crowds.

"At the moment Bus 1 is taken over by the police, Bus 2 will be ready to depart Bravo. But it will depart only after receiving communication from Alpha. At Alpha, during the time Bus 1 is being loaded and departing with children for Bravo, our lead investigative specialist, Robert Earle, will be summoning more girls to come to this location," he said, pointing to the square on the white board representing House C, the rented facility inside the village.

"So the ones who did not make it on Bus 1 will be gathering inside House C. Once inside House C, they will not be permitted to leave; this includes the children and the brothel keepers and pimps."

The plan was to move the children into one or more of the small bedrooms of the brothel, then take the pimps, by force if necessary, to another room guarded by our security officers, to be held until the police arrived.

"Once we get the communication that Bus 1 has been taken over by the police at location Bravo, Buses 2 and 3—a twenty-five-passenger bus and a police minibus—will depart for Alpha.

"Upon arrival at Alpha, the Cambodian police will immediately overwhelm House C and take protective custody of the children, and they will arrest the suspects we have restrained inside this area. At that point they will begin to load the children onto Bus 2.

"Then Robert Earle and I will go into the village, to the nine other locations we have identified, and begin to search for additional suspects and victims. The police will be preappointed to these locations awaiting instructions as to which house to enter. If additional suspects are located, they will be immediately transported back to Alpha and placed on a separate bus from the children so they have no interaction with any of the victims. Police will be assigned to that location to secure the suspects."

"Bob, what's the travel time from Bravo to Alpha?" I asked.

"Seven kilometers, takes about fifteen minutes."

"Will there be anyone from IJM to ensure that there is no communication between the suspects and the victims at that time?" Kayrn asked.

"Yes, there is one IJM person appointed at that location according to the operational plan to ensure that there is no contact of the children by the suspects."

"How long will we have to wait and hold House C secure until Bus 2 arrives?" Robert Earle asked. "It could come right away, couldn't it, so we wouldn't be stuck holding that location for a very long time?"

"No. That's a good point," Bob answered. He drew on the white board again. "It's important to remember that at this point the ruse is still in play, up to the time that Bus 1 drives into the gate and is overwhelmed by the police. We can't take even the slightest risk of the buses passing one another en route and having a suspect call back to the village, saying, 'Hey, it looks like something's going on at the village, get ready!'

"So the Cambodian police officers on board Bus 2 will be waiting outside location Bravo and will not depart until they know the suspects have been taken into custody. If they are needed for some reason to help maintain security at Bravo, we want them available to do that. As soon as the suspects are safely in custody, Bus 2 can depart from Bravo and head to Alpha."

I did some simple calculations in my head and could understand Robert Earle's concern. If it took the first bus fifteen minutes to get from Alpha to Bravo, then fifteen to thirty minutes to ensure that the suspects were securely in custody, then another fifteen minutes to drive Buses 2 and 3 back from Bravo to Alpha, he and Bob could be in the village for an hour or more, waiting for the opportunity to spring the second half of the trap. And a lot could happen in an hour in such an unstable and volatile setting.

As if reading my mind, Bob added, "Just for safety and security, there will be two additional minibuses on the main road outside the village, Buses 4 and 5, and they will have a small contingent of Cambodian police on board, ready to respond anywhere in the village, as needed, and extract anyone who may need help.

"When it's determined that those police are not needed in Svay Pak, and that the operation is well in hand, those buses will be dispatched to location Whiskey, to arrest Mamasan Lang and to recover the children involved in that operation."

That's when I asked Bob, "What's the plan if something goes wrong on Bus 1 on the way to Bravo?" I was concerned about the kids' safety if one of the suspects had a gun.

"We will request that the police have checkpoints along Route 598, so officers will be available to follow the bus or stop the bus and assist the victims and staff if something goes wrong," Bob answered.

One of our operatives asked, "I don't know if you have security measures in place if something happens inside Bus 1, if the guys are tipped off. Could we have some police officers following that bus in unmarked cars, so if anything happens they can take them out?"

"That's fine," Bob answered. "We can ask for a plain-clothes police intercept somewhere along here," he said, pointing to the white-board map. "At the eight o'clock briefing, I'll need from you all the information about your bus.

Get the registration number, the color, the size, the style, the color of the curtains inside the bus, and deliver that to me at the briefing, so I can make a request that they put police officers on motos along Routes 598 and 5 with a description of the buses to look for.

"Also, we need to be prepared in the event that someone from one of the brothels decides to follow the bus. They may want to ensure that everything is happening according to plan. We don't want that suspect tipping off the rest of them back at the village, so we will have a chase car available to take care of that person to ensure there's no further communication with anyone in the village."

"At what point are they going to know that they're not going to the fake Bravo location they saw?" I asked.

"We didn't have time to do that decoy run with them, so we don't have to overcome any of that information," Bob answered. "There's no reason for them to suspect anything other than what we've planned with them.

"The element of surprise—the ruse—is still our best defense," Bob said.

"Who has a command relationship with the man driving the bus?" I asked.

"We have a brand-new bus driver, an undercover police officer we've never met before. So we are going to ask the driver that we used last time to sit in the pilot's seat and direct the new bus driver to Bravo, so that nothing goes wrong," Mosier answered.

"How do we make sure the bus driver or the pilot doesn't overshoot Bravo?"

"One step we've taken is to spill a large quantity of white paint on the street in front of Bravo, for easy location," Bob answered.

"That white paint is gone this morning," Will Henry said from the back of the room.

"Then we'll post someone across the street to flag the bus driver in at the last moment," Bob said. "He can pose as a moto driver parked out on the street and make sure the bus driver turns into the gate at Bravo."

Around the room, the fatigue was noticeable. First one staff member, then another, rubbed his eyes or yawned. It had been one and a half weeks since we'd landed in Phnom Penh, and these people had worked diligently to make all the moving parts and pieces of this operation come together. I was exhausted myself. It's tempting in these settings to not sweat the details and assume the best. But things never go as you think they will, and they frequently go a lot worse. Now was the time to discuss each of these contingencies and see what our response would be.

We had worked so hard to get to this moment. Now it was launch time, and there was no guarantee that all this work and struggle and heartache over three years would accomplish any of our goals. In fact, now that a large circle of the Cambodian police had been thoroughly briefed on the precise details of the operation, the entire endeavor could have been rendered utterly void overnight through a simple heads-up from a police lackey to his friends in Svay Pak, friends who could easily reward him with a couple months' salary for his trouble. But we were sure going to find out soon.

And that was the great overriding weight of this moment. In a matter of hours, the question we had been thinking about, sweating over, pouring ourselves into was going to be answered—one way or another. The tortured children we knew by name were going to be either rescued or dispersed into the impenetrable darkness. The pimps and brothel keepers were going to be apprehended, arrested, and taken to jail, or lost into the warrens of Svay Pak, only to bide their time until it was safe once again to reopen the rape factory, inoculated against our operations. Either way, we had now put our boat into the swift current and it *was* going to go through the swelling rapids, to emerge intact with all aboard or shattered and emptied into the churning foam on the other side.

Sitting at that last morning briefing, I had no premonitions of success or glorious night visions from the Almighty. I had vivid mental pictures of what was happening to those girls. I had a confidence that we had thought this through as rigorously as humanly possible, and I had a conscious record in my mind of what certainly seemed to me multiple miracles that had brought us to this point. I also firmly believed that what we were trying to do was, by God, the right thing; we had prayed continuously for his favor and wisdom and leading. For me, all that added up to a reasonable basis to say to my team: "Go." But it was no guarantee that we would not meet defeat, waste, and even tragedy. This, I know, is a fallen world. My faith tradition is populated with as many martyrs and suffering servants this side of eternity as triumphant victors in the affairs of such a world. But either way, for each and for us, there is God—larger, deeper, farther, closer, and true. This, I believed, we had been given. But that was all. And with that in hand, the right thing was "go."

We wrapped up the briefing with long lists of assignments that had to be completed by 11:00 A.M. Eighty Cambodian National Police officers had been assigned to us for the day, and their commander would be ready to go over final instructions with Bob in about an hour.

I offered a very brief prayer. In truth, the prayers had been said. As Jesus said after prayer in Gethsemane, "Let us be going."

CHAPTER 44

THE PARTY BEGINS

Between the end of the 6:00 A.M. briefing and the beginning of the raid operation, all of us who were not participating in the tactical police briefing had spent the morning trying to equip Bravo to receive the girls we hoped to rescue by the end of the day. In a few hours we had to scour Phnom Penh to round up scores of checklist items necessary for scores of little girls to camp out comfortably and securely for several days: sleeping mats, clothes, sandals, toiletries, water, catering, television, VCR, kids' videos, crayons and paper, toilet paper, towels, soap. And of course teddy bears.

That exercise in itself was somewhat comical. Imagine a team of Westerners running around Phnom Penh in the early morning trying to buy forty of everything a little girl or a young woman might need. They endured the strange looks of shopkeepers and salesclerks as they rushed around stores, saying, "I'll take this toothbrush. Do you have forty of them?" "No, that's not a teddy bear; that's a dog, and it's not very attractive. Do you know where I can get more teddy bears?"

———

Robert Earle had stayed up all night taking care of last-minute logistical details he was responsible for in the rescue operation. He had also spent considerable time praying for success and safety for all involved. At the briefing meeting and afterward, Robert drank enough coffee to stay wide awake, but as the time drew closer to leave for Svay Pak, caffeine became unnecessary. As adrenaline took over, his senses were at peak performance, even though, or maybe because, he knew his own life was in danger. After all, this was the day the people with whom he had been building relationships in the brothel community would find out who he really was. And they weren't going to be very happy about it. Especially the pimp who had told Robert if he came back, he would die. Even so, before the operation really got under way, Robert grew so hot and uncomfortable in his bulletproof vest that he took it off. "I didn't need one more distraction to take my attention away from the task at hand," he said. "I couldn't afford the risk of that distraction."

Recently the pimps had told Robert that it was unlikely the brothel owners would let the very young girls leave the village, that is, the five- to seven-year-olds, maybe up to ten-year-olds. They had never allowed it on previous requests, because they like to keep tight control of their "property." If the girls have intercourse for the first time, their keepers lose out on a great deal of money—the premium price they can demand for a girl's virginity.

So five Western men arrived at the village around 1:00 P.M. and approached House C: Robert Earle, Bob Mosier, Ted Haddock, and Rich and Mitchell, the two guys from NBC. They entered the building hoping and believing that the girls ten years of age and older might leave and go to location Bravo, while the younger ones would stay and need to be rescued here.

It was a single-story concrete structure with a concrete floor and solid walls, divided in half by a sixty-foot hallway that connected the only two doors in the building. On each side of the hall were three rooms, usually used by girls to have sex with customers. The place was quite dark, lit by single bulbs in most rooms. Each room had a fan mounted to a wall, to help mitigate the poor ventilation in a very hot climate.

The customer rooms held dirty, worn beds that you wouldn't want your dog to sleep on. This was not the type of establishment that changes the linens between guests. The beat-up old furniture throughout the house had certainly seen better days. Walls covered with photographs of Asian girls in various stages of undress set a salacious tone.

On his first undercover trip into the brothels of Svay Pak, Robert Earle met Victor, a pimp and community leader of sorts. Victor was actually in charge at the first brothel that Robert and Mark, the former U.S. special forces guy, were led to in the dark alleyways when they first rode into Svay Pak.

Victor's social status was evident as he gave orders to younger pimps, who obeyed immediately. He carried himself proudly, as though he had accomplished something for which he should be admired. After cataloging Victor and the girls in his charge on that first undercover videotape, Robert had left that brothel hoping he'd meet this pimp again.

The only person who seemed to outrank Victor on the social ladder of Svay Pak was Kha, the self-appointed chief of the village, and Victor's would-be partner in preparing this party for Western sex tourists.

Robert had called again this morning, confirming that the group was on its way. When Robert walked through the door leading a group of Western men carrying party supplies, toys for the girls and drinks for all, the two men greeted Robert like an old friend.

Robert remembered, "They were just so excited to see us after all the talking and preparation I had done with them."

The warm greeting he received actually helped set aside some of Robert's anxiety in those first few moments. Imagine yourself in his shoes, carrying off a hoax like this to try to capture the people standing before you and rescue dozens of girls who right now were just a few yards away. Robert knew that when he walked in he could find that the police had already tipped off these bad guys, and if so, he could be greeted with life-threatening violence.

"So, are the girls still available today?" Robert asked, holding his breath, waiting for the reply.

The rest of the day's activities, the whole operation really, hung on Kha's answer. If he said no, that would mean a tip-off had occurred and no girls would be rescued today, maybe not for a long time. It could also mean our team was already in danger.

"Yes, yes, they are ready," Kha answered. "They be here in a minute."

The words were a huge relief for Robert, but he took it in stride and pointed to a room near the front. "We'll set up our party in there," he said, both to the brothel keepers and to his friends, who now stood behind him with their arms full of party props. This "mini-party" with the team of five was being set up for two reasons: to establish this crew as the "advance team" for the much larger group of sex tourists waiting back at a rented house, and to provide an activity to occupy time between the departure of Bus 1 and the arrival of Bus 2. He felt as though his life had been protected, even though a few people in the village had turned against him and threatened to kill him. Apparently Kha and Victor were blinded by the dollar signs in their eyes, as we had prayed they would be. And now they welcomed into this house the investigators who would send them to jail today if everything worked out right.

"Come on in, guys; bring the drinks and toys in here. Kick back and relax for a while. The girls will be here shortly," Robert said casually.

In a few moments, the first two girls walked in the back door. Robert breathed another sigh of relief. And they kept arriving, one or two at a time with the same painted-on smiles they always wore, until about twenty girls were in the house, lingering around the party room, and around Robert.

He was delighted to see so many of the faces he recognized. On previous investigative trips he had learned their names and ages, and they recognized him, too, because he had brought them presents on his earlier visits. These were the girls whose photos he had been looking at for months, whose names he had read over and over in the investigative reports, whom he had prayed for personally and we had prayed for as a group.

"It was like the girls were walking on treasure without knowing it," Robert said of that moment. "So close to rescue and freedom and leaving a life of slavery and oppression that they had grown used to. They expected it to be just like every other sex party they had experienced, where they would be treated in horrible, cruel ways." But these girls had just walked into the closest thing they would ever know to hope.

As he took mental inventory of the girls, he saw Linh and Mychau, the sisters who had most captured his attention among the victims he had documented. The only immediate problem was that there were so few men for all the girls. They really didn't have enough guys to keep them occupied until we could get them out of there—five Western males and fifteen to twenty girls between the ages of five and fourteen. This would turn out to be a bigger problem than Robert even feared at the time.

"The rest of the guys are waiting back at the house," Robert told Kha and Victor standing in the hallway. "Can we get the other girls here to load up the bus and head over there?"

"No," Victor answered. "None of the girls can leave the village now. Word is going around the village that an NGO is operating in Svay Pak."

Robert's pained expression told Kha and Victor how he felt even before he spoke. "But I've got all these guys, paid all this money, made all these promises; how can you do this?"

"Sorry, it's not just our girls. None of the others will let their girls go from the village," Kha answered.

Robert knew they felt bad; he could see it on their faces. He had spent the last two months building a friendship with these men that they thought was genuine. He had brought them gifts, including the soccer balls for Victor's soccer team, and they had given him presents. They had even shared dinner twice in Phnom Penh, Robert's way of further earning their trust, building the rapport.

"I understand they're nervous, but isn't there anything you can do? Can't you vouch for me? Tell them you know me?"

"No. It's just not possible now."

After a few more moments of intense but careful persuasion, Robert realized there'd be no budging. Kha, Victor, and the other brothel keepers would not be changing their minds. Robert needed to talk with Mosier.

"Well, I'll need to tell my guys what's happening. I'll be right back."

After a careful conversation with Bob in the party room that lasted less than a minute, they decided Bob, as an angry customer, should also try to persuade Kha and Victor to change their minds.

"What's going on here?" Bob asked as he came out into the hallway. "We were told our friends back at the house would have girls brought to them, so they wouldn't have to come here. Can't you just talk with their managers and get them to change their minds?"

"We talked already. It's no use. Girls cannot go. Friends must come here. Sorry."

Bob and Robert turned and walked away slowly, not just pretending to be frustrated and angry. They talked quietly about what to do next, and during the delay some of the girls who had come into the house started wandering back out the door. As Bob and Robert talked, and as Kha and Victor stood watching the conversation, it was discouraging to see nearly all the gathered girls begin to leave. No one made an attempt to stop them because they couldn't block the door or refuse to let the girls out—yet. It added pain to Robert's discomfort during this delay when he saw Linh and Mychau walk out the door, too.

These two were sisters, ages ten and six, respectively, who were sold for sex by their parents. Robert had visited them a couple of times in the shack where they lived with their parents. Each time he had brought them gifts, and each time he had asked if they were still virgins. (What he was really asking was if they had been forced to perform oral sex on customers or if, as of yet, no one had purchased them.) They had always answered yes, they were still "virgins."

Today when the girls arrived, Robert's heart jumped because these were the two little faces that had haunted his dreams and stuck in his mind since he'd first met them.

Much like certain kids seem to stand apart from the class for a teacher, Linh's and Mychau's faces had stayed with Robert. He had greeted them and they smiled, seeming genuinely happy to see him. He asked them, "Still virgins?" but he didn't get the response he had been hoping and praying for. Each girl held up fingers, as if telling her age, but instead of years the fingers represented the number of men she'd been forced to have oral sex with since he last saw them. Now his heart broke as he watched these two little ones walk out the back door, and he knew he might never see them again.

Quickly Bob and Robert decided it was time to move to Plan B—a one-phase operation rather than two. They would break off negotiations, call in the police, and get as many girls as possible into the rooms with our guys to wait until the officers arrived.

When they told Kha and Victor that this arrangement would be okay—to hold the party in the village—the call went out in the village for the young girls to return.

"We'll just have to call and let the guys back at the house know they should come here," Robert said. How true the words were. But rather than more customers, the "guys" wore uniforms and badges and carried weapons.

Bob called Will Henry to tell him it was time to bring in the officers.

"Okay, guys, time to party," Robert said as he entered the front room where the "customers" sat. Many of the girls who had left were now easing back into House C, milling about in the hallway outside the party room. Some of them had begun to open the toys and they giggled as they blew bubbles into the air.

"The other guys are going to have to come here now, so we need to make room for our friends. Everyone take several girls into a room, and you can stay there until the others arrive. Got it?"

Eye contact and nods showed the men understood. Plan A shifted to Plan B, and now each knew what to do.

"Ted, you take this one, and this one, and these two into the room on the right. Mitchell, you take these three; Bob, these two right here; Rich, here are one, two, three for you; and I'll take these four with me." Sadly, Linh and Mychau were not among the girls who had returned. Many of the little girls wanted to go with Robert because he wasn't a stranger and he had always been nice to them. They had seen him on several occasions, and he always brought them candy, toys, dolls, or dresses. (Even the clothing had evidentiary value, because Robert had written his initials on the tags.)

Each of the Western men now sat in a closed room with young girls around him, each man trying to keep them occupied by playing with the childish toys he had brought, toys the kids should have been occupied with at this age. The men fully expected to hear the arrival of the police at any moment, so they geared up emotionally for what they were going to do when the time came.

Meanwhile, back at the control room at Bravo, Will Henry's cell phone rang. After confirming the order to bring in the cops, Henry sprang into action. As soon as he hung up the phone, he went to talk with the police commander.

"I just spoke with my boss. He wants us to go to Svay Pak. The first plan has broken down and now we need to go in," Will said, then waited for the translation.

The commander replied, "No, we don't need to go. It's all right."

Keeping his composure, Will said, "Yes, we do. I just spoke with him. He wants us to go in now and conduct a raid. Let's go."

Again, he waited for translation.

"No. We have it under control. We don't need to go. Everything is okay."

"What do you mean, it's okay? If you don't go now, I'm going in without you," Will answered, frustration growing, knowing that precious time was slipping away. He went out, got into the bus, and got the driver ready to go.

"Wait," the interpreter said as he walked quickly to the bus. "Just a minute. I can tell you why he said it's okay. He has about sixty undercover officers, Khmers, in the village already. Your men are not in danger. But he will send his uniformed men with you now."

As the officers filed onto the bus, Will handed them packets of information that included maps of the village so they would understand exactly where they were going and what they needed to do. The writing on the maps had been translated into Khmer. As they rode to the village, Will gave instructions to the officers through the interpreter.

CHAPTER 45

THE RAID

Back in Svay Pak, some of the guys were buying time by teaching the girls English ABCs. Others taught them how to count in English as they waited and waited and waited. In Robert's room, he found it much like managing a classroom of kindergarteners. First one girl would want to play with the bubbles, then another would get angry that she hadn't had a turn, so she would try to take them away.

About every ten minutes, Robert came out of his room to make sure the pimps were still there. Was the house still secure? Yes. Victor had placed a padlock on the back door of the house as was standard practice while customers were inside with the girls. And Robert had secured the front door with an industrial-strength plastic tie, telling Kha and Victor, "I don't want any other customers coming in here and taking our girls away."

The team had been keeping the five rooms of girls in line and entertained for thirty to forty minutes when Robert popped out of his room again. Were they still secure—sixteen girls, two perpetrators, our staff and the NBC crew? He checked the front door. This time, he was shocked to see Victor's mother, who owned the house, appear from the kitchen with a meat cleaver in hand. She walked straight to the front door and sliced the plastic lock off, mumbling something about this being her house and she could go out that door if she wanted to.

Praying for quick police response, Robert reentered his room. And within minutes an eerie sound broke through the concrete walls of House C. It was the sound of screaming, as if the whole village had erupted in panic at once. "The sound reminded me of an air-raid alert over London or something, with a whole city screaming and running around in panic," Robert said. Even the girls joined in the chaotic chorus.

Because our guys didn't speak the language, they didn't know if all the townspeople, including the girls, knew what the screaming was about. They all stayed in the rooms and first tried to secure the girls so they didn't get away. All except Robert, that is. He quickly bolted from his room and took up his predesignated position blocking the front door. When he turned around and looked down the long hallway, he saw Victor fumbling with the key to the padlocked back door. Not seeing Bob, Robert ran the length of the building toward the back, watching as Victor succeeded in removing the padlock. In an instant, Victor had opened the door and was halfway out when Robert reached him. Slamming the door into him, Robert wedged Victor in the doorway. The two wrestled, and Robert wrapped an arm around Victor's head, securing a tight headlock.

Robert noticed the look in Victor's eyes: fear turned to confusion. He couldn't understand why this businessman, his friend, was preventing his escape. Was Robert just mad that the police were here, thinking that Victor had set him up? Over the course of the investigation, Robert had been bringing gifts to Victor, Kha, and others to win their trust and affection. When Victor had told Robert he didn't have enough money to buy his fiancée a ring, Robert had picked up a ten-dollar ring at the market and given it to Victor the next time he was in Svay Pak. Now Robert was holding him by the head, preventing his getaway. Robert was sure Victor would have fought much harder if he had known Robert had set the trap.

Then, without warning, the lights went out and they were plunged into darkness. Only the sun shining through the door space held open by Victor's body cast light into the room. From the shadows, Bob emerged. Seeing Robert wrestling with Victor, he approached, pepper spray in hand. As Bob sprayed Victor's face to subdue him, Robert let him loose so he wouldn't be debilitated by the chemical, and he ran back to take up his position at the front door of the brothel. As he arrived at that door, he saw a uniformed police officer taking up a position. Knowing he wouldn't be needed there, he ran back to help Bob.

He could see through the open back door that Bob was wrestling with someone else. As Robert approached, Bob heaved the suspect back inside. Now, instead of pepper spray, Bob held his retractable baton in one hand as he tugged the perpetrator out of the way. Robert couldn't see Victor, but he assumed he was somewhere in the house hiding; the pepper spray would have made it nearly impossible for him to run or walk away. But there was no time to worry about him now. It was time to try to rescue the girls.

The effort was complicated by the fact that the lights were still out, it was oppressively hot, the girls were now all screaming at the top of their lungs, the investigators were drenched in sweat, and the air was filled with pepper spray residue. Add to this melee the arrival of armed police officers who had not met our investigators and Robert's memory of a large meat cleaver in the hands of Victor's mom. It did not yet seem like a very safe place to be.

When Robert had left his room, the girls in his care had scattered and hidden in closets and under beds. No doubt they had been told horror stories about what happens to little commercial sex workers when the police get hold of them. It was certainly in the best interest of their handlers that they never get caught by the police.

At the time the screaming started, there had been about sixteen girls in the house, but several of them had run away in the pandemonium and darkness, while others hid inside. More would have escaped if it had not been for the quick thinking of the *Dateline NBC* cameraman, Mitchell. He had pulled his camera out of his bag and started shooting as soon as he heard screaming. When Bob was wrestling with the criminal at the back of the house, Mitchell noticed several girls running toward the back door. Bob yelled for Mitchell to save the girls, so he dropped his camera and grabbed two of them, preventing their escape.

Mitchell became a hero to our staff in that moment for giving up a portion of the story in order to participate in the rescue of little girls. After hearing all he had heard in the interviews, he understood the importance of freedom. In an instant, he knew that those little ones were more important than the story, and he moved to take action.

CHAPTER 46

A FACE IN THE CROWD

The police had secured the building, though some perpetrators and victims were still hiding inside. Robert went to the police commander, asking for five policemen to help him quickly scour the village. The commander responded, "Just wait; just wait," and he went to get permission from his superior. Robert went to another officer who looked as if he was in charge and asked the same question, but got no response. With the police evident in the village, he knew it would be only a matter of moments before the girls would be gone forever. And it was almost more than he could stand.

Inside House C, all the remaining young girls were secured, seated on a worn red sofa in the former "party room." Because the house was still dark, Bob and police officers had searched the house with flashlights and found girls hidden everywhere. When he got to a back room, Bob pulled out a sofa and found Kha tucked underneath, hoping to avoid capture. Bob delivered him to the police. As they combed through the building, though, there was one person missing—Victor. He had somehow made his escape in the chaotic darkness, and we still don't know how. We can only hope that a close brush with justice, and potentially many years in prison, will cause him to rethink his profession and prompt him to pursue another career that does not harm innocent victims.

Robert now looked for his favorite informant, Ba, who had been with him on nearly the entire investigation thus far. He had counted on Ba's services as a translator to speak to the police, to the children, to look for more kids, and to generally help him navigate the village. But Ba had run away, fearful that he would be caught in the police web and sent to prison for his role in aiding these Western pedophiles.

Robert hoped Ba had kept the radio he'd given him.

"Ba, do you read me?" he called, then waited for a response.

"Yes, I hear you."

"Ba, I need you to come back, and I need you to trust me that you're okay. Everything will be all right. You know me. It's no problem for you; you come back here. Trust me."

Robert had no way of knowing what Ba would do. The son of parents who had been killed by the Khmer Rouge, Ba was a poor moto-taxi driver who had been lured by extra cash into bringing customers to the brothels of Svay Pak. He had formed a deep, loyal bond with Robert over the past two months, and it proved to be the motivation he needed to return. When Robert saw Ba approaching the house, he went to the doorway and motioned for him to come inside. He looked Ba in the eye and said, "We are police. I need you to help me find more children. Are you willing?"

Robert was asking Ba to make a snap decision: Was he for us or against us?

"Yes, I will help you," he answered.

By coming back and agreeing to help, he sealed his own good fortune. If he had run, he would have been subject to prosecution, and we had a wealth of evidence against him.

———

A crowd had gathered outside House C. About three hundred people from around the village had come to see what was happening to their cronies. They could certainly hear the girls inside the house, still crying and pleading for mercy.

To disguise his identity, Robert donned a baseball cap, sunglasses, and a surgical mask so no one would recognize him and try to harm him. He was still inside the house, looking out into the crowd, when he spotted a couple of offenders. He saw one man who had claimed to be a policeman, now in plain clothes, who had taken a bribe from Robert to keep other police off his back. Quickly Robert grabbed a Cambodian policeman, pointed through the doorway at the guy and told the officer to arrest him.

"I need to go get authority," he said and walked away.

While Robert waited for the officer to return, he looked back out into the crowd with the hope that we would be able to capture another bad guy in this operation. His hopes faded when he couldn't locate the corrupt policeman in the crowd.

The officer returned with a colleague and announced that he had received the authority to make the arrest. Robert scanned the crowd again. "There he is!" Robert said, pointing into the mass of people.

The man had moved to a new location in the crowd, but Robert could easily see it was the same guy. He was wearing a baseball cap, and Robert continued pointing and describing him, but the officers couldn't determine exactly which person was the criminal. "Come with me," Robert said and walked out into the sunlight.

Onlookers now stared at this Westerner covered by cap, sunglasses, and surgical mask, slowly leading police to a very specific part of the crowd. As Robert pointed toward the corrupt cop, the man suddenly realized he was the subject of this curious activity and in an explosion of movement made his getaway. He violently pushed people down, ran over them and away from the crowd, hurdling benches and running across tables in his attempt to escape. Robert's instincts kicked in, and he took off in pursuit, all the adrenaline and stress of the day pumping through his veins along with the desire to see the perps captured.

Robert broke through the crowd with the police on his heels and sprinted down the open street. When the perpetrator rounded a corner at the other end of the street, Robert lost sight of him momentarily. Seeing the chase from a distance, a Cambodian police officer ran to cut him off. As Robert also rounded the corner, he saw the police officer step out from behind a building as the crooked cop approached. The officer whacked him in the chest with the butt of his rifle, laying the perpetrator out flat on his back in the dust.

The other officers quickly arrived, handcuffed the suspect, and marched him quickly back to House C, the man's feet barely touching the ground as they went. Robert stayed close and followed the officers back through the mass of people. He noticed a couple of low-level pimps watching him, but when he looked directly at them they quickly disappeared into the crowd.

CHAPTER 47

EXPANDING THE SEARCH

Back inside House C, it was time to load the victims on one bus and the perpetrators on another and get them out of the village. We had secured ten of the younger girls, and we knew that the police officers were about to search the village for other victims. Our guys still didn't know if anyone in the village would be bold enough to bring out weapons to try to harm them, so they were extra alert as they took the girls outside to the waiting bus. One by one, and sometimes with a girl in each arm, our men carried the victims out. The fact that they were being taken away from everything familiar to them caused another dam of tears to break and the crying started afresh.

Remember what Sharon Cohn said about holding the hand of a little girl when you walk out of a brothel—that the power of God in that moment will drive you to your knees in worship? Our investigators experienced a similar emotion as they took the girls out of the brothel that afternoon.

Robert Earle said, "One of the greatest moments of my life was carrying a little six-year-old girl named Lanah out of the brothel, into the sunlight of the bus, off to safety, to hope, to freedom, to everything we had worked for so long to achieve."

These girls had not just been carried from a building to a bus; they had been carried from abuse to safety. From oppression to freedom. From a world of evil and injustice where children are treated with brutality and forced to endure the whims of the perverted, to a world of hope where caring people would provide them with the nurturing they deserved. The bus carrying ten young girls rescued from the brothels of Svay Pak pulled out of the village toward the police station, where their cases would be documented. Then they would be delivered to our location Bravo, which we had set up as a transitional safe house until we could place the girls in qualified aftercare facilities.

The police had apprehended a total of twelve suspects of sex crimes against children. They had been loaded onto a separate bus, also headed for the police station. One positive outcome of the change from Plan A to Plan B was that the children didn't have to ride a bus with their abusers. So my earlier fear about pimps on the buses with guns had thankfully not become an issue.

———

Now, more than an hour and a half after the screaming had begun echoing through the streets and alleyways of Svay Pak, the village was strangely quiet. The dust had settled; the smell of pepper spray had dissipated. Many had returned to their dwellings. Others gathered in small groups, no doubt to talk about what had happened and how it might affect their future.

Someone told Robert Earle there was still one bus left to take back anyone else he could find. So with Ba's help he rounded up five officers and explained where he wanted to go, what he wanted to do.

In the meantime, other officers had begun their own raids on brothels where older girls were held. As he watched the officers struggle with locks and doors, taking five to ten minutes to get in despite their cutting through padlocks with bolt cutters, Robert knew they wouldn't find anything. And he felt heartbroken. It was all he could do to keep his composure. He remembered back to the first week of his investigation when he had documented more than forty cases of girls under the age of fifteen, and he knew the majority of them had slipped through their fingers.

Nevertheless, he mustered what strength he had left and led his small contingent of officers through each location he now knew so well. Each one was empty.

As Robert led the officers down one of the same alleyways he had walked through on his first night in Svay Pak—now much less intimidating in the light of day—he happened to look to his right, into one of the dark little shacks. Sitting there staring directly at him was Vicana, a fourteen-year-old girl who had been offered to him for sex. When she saw that Robert recognized her, Vicana got up and ran out a side door. Robert ran after her, straight through the living area of this balsawood, tin, and plywood shack, and out the same door. He chased Vicana a short distance, caught up with her, and grabbed her. In English he told her that she should come with him, and she did.

Out closer to the main street, the police did locate two groups of victims in the brothels they unlocked and searched. Twenty-seven girls from those places were transported to the police station so they could also be documented and taken to the safe house.

As they walked past another dwelling, Robert spotted one of the principal offenders, a woman who had trafficked two girls in from Vietnam and offered them to him for sexual activity. Robert had videotape of his dealings with this woman, a video that would turn out to be a cause for significant drama when the case went to trial. But for now, Robert led the police straight to the woman and had her arrested.

Before leaving the village that day, Robert went to the home of Linh and Mychau, whom he had earlier seen in House C, but who left and never returned. Not surprisingly the girls were not home, nor were their parents, though another younger couple was in the house. After searching the small shack, Robert turned to the couple and said, "Linh and Mychau are too young to sell. Tell their parents that. It is wrong! You pass that on for me!" Then he turned and walked out.

Robert got on the bus with the one girl and the one offender and rode to the police station in silence.

A total of thirteen suspects were caught in the net of the Cambodian police or IJM staff that day in Svay Pak. Of those rounded up and placed on a waiting bus, four were immediately familiar to us. We had in our possession videotaped evidence of their involvement in criminal activity earlier in the operation and on the day of the raid. We had documented several other perpetrators, but they eluded the police and us during the raid, along with Victor.

One of those arrested was Kha, the first person Robert Earle had met on his initial trip into Svay Pak with Mark, the special forces guy. Kha, who was more or less responsible for gathering the girls into House C, was arrested there at the time the police began the raid.

Then, after the initial raid and as Robert combed the rest of the village with the Cambodian National Police, he located two women who had also been documented participating in criminal activity by our undercover investigators. We suspected one of those women was the trafficker, the person who actually found and transported girls to Svay Pak and sold them to the brothels. The other woman had offered her house to be used to exploit girls. To gather evidence against her, we had taken two very small girls, ages five and six, and asked if we could use her house for the purpose of performing sexual acts with them; she had willingly consented.

The fourth perpetrator we knew was the man Robert had chased through the crowd; claiming to be a police officer, he had offered to protect Robert and his friends while they conducted their sex party with these girls.

The other nine suspects had been arrested based on the Cambodian police and prosecutor's own investigation on the scene. They were collected by the police during the raid and each one was officially arrested and booked at the jail.

As part of her overall responsibility for the mission, Sharon now had the critical task of making sure the kids were safe, signed over to IJM, and kept together but away from the perpetrators during the confusing hours after the raid. These actions provided for a little drama and quite a bit of shuffling around as the suspects were delivered to the police station not too long after the girls had been brought in.

The girls were all sitting inside the station, stunned by all that had happened that day, yet beginning to calm down as they realized they weren't in trouble or about to be thrown in jail. Then suddenly one or two girls pointed out the window and spoke loudly. A few began to cry again. The bus loaded with arrested perpetrators had arrived, and the suspects were being lined up right outside the window of the room in which the girls were being processed. The perpetrators stood there, some of them looking through the window right at the victims.

Though she didn't speak the language, Kayrn realized what was happening and acted quickly to get the perpetrators out of sight. One of our people hung a blanket over the window to block the view so the girls wouldn't have to see their former captors in these very tender moments and hours after their rescue. The girls quickly began to calm down.

But the powers of evil weren't done with this case, and at least one of the suspects now in custody would go to great lengths to regain her freedom.

CHAPTER 48

SAFE AT BRAVO

Throughout the morning, I had been monitoring events at Bravo, the large multistoried home with a fenced-in compound that we had rented for the ruse as the site for the supposed sex party. It was also intended to serve as the initial processing center for the perpetrators and as a transitional safe house for the victims while long-term aftercare arrangements were finalized. During the raid Bravo was also our communications and operations center; and Sharon and I and other IJM team members monitored developments in Svay Pak through radio and cell-phone communications throughout the morning.

It was an almost unbearably agonizing morning for me. As 11:00 A.M. approached, I knew the team was heading into Svay Pak; as 11:00 A.M. passed, I felt time enter that borderless oblivion where points of reference and proportionality are lost in the pounding of the heart. It's the same way time loses all meaning when you've lost a four-year-old child in a public place, and in the midst of all your scurrying you can't tell if she's been out of your sight for five seconds or fifteen minutes. All you can feel is the sweat and nausea of desperation. You sense and know that what is going on *right now* in a place you cannot see is very, very important. I felt as if I had scores of little girls, who were out of my sight, who desperately needed to be found, and my only job in that moment was to wait. And so we waited. There was very little conversation, a good bit of pacing, and relentless prayer.

Then, in a moment, we got our first word from Will. And that initial report was devastating. It appeared that the pimps were spooked and unwilling to put any kids on the bus to Bravo. No kids. Zero.

Okay, I said to myself, hitting the mental switch of analytical processing that sets the overwhelming-but-unhelpful emotions of desperation, agony, and heartache in a sealed compartment, out of the way. *How do I now manage complete failure? How do I advise the team? What can be fixed? What will be the avalanche of problems that now descend? What do I most urgently need to know to find what can be salvaged?*

The urge to immediately wade in on the ground felt overwhelming, but I knew Mosier was on the scene, processing precisely the same questions in hyperdrive and making every possible tactical fix. My confidence in his judgment and speed was so absolute that staying put was actually bearable.

Then word came, just that quickly, that about a dozen of the very young victims were secured and on the bus.

Oh, thank you, God; thank you, God, my soul called out. *Thank you, Jesus.* A great wave of reverence and awe surged within me and overwhelmed me. *Who are we to be included in such a thing?*

I had been praying for days from a folded-up piece of paper showing forty faces of little Svay Pak girls captured from our undercover video and listed by the names they had given. And now God had given us a dozen. *It is enough. It is good,* my heart exclaimed.

But where are the others, O God? I prayed. My heart ached.

Sharon and other team members headed to the police headquarters, where the dozen little victims would have to be processed and where any arrested offenders would be booked. Sharon and her team would make sure that the processing of both the children and the offenders was done as properly and effectively as possible.

I remained at the operations center to await and pray for further developments. Then, just as suddenly, word came again that more than two dozen additional girls had been rescued and were also on a bus headed to police headquarters for processing.

I was thrilled beyond words. Again, all my soul could say was *thank you* to the God who had granted such a miracle. I felt so very small to be in the midst of such a great act of goodness as it moved across Phnom Penh.

Soon I was able to get Mosier on the cell phone. "Well done, brother. I am so thankful. Way to go. Guess it's been a tough morning, but I hear we've got kids on the buses. What's the status on ground, Bob?" I asked.

"It wasn't pretty, Gary, but we got about three dozen girls out." He was breathing heavier than normal. "The police have arrested about a dozen suspects."

He gave me a brief assessment of the sweep actions that were continuing through the Svay Pak brothels to try to find more girls and more perps. We decided I should come over and check in with the operational team in Svay Pak and get an assessment. Will Henry had briefly come back to Phnom Penh after the initial raid, so I jumped on my motorcycle and he provided escort to the village. When we arrived the streets were choked with vehicles, onlookers, and scores of police. Mosier gave me a quick briefing, and I took a look at some of the suspects taken into custody. Then I joined Mosier and Henry and our Cambodian police colleagues crawling through sweeps of the remaining brothels. Each confirmed our original planning assumption about the speed and sophistication by which the brothels are able to lock down and evacuate when there is a police threat. The victims and suspects you don't get in the first few minutes, you generally don't get at all. These brothels were empty, with only the artifacts of the sex trade and a hasty exit left behind.

Because of the elapsed time, and the near-certainty that word of the raid would have traveled to the brothel communities of Phnom Penh, we called off the raid on "Whiskey" that was part of the original plan. We'd have to come back for Mamasan Lang at another time, or leave her to the Cambodian police.

I rode back to Bravo with Ted and checked in by cell phone with Sharon, who was managing an indescribable chaos at the police headquarters. About three dozen exhausted and traumatized child victims awaited all manner of confusing registration procedures in close quarters with more than a dozen suspects and unwanted hangers-on loitering about, awaiting booking and shamelessly seeking to interfere with the children. Sharon, Kayrn, and Shannon worked with some of the NGO partners that had joined them to have the girls quickly processed and back on buses to Bravo, where they were to spend their first night and next few days until final placement in long-term aftercare.

We faced a host of intimidating challenges in simply getting through the first night. The first and most obvious was the management of nearly forty traumatized, Vietnamese-speaking child victims of severe sexual exploitation. Second, there were very significant security threats. We expected that the pimps, brothel keepers, and exploitative family members who had evaded arrest would descend upon the house and interfere with the children, even seek to break them out or attempt to intimidate everyone involved with some show of violence. It's amazing how something as simple as a bullet through a window can dampen everyone's enthusiasm for a project such as this.

There were scores of critical things to think about in taking on the care and security of these girls. Fortunately we had been discussing and planning for such an event for months with many experienced friends and consultants, but the broad array of challenges and contingencies felt quite overwhelming as we received word that the first bus of little ones was on its way to us.

Somewhat comically, our first challenge was to get the Cambodian police force to tone down all the sirens and extravagant police escorts accompanying the bus that were making it impossible to be the least bit discreet about where we were taking these girls. Fortunately, a few well-placed phone calls managed to call off the parade.

Shannon Sedgwick Davis was on the first bus with the dozen smallest children, almost all between the ages of five and ten. As they approached Bravo, Shannon gave me a heads-up by cell phone. I unlocked the massive front gate to the walled compound and let the bus in with its plain-clothes police security detail on motorcycles.

Dusk was spreading its cooling shadows over the compound. A peaceful evening of surprising quiet had settled over the courtyard as the bus eased its way in, opened its heavy door with a hydraulic whoosh, and unloaded its precious cargo. Off stepped a line of tiny girls, most looking about the size of the kindergarteners who step off the bus at my son's elementary school. They were chatting quietly and clutching gently at one another as their small bare feet first touched the ground and they looked up at this new big house. Within a few moments they spotted on the patio the colorfully wrapped baskets with teddy bears and toiletries. Once the interpreter had convinced the girls that the teddy bears and goodies were really for them, a marvelous pandemonium of little-girl laughter filled the courtyard. The softest sunlight of the day cast a sublime glow over these girls as they forgot themselves for a moment and shared the unfettered glee of soft and pretty things that someone had prepared just for them.

The moment wasn't indicative of miraculous healing or of the long and difficult road of recovery that lay before them. In fact, it wasn't indicative of anything. But it was true and it was beautiful, and I got to be in that courtyard to see it. Here were a dozen tiny Vietnamese children who had been forced into dungeons of sexual molestation, sadistic torture, and unspeakable acts of cruelty with no hope of escape and no one with any plan to make it stop. And now here they were—where I would want my own children—in a safe place where they might be loved and cherished and cared for.

While we awaited professional staff, medical personnel, and skilled volunteers from partner nongovernmental organizations to assemble at Bravo,
Shannon and the interpreter helped the girls settle in and get sorted out in
their new space. As men in this setting, we had to maintain an appropriate distance from the girls at all times, and I was so grateful to Shannon for the way
she pushed past her exhaustion and poured herself out in games and play with
these little ones in their hours of unimaginable dislocation and distress, especially when there just wasn't anyone else to do it. Sharon, Bob, and all the
other IJM team members were at the police station working on tasks related
to the other girls awaiting processing and the dozen suspects who needed to
be interviewed and charged. The personnel from partner NGOs would take
some time to gather at Bravo, and yet here we were right now with a dozen
needy girls to look after and another two dozen on the way.

Indeed, as the darkness of night finally descended, the second bus arrived
in the compound with another twenty-five girls rescued from Svay Pak. Most
of these were young teenagers, between the ages of twelve and seventeen, who
had been subjected to overwhelming nightmares of sexual exploitation, some
for a very long time. Sharon and Kayrn arrived with these girls as well as a
counselor and social worker or two. We were so profoundly thankful for these
friends who had dropped everything to rush to the aid of these children. But
soon the circumstances began to feel crushing.

We were all utterly exhausted, physically and emotionally, having run on
pure adrenaline, desperation, and passion for days. Now we were in a house
with thirty-seven abused and traumatized children, with the youngest ones
starting to melt down (wailing, to be exact) in fatigue and anguish and trauma,
and the oldest ones expressing their own anguish and capable of acting out
with significant mischief. What in the world were our exhausted, small IJM
team and overtaxed nongovernmental friends supposed to do with all these
kids? How were we supposed to care for them, keep them secure, and walk all
of them through the very difficult criminal justice processes necessary for
bringing their perpetrators to justice?

Eventually, by 11:00 P.M. that first night, most of the girls had exhausted
themselves and were fast asleep. A female interpreter or social worker slept in
each of the rooms where the girls rested by the dozen. Mathew, in the first-
floor operations center, setting up security, would spend the night at Bravo.
We had posted armed police sentries inside and outside the compound, and a

local human rights NGO helped with two supplemental unarmed security guards.

We needed a senior staffer from IJM to stay at Bravo that first vulnerable and critical night, and I offered to pull the first night's watch. I knew that Cohn and Mosier were beyond exhaustion. Although they had the stamina to stay, I knew that much more was going to be required of them than of me over the next day and the days that followed. So I was eager to have them get at least one solid night of rest at the hotel, especially after all they had been through. I was also nervous about the vulnerabilities of that first night. I was well acquainted with the 24/7 commitment of the brothel keepers to retrieve their property, and I wanted to be there myself to watch who walked through the gate, to make sure the guards stayed awake, to make sure that some older girls did not seize their rescue from Svay Pak as a chance to run away before they had any idea what might befall them. I wanted to be there myself, motivating our police colleagues if any of the perps or their cronies sought to intimidate or threaten the girls or those associated with their rescue.

So I camped out in the front living room, where I could watch the front gate, check on the guards, and watch the staircase up to the girls' rooms. I won over the police sentries and the security guards by fetching them bottled water and food (of which they had none on their own), and walked around every thirty minutes or so to check on the police officer I had positioned in the back to make sure he was awake and still in the precise spot where he had been placed.

I set the alarm on my watch to go off every ten minutes to make sure I didn't fall asleep. But adrenaline and the profundity of the day's events left my mind and spirit with much to mull over. The long night passed without incident, and the slow morning hues of light emerged again to give shape to the courtyard with whispers of God's generous love shed abroad.

It was, indeed, a new day. A new day for the victims of Svay Pak, but a new day as well for those who hoped to continue in the commerce of rape. Having secured the rescue of these girls, we were looking to drastically increase the price the Svay Pak operators were forced to pay for their brutality. We were already all too familiar with the price the victims had to pay.

CHAPTER 49

EVERY DAY COUNTS

Sometimes people see crying kids and the untidy, dramatic moments of a rescue and wonder whether it's worth it. I've come to think that much of this paralysis and lack of urgency stems from the difficulty people seem to have in comprehending the reality of what is happening to these children inside these places.

In the days and months following the raid in Svay Pak, we would learn many of the gruesome details, not only of how these specific girls were brutally molested by sex tourists and sadistically punished by the owners for not smiling or cooperating enthusiastically enough in their abuse, but also about the way they were rented out to internationally wanted sadists who specialized in the torture and humiliation of their victims. In most cases all of this was done with the complicity of immediate or extended family members. Some people see only the hardships of the intervention action and lose heart largely because they have not been forced to watch the torture the children endure behind closed doors every day. I think if they had to watch it, they couldn't possibly fail to act.

As experienced professionals who work with child protective services in America know, it's never a pretty scene when you have to pull a child out of a home of sexual abuse. Of course important things can be done to reduce the trauma to the children (procedures rarely followed by law enforcement in the developing world), but you are rarely going to eliminate confusion and trauma for the children, especially if the abusive family members are aggressive about trying to keep the child. Although the children may be confused, fortunately the professionals assigned to these extremely difficult tasks are not, and they get the children to safety.

Another aspect of the suffering these children endure out of sight (and therefore out of mind) is introduced by the vicious and overwhelming reality of HIV-AIDS. If people understood that these children are not only being sexually abused but also forcibly infected with a deadly virus, they would, I think, be seized with a greater sense of urgency to get them out and get them out now.

Sadly this is an all-too-vivid reality for my colleagues around the world who work feverishly to get these girls out but sometimes know they have arrived too late. I remember when Indian colleagues were looking after Nandi, a rescued teenage girl.

Nandi held her silk scarf over her mouth. Her body had become so sore and sensitive that even the soothing breeze of the ceiling fan burned her lips. HIV positive, Nandi had developed large sores on her legs so painful she could not sleep at night; she only grew more and more weary with each passing day. She struggled against overwhelming waves of depression, despair, and loneliness. Added to her physical suffering was the emotional pain of knowing how she came to be in this situation. Her father and his mistress had sold her three times into brothels.

Although IJM operatives working in India had rescued Nandi from the nightmare of forced prostitution, she reminds us that the work doesn't stop there. Even when young girls are placed in safe facilities staffed with caring people, their chances of a long and healthy life have already become diminished. Many of the girls we rescue are destined, like Nandi, to fight against AIDS. After serving ten customers a day for six months, these children have experienced eighteen hundred sexual encounters with men who have no regard for their health or their future.

When IJM staff met with Nandi in December 2003, she was in such pain and despair she wanted to die. One of our social workers assured her that we were here to stand beside her no matter what. After a couple of hours, Nandi said she wanted to live, holding to the promise that things could change and she could get better. Then IJM social workers and aftercare partners helped to provide Nandi with the love, support, and medication she needed.

Recalling her rescue, Nandi only asked, "Why didn't you come sooner?" Her downcast eyes spoke volumes about why every day counts, for every day the oppressor had hurled an assault against her body, rolled the dice with her immune system, beat lies against her soul, and, in no small way, unleashed a fistful of fury against her very Maker.

Nandi died in March 2004 from AIDS-related diseases. IJM staff members were there with her during her final hours, offering love and support to Nandi and her sister. One staff member in particular, Ted Haddock, had become a dear friend to Nandi. When others would mention Ted's name, she would smile and clutch the cross necklace he had given her.

Again, this is the reason for the urgency of our efforts to get the children out. It is also precisely why we were now so eager to make sure the suspects arrested in Svay Pak were properly prosecuted for their crimes, so they could no longer hurt other vulnerable girls and so other brutal entrepreneurs in the child-torture business would find the risks too great. Although we know that Nandi can finally rest in the arms of her loving Creator, every day counts for the millions of other children and young women trapped in brothels around the world and those who have not yet been exploited. That's why there is a very special joy when we feel as if we showed up in time, as we found in Elisabeth's case.

CHAPTER 50

IN THE PRESENCE OF GREATNESS

Elisabeth was seventeen, the oldest of seven children from a poor family in Southeast Asia. Her father, a day laborer and agricultural worker, was regularly but not always employed, so the family never had extra funds, only just what they needed to get by. A bright girl with a special, peaceful quality about her, Elisabeth was a good student who had completed tenth grade at her nearby school. She grew up in a Christian home and enjoyed attending church with her family. She dreamed of attending Bible college one day, but she knew her family would never be able to afford it. So she started looking for opportunities to make money to save for college and, more immediately, to contribute to her family's meager income, as children often are expected to do in her country.

One day Elisabeth ran into her mother's cousin, who told her there were jobs available in a neighboring country where she could make good money. Because of the aching poverty of the area, it was not uncommon for girls to travel out of the country for economic prospects such as this. Though she was nervous about leaving the security of her village, her family, and her country, she decided to go with this woman for the opportunity it could provide.

Thinking there would be security in making the trip with others she knew, Elisabeth traveled with two girlfriends also looking for work. After a grueling, six-day journey by truck, they arrived at a house where they stayed for one day, along with many other strangers. This house appeared to be a holding facility where agents for employers came to meet prospective employees from outside the area. A number of agents came by, playing the role of smooth-talking recruiter, promising the girls jobs in the textile industry, restaurants, or domestic work. Elisabeth and one of the girls liked the way one of the agents described the work, so they decided to accept his offer to work in the food-services industry.

While traveling with this agent, they were stopped a number of times by officers at border checkpoints, because there was a lot of illegal travel between these two countries. Each time they were checked, their agent made a phone call, and then they were allowed free passage.

The same agent transported Elisabeth and her friend into a large city, to a brothel, but the girls had no idea what kind of facility this was. The man spoke briefly with the brothel keeper, received his payment—his bounty for delivering the girls—then left. The girls felt the natural emotions any teenager would experience in a setting like this, far from home in a brand-new environment, an unfamiliar culture, where most people didn't speak their language.

Nervous, but still excited about all the future held for them, the girls were taken inside by the brothel keeper. He was clearly trying to communicate with them about their jobs, but the girls couldn't understand a word he said. Another woman in the house stood by, observing the situation for a while. She recognized the language the girls spoke, as she was from their home country, so she stepped over to clarify their work assignments. She told Elisabeth and her friend that they were here to have sex with customers.

The girls were horrified. This couldn't be happening. They were here to work in the food industry. There had to be some mistake, some grave misunderstanding. But there was no way out. They were stuck in a country far from home, illegal immigrants who couldn't even go to the police for help for fear they would be arrested. And they didn't speak the language anyway, so even if they ran away, there was no way to seek out help, no way to get back home again. They were trapped.

The brothel keeper asked Elisabeth if she was a virgin, hoping she would say yes, therefore becoming a precious commodity he could sell for an exorbitant price. When he found that she was indeed a virgin, he took his time searching for the customer who would be willing to pay the highest price to rape this sweet and frightened girl. Dreading the inevitable, Elisabeth clung to her one source of comfort, her Bible. For solace, she spent hours reading Scripture and praying.

Then, about a month into her stay at the brothel, Elisabeth's nightmare came true. The fee exchanged for Elisabeth's virginity was around $240. And though she was told she would receive some of that money, the brothel keeper later told her that she would get none of it; that he had used Elisabeth's portion to pay the agent's fee for bringing her here.

And so began her seven long months in the brothel, during which she was forced to have sex with several customers a day. When she wasn't required to be with customers or to sit in the viewing area where men selected the girls they wanted, Elisabeth sat in her room, Number 5, and read her Bible. Elisabeth had written many verses on the wall of her room, the most prominent being Psalm 27:1–3:

> The LORD is my light and my salvation—
>> whom shall I fear?
> The LORD is the stronghold of my life—
>> of whom shall I be afraid?
> When evil men advance against me
>> to devour my flesh,
> when my enemies and my foes attack me,
>> they will stumble and fall.
> Though an army besiege me,
>> my heart will not fear;
> though war break out against me,
>> even then will I be confident.

She tried hard to be a shining light inside the oppressive darkness of the brothel. At first she often sang and prayed aloud, until her roommates told her to stop. "God doesn't see what happens to us," they told her. "There is no use. God won't help you."

So, for the most part, Elisabeth kept to herself, remaining hopeful by reading her Bible and calling out to the God of mercy for help. And help was on its way.

IJM investigators met Elisabeth while conducting a routine investigation of brothels in the area, looking for underage victims. Over the course of a couple of weeks, one investigator, Eugene, built a friendship with her. Because he didn't exploit Elisabeth, Eugene earned her trust during conversations recorded by undercover cameras in a hotel room.

At the same time Eugene and his colleagues were gathering information from Elisabeth, they were also encouraging the appropriate authorities to raid the brothel. And though the IJM staff people felt they were making progress toward this goal, they could get no firm commitment from the local police. They just didn't know if or when anything would happen to get Elisabeth and the others released.

Elisabeth had told Eugene that she was planning to escape along with two of her friends. She even had a firm date for the escape, May 1, and since it was late April, Eugene knew we needed to act quickly. He was well aware of the dangers she could face as an illegal immigrant alone on the streets of a city where no one spoke her native language. Our staff had heard about other victims in the sex trade who had tried to break free from their captors. The outcome was seldom positive.

Eugene went back to the brothel and picked up Elisabeth a second time under the guise of a normal transaction in which she would stay out all night with him and be returned to the brothel by 7:00 A.M. But, thankfully, Elisabeth would never return to that brothel again. She was taken to the IJM office to meet with a social worker and other IJM staff. She clearly expressed her firm desire to get out of the brothel; she hated it there and couldn't wait to leave for good.

We arranged aftercare housing for Elisabeth, and she was checked in that night, happy to be free from the repeated sexual abuse. Soon after she arrived at the aftercare facility, she wrote a familiar passage of Scripture on the wall of her room. "The Lord is the stronghold of my life—of whom shall I be afraid?"

When Eugene knew Elisabeth wouldn't be returned to the brothel by her curfew of 7:00 A.M., he and Bob, another staff member, developed a ruse that would buy a little more time before the brothel keepers got suspicious. They were still hopeful that the police would agree to a raid on the house, and they didn't want the perpetrators to be on alert. At around 2:30 P.M., Bob went to the brothel to talk with someone about Elisabeth.

A male brothel manager was sitting outside watching television when Bob approached. "Hi. I'm a friend of the foreigner who took Elisabeth out last night," he said.

As soon as he heard the girl's name, the manager became extremely animated. "Where is she? He take out girl and not bring back! If you look for her, I don't know where she is!"

"No, no. That's why I'm here. Everything is okay," Bob answered. "My friend has taken Elisabeth on a road trip for a couple of days. I tried to reach him myself, and his cell phone was out of range. Then his car broke down, and he finally called me on a landline and asked me to come explain things to you. He didn't want you to worry about Elisabeth, because she is all right. And he wanted me to give you some money for the extra day."

After he received the money and the explanation, the brothel manager was extremely pleased. He thanked Bob, tucked the money in his shirt pocket, and returned to watching TV.

It's all about the money.

The second day after Elisabeth was set free by Eugene, police raided the brothel where she had lived. Twenty-eight girls and young women, seven of them minors, were found in the brothel that night.

Back at headquarters we rejoiced to know that other victims had been set free in addition to Elisabeth, and we hoped the police would have the good sense to help the victims find appropriate aftercare. We knew what a challenge that could be, and we prayed for people to step forward and lend their support.

While rejoicing that Elisabeth and her friends had been rescued, we received sad news of other girls in this Southeast Asian country who had tried to escape from sex slavery. We knew of around 150 victims in a single brothel in the northern region of the country, and we had delivered that information in intervention reports to the authorities. But we were unable to get police cooperation for a raid.

A couple of months later, I met with the ambassador to talk about that brothel and other important issues. A few days after our meeting, an escapee from that very brothel was brought to authorities. You may remember I mentioned her earlier. Her name is Achara, and she told us about the two girls who escaped from the brothel, only to be tracked down by police and returned to the brothel keeper. He made an example of them by beating them, binding them with a rope, and shooting them for all to see, as a deterrent to any who might think about trying to escape in the future.

Make no mistakes about the viciousness of the people who buy and sell children, particularly if they are making enormous amounts of money doing it. Whoever threatens that flow of cash into their pockets had better be very careful, and they'd better be ready for a serious fight. Really, what is one more life worth to these people? Taking the life of one innocent girl will cause them to lose the money she might bring in from customers, but they look at it as an insurance premium. Give up this one, or these two, and ensure that the other eighty, ninety, or one hundred victims won't try to escape. And it works, most of the time. As with the girl we had just met, though, some would rather risk death than live through one more day of indescribable abuse.

Elisabeth spent about five months in the aftercare facility, then she was repatriated to her family. Our staff has been in contact with her since she has returned home. Elisabeth is doing well and planning to start her college education soon. She wants to study government, English, or physics.

It's hard to describe the lasting impact Elisabeth has had on IJM staff members who have met her. Sharon explained, "Elisabeth's story is profound because Elisabeth is profound; because being with Elisabeth gives you the impression that you're in the presence of greatness. There is a peace and a presence about Elisabeth that makes you remember her. Everyone who meets her will tell you she does that to them. It's how God manifests himself in her." She is, indeed, a very special young lady, who never took her eyes off her Father in heaven, even as she suffered horrible abuses.

There's one thing you should know about the way we rescued Elisabeth. We did not "buy her out," as some do. That approach is problematic for several reasons: Primarily, it doesn't support our goal to help prosecute the perpetrators. Such prosecution is difficult without police cooperation, though, and once the victim is out, it is hard to get police involvement because they don't perceive it as an ongoing crime. If the child has already been rescued without police participation, they are often hesitant to get involved in the case.

There's another extremely important point of definition. Put in fairly crass terms, what we did with Elisabeth was "rent" her out for the night, under the ruse that we were paying for sexual services, then we simply didn't take her back. During our second conversation with Elisabeth, we made arrangements with an aftercare facility that helps girls in precisely Elisabeth's situation. It was her desire and her request that we help her to escape from the brothel, so we did.

There are some who advocate buying the children out of the brothels. They find out where kids are being sexually exploited; they go to the brothel keepers and negotiate a price to buy out the victims. On the surface, it's good to get innocent girls out of horrific situations. No one would argue that they should stay. But if you look only at the economics of the situation, this approach is adding a financial incentive to the traffickers to go out and acquire more girls. When rich, humanitarian Westerners will come and buy the girls outright for a fee roughly equivalent to their four-week revenue stream, all the traffickers have to do is replace the one bought out within four weeks, and they've increased their profits. How many more innocent girls around the world will then be taken against their wills into the dark, seedy underworld of sex trafficking to be abused day after day?

These people see the children as nothing more than cattle to move through their systems in order to make more money. And they'll just keep buying and selling children until the supply runs out, which is never.

An equally important flaw in the system of buying out girls directly from the perpetrators is that this approach forces no transformation of the sex-trafficking community. Remember, our approach at International Justice Mission is fourfold: (1) Free the victims; (2) prosecute the perpetrators; (3) secure places of safe aftercare for victims; and (4) transform communities so the injustice isn't acceptable or worth the risk any longer.

If you simply buy out children without taking the extra steps involved in prosecuting the people who profit from their torment, you can't possibly hope to transform communities that foster the abuse. Only when traffickers, brothel owners, and pimps see their comrades sentenced to fifteen or twenty years in prison will they begin to look for a legitimate, legal line of work. I am afraid that the wholesale buying out of girls may serve only to entice more bad guys into the business, because it begins to look even more lucrative. The more effective approach for ridding forced prostitution from the face of the earth is to stop both the supply and the demand for the sex-trade industry.

Working within the legal system to prosecute sex customers wherever feasible will also help to reduce the demand. When sex tourists find they cannot hope to continue their brutal practices unhindered, they'll think twice about traveling to remote parts of the globe to find children to abuse. Maybe they'll get help to address their aberrant behavior and stop altogether.

Several months after Elisabeth's rescue, we videotaped a conversation in which she thanked IJM staff and friends: "Thank you very much for helping me to go to school and praying for me. Thank you so much for everything you've done for me."

But this girl who had seen so much ugliness firsthand did not stop there. "I have faith in God. He has never abandoned me. Before, when I had problems, I was discouraged. I thought God had left me. Now I know only God can help. My faith is much stronger now."

Then she offered a request that we pray for other victims—*and* for those who victimize them. "I want people to pray for the victims of trafficking. But also pray for the traffickers. Pray that they would change their ways. Pray that the victims would not believe the lies of the traffickers. Pray for the families of the victims, and pray for the Christian victims, that they don't lose their hope in God.

"It's grace from God that people have come to help me. It's from prayers that God has sent people to help me. I would tell people to keep praying for me. . . . Pray that God will use me, and that I can serve him."

CHAPTER 51

AN ASTOUNDING CONTRAST

At the Phnom Penh safe house the morning after the raid, the tone was entirely changed, thanks in part to Operation Teddy Bear. Each girl had seemed excited to receive her package of personal items, new clothing, a toy, and the symbolic teddy bear. What a miraculous, moving change happened overnight with these precious little ones. To see them outside in the courtyard of the safe house, dressed in new clothes (one with a bright picture of the cartoon character Tweety Bird emblazoned across the T-shirt), laughing and trying out their Hula-Hoops to see who could keep them twirling the longest—it looked like a Cambodian girls' school on holiday.

Their smiles and laughter were such an astounding contrast to their wailing and tears of the day before. Our staff women and NGO counselors and social workers had spent hours with the girls, holding them, comforting them, communicating in actions rather than words that they were in a safe place where no one would hurt them. People talk about the resilience of kids; I've seen it firsthand, over and over again in ways that overcome the great temptations to despair. Of course I had also witnessed around the world the difficult months and years of healing that lay ahead for girls such as these. But the process of restoration was having a good first day—here in this good place—and I was so thankful.

Of course I was also completely exhausted. While the little ones had certainly rebounded from the previous day, I was fading fast. My colleagues assembled throughout the morning to relieve me and take on a very taxing day of looking after the girls and processing them through difficult interviews that were required by the police for prosecution purposes. But before taking my first break from Bravo and heading to the hotel for a desperately needed hot shower, there was one more delightful surprise awaiting me.

I was sitting off to the side in the courtyard, watching the little munchkins fooling around. I had four young children of my own about their age at home and recognized the universal antics of children at play. There were spunky ones who definitely made themselves seen and heard with pranks and high drama, and quiet ones who occupied themselves with little projects of paper and crayons. One of the spunkster drama-queens was a tiny little girl named Lanah. She had a big, winsome smile and a mischievous twinkle in her eyes. She was full of jokes and dances and silly play.

"You recognize that one, Gary?" Will Henry asked me with his enormous arm around my shoulder. He pointed to Lanah. "That's the girl from the video. The one you've been showing everyone for the past year."

Of course. He was referring to the shocking image he had collected in his first undercover mission in Svay Pak the year before. It was the picture of the little five-year-old being picked up on the hip of another girl and being offered for sexual services—an image I had shown scores of times to members of Congress, ambassadors, television producers, and any other mover or shaker I could reach with the story of sex slavery in Cambodia. This little Lanah was the one whose suffering had mobilized so much global power, and now here she was safe and free before my eyes.

But that had been more than a year ago, and what were the odds of finding her again and rescuing her now as one of the thirty-seven? I couldn't believe it. It just seemed too good to be true. But then sometimes it turns out that the very best things are indeed true. I compared pictures and, for sure, there she was. *Oh, what a prize,* I thought. *Oh, what a kind gift from our heavenly Father that he should provide such encouragement.* I was already wrestling, as much of the team was, with the thought of all the girls we knew who had not been rescued on this raid. But from this little Lanah there was a voice that asked, *Isn't my rescue good enough? Isn't the miracle of my preservation and release worthy of great joy and celebration?*

Oh, indeed it was. It was good, and it was enough. And reverence and awe descended again. We would take away from this Svay Pak operation much grief and sorrow over those girls who remained lost to us, but we would also take away an experience of joy and goodness that said, "Each of these is worthy. Each of these is made in the very image of God and to the extent we have extended such love to even one of the least of these, we have extended such love to the very Maker of the universe. And we, for a moment, could experience the eternal resonance of why we existed on the earth at all."

In the coming days the local and global presses would begin to articulate the significance of the intervention.

Cambodia Daily (March 31, 2003): "13 Arrested in Brothel Raid"—Police arrested 13 suspected human traffickers and rescued 37 trafficking victims—some as young as 5—on Saturday in what is considered to be one of the largest brothel raids in recent years. Acting on information gathered by a US-based NGO and under pressure from the US State Department to improve its record on trafficking, the Ministry of Interior closed down at least eight Svay Pak brothels and arrested 13 brothel workers from Vietnam suspected of involvement in the international flesh trade.

New York Times (April 2, 2003): "Sex Arrests in Cambodia"—A Cambodian court charged 13 Vietnamese today with human trafficking and conspiracy in the sex trade after the rescue of 37 girls from a brothel village over the weekend. The suspects were arrested and the girls were rescued in a weekend operation in Svay Pak Village, seven miles north of the capital, Phnom Penh. . . .

BBC News (May 7, 2003): "Cambodia Brothels Under Threat"—Cambodia's most notorious red light district, known as Svay Pak, has been a virtual playground for sex tourists and foreign pedophiles for over a decade. . . . But one week after a police raid on the brothels, the area looks more like a broken-down theatre set after a performance, than the thriving brothel scene it used to be. In the raid, the authorities arrested 13 suspects and rescued nearly 40 trafficking victims, some as young as five years old.

CHAPTER 52

MIXED EMOTIONS

These little girls in location Bravo were finding joy in just acting like kids. One came near to where I was sitting on a sofa and began rolling a white paper tube back and forth with Ted Haddock. She would roll the tube to him, and he would gently kick it back to her. It was so simple. So everyday.

I watched our staff and the nongovernmental organizations' counselors and social workers playing with the girls, drawing with them, singing songs, and, most important, smiling at them—just looking them in the eyes and smiling genuinely out of love and compassion. I wondered how often someone had looked in their eyes and given them a loving smile in the brothels. And the thought caused my heart to ache.

Robert Earle had spent more time than anyone else in the brothels of Svay Pak, documenting the girls who now played freely in the safe house. In Bravo after the rescue, he noticed that a few of the girls seemed quite nervous around him. Through a translator we learned that some of the girls recognized Robert as a customer; they remembered him coming to buy them when he was undercover. Now they couldn't figure out what he was doing here.

This was a significant oversight on our part, and we acted quickly to make amends.

When the translator explained to the girls that Robert had pretended to be a bad guy to help them get out of the brothels, their tension eased visibly. One of the girls stood up, walked across the room, and gave Robert her teddy bear, her only real possession in the world.

There was another ache in all of our hearts that day that equaled the joy we experienced over the freedom of the thirty-seven girls we had rescued.

We knew there were other girls we had left behind in the brothels of Svay

Pak. We had documented forty girls in our undercover investigations. We knew their names and their faces. We had captured still shots from the video footage and printed an I.D. document so we could compare names and faces once we got the girls out. I watched as one staff member flipped through the pages of the document; there were circles around several of the girls' photographs. These were the ones we couldn't find. The ones who were left behind. The girls for whom our hearts were breaking, even as we rejoiced over the girls who were freed.

———

The day after the raid was challenging for Sharon in other ways. She sat through all the police interviews at Bravo with each of the littlest girls, about ten of them under the age of ten. One of the police investigators was a gracious man who acted with compassion toward the girls. Another police investigator tried to treat these little ones as suspects in a crime. He was rather harsh and abrupt, telling one of the smallest girls, "If you don't tell me the truth, your parents will go to jail."

It was strenuous sitting through the interviews; first, because it was so oppressively hot and humid; second, because of the double translation that was required for Sharon to understand the policeman's questions and the girls' answers. The officer would ask a question in Khmer, then one translator would translate into Vietnamese for the victim and English for Sharon. You can imagine the tedium of that process, particularly after the stress and adrenaline rush of the past thirty-six hours.

The frustration grew for Sharon when many of the girls were simply unable to clearly articulate what they had experienced in the brothels. It was just too shameful and embarrassing for many of the girls to verbalize what they had seen and done behind the barred doors of the brothels. Of course it was important that a number of the girls were able to describe concrete pieces of the sadistic horror they had been through, but as they did so, the pain of having to listen to it was almost unbearable for Sharon.

Add one more frustration to the heat and the double translation and the lack of information from many of the girls—the constant ringing of Sharon's cell phone. Team members in Cambodia needed her direction or answers to questions, then there were calls from the Cambodian government, the U.S. Embassy, and other NGOs. Even though each caller had a valid reason for reaching her, Sharon had no time to focus on anything but getting through the grueling victim-interview process.

After the interviews were completed, Sharon needed to take a break.

"All I wanted was a few minutes to be left alone," she said. "I really needed a quiet place where I could get away. I just couldn't get my mind around what had been done to the kids. Will was very adamant that I not leave the compound because of a run-in I'd had outside the safe house with one of the women from the brothel community. I had been very aggressive with her, because I thought she was coming back to try to get some of the kids. I got in her face and though we didn't share a common language, I expect I was quite clear that she would not have any communication with them whatsoever. Will's concern was that I might have some difficulty if I met her again."

And that could have been very dangerous. So, because she couldn't leave, Sharon walked outside to a quiet place near the wall. "I stood there on the edge of the compound trying to collect my thoughts, settle my nerves, catch my breath. Within minutes, one by one, each of the little girls silently came out and just stood there next to me. As I turned, I saw that they were just looking at me with these enormous eyes. And then one would start to cry. Then another girl would come out with a tissue and dab the eyes of the others. But these girls are so tiny, the tears were just popping out of their eyes rather than running down their faces."

Then they started saying, "Please, go home. Go home now. Go home now."

"I knew they wanted to go home, but I also knew they couldn't go home, and that there were such limited options for them. And after hearing all that had been done to them, I just didn't know what to do.

"I couldn't communicate with them at all because we didn't have any common language between us. So I spoke to them in English anyway: 'You've got to trust me. There are people all over the world praying for you right now. We'll work all this out; just trust a little bit longer.'

"I was just pleading with them and crying with them; it was really an upsetting scene."

Sharon finally dialed her cell phone and asked someone to please come out and take the girls back inside. And another painful moment passed.

"I was quite bewildered just then," Sharon said. "That may have been the single most difficult moment of the entire mission for me."

CHAPTER 53

MORE THAN A COINCIDENCE

After returning to Washington, Sharon Cohn was responsible for ensuring that the case against the exploiters progressed well. We had set up a partnership with a local nongovernmental organization to monitor the prosecutions and to provide information to us back in Washington as the case wound through the judicial process.

In May, Sharon and Rebecca Kipe, IJM's case system manager working out of our Washington headquarters, went back to check on the girls, inquire into the status of the prosecution, and meet with the investigating judge. In the Cambodian legal system, there is an investigating judge and a trial judge. (Theirs is an inquisitorial-based French system, not the adversarial-based British system used in the United States.) The investigating judge has the case for up to six months before it goes to trial; he is responsible for gathering all the evidence that will be used at trial.

While in Phnom Penh, Sharon and Rebecca went to the courthouse to deliver to the investigating judge a specific tape in the hope that it would provide the evidence he needed to hold and prosecute the four suspects arrested on the day of the Svay Pak raid. In God-ordained timing, the day Sharon and Rebecca met the judge, five false witnesses were being brought in to testify on behalf of the female sex trafficker, Hay Kamlim. These false witnesses were there to corroborate the story that the woman was a makeup salesperson in the village, and that she had no ties to sex trafficking.

"The evidence of the police is not very clear. It's all very confusing," the judge told Sharon and Rebecca. "It doesn't appear that all these people were involved in the trafficking business. In fact, five people are here today to testify on behalf of one of the accused to show that this person is not guilty. Would you like the opportunity to interview these witnesses?"

Sharon didn't immediately recognize the suspect's name, and she was caught off guard by the judge's offer to interview the witnesses. Nonetheless, she accepted the offer at the pleasure of the court and watched as the one man and four women came forward to state the case for the defendant.

One by one, the witnesses brought false testimony on behalf of the accused, whom Sharon had, in the intervening moments, discovered was one of the perpetrators IJM investigators had captured on undercover video—and had included in the intervention reports sitting on the judge's desk.

"We had recorded her on videotape as clearly as we had recorded anyone," Sharon said, "offering girls to customers for the purpose of performing sex acts with them. In fact, she had trafficked the girls herself just days before from Vietnam. She was clearly knowledgeable about what they were being offered for."

So our staff listened to the witnesses' testimony and were allowed to ask them questions. "Their answers made it clear that there were inconsistencies in their stories, and that they were telling fabrications," Sharon said.

Then Sharon showed each witness a picture of the perpetrator from IJM's investigative report to let each one know that she knew what Hay Kamlim had actually done. She and Rebecca also took photographs of the witnesses, so they could show them to some of the girls and determine if any of these false witnesses had been involved in trafficking themselves.

When all five witnesses had left, the judge said, "So you see, I can't possibly hold her. It's clear that she was not involved." He had not yet seen the video implicating the suspect. Sharon immediately showed the judge part of the video clip implicating the woman he was about to set free. It was important that they watched the video together so that both IJM staff and the judge knew what the other knew about the case. The evidence was on the table now—Hay Kamlim clearly offering the trafficking victims to IJM investigators for money.

"It was quite a God-timing thing," Sharon said later. "Those false witnesses could have come in any other day, and that perpetrator would have been released. But we were there in Cambodia, halfway around the world, checking on the girls; that day we happened to drop by with a packet of evidence for the judge that included videotape of that specific suspect."

Though the judge didn't make any statements after watching the video, there was a sense that he felt the evidence was sufficient to hold the suspect over for the second phase of the trial before the trial judge.

Sometimes our staff members receive "emotional wages"—huge bonuses—from the victims we exist to serve. Much more lasting than any amount of money, these gifts remind us all why we do what we do. After they had returned home from this trip, Sharon and Rebecca received such a gift, the following note from the little girls of Svay Pak:

> *Hello Sisters Sharon and Rebecca,*
>
> *How are you doing? We are here fine and had many lesson to learn: English, Khmer and Vietnamese and many other.*
>
> *Here all the mother and father and sister in the Center love us and take care of us. But we also wanted to go back home.*
>
> *We miss you alots. Do you missing us?*
>
> *Send our regard to the other sister. Okay we stop now, we miss you.*
>
> *10 of us.*

CHAPTER 54

PRESENTING THE CASE

Sharon went back again in October 2003 to check on the case, the victims, and the work of IJM in Cambodia. We were planning to open an office in Cambodia, and she was there to meet with nongovernmental organizations and check other set-up details. At a meeting with one of the NGOs, Sharon discovered that the trial for the Svay Pak suspects had been set for the following week. IJM had never been advised of the trial date.

Sharon had planned to go on to Vietnam and then India for a meeting at the embassy in Mumbai. But those plans quickly changed. She needed to be at the trial, as did Robert Earle, the lead investigator in Svay Pak, who would need to be prepared to testify. Staying in Cambodia, Sharon arranged a meeting with the second judge, the trial judge.

A level of separation and decorum is required between lawyers and judges, so Sharon approached the trial judge officially through a court monitor. "Your Excellency, could we be of any assistance to you during the trial? Would it be of any help if our investigator was available for you? Would it be helpful for you to have the undercover video that we collected in the cases of four of these perpetrators?" Sharon asked the judge.

"Yes, we would like your investigator to be available for the trial," the judge answered.

"Well, I would be bringing him here from another part of the world just to testify for this trial," Sharon mentioned, hoping to add a little more weight to the testimony Robert would provide.

The trial judge also told her that he had already received all the undercover tapes from the investigating judge, so he wouldn't need those from us.

There's one positive side to the trial system in Cambodia. Trials don't last more than several hours, because the investigating judge has already processed all the evidence that will be used in the case, so there's no need for a long, drawn-out courtroom battle. Also, trial dates don't move once they're set, as they do in so many other parts of the world, where suspects can see their court dates getting bumped to later dates over and over again.

In the short time they had to prepare, Sharon and Robert carefully went over the details of each case, the relevant Cambodian laws that had been broken, and the appropriate responses to questions the defense might raise. Sharon walked Robert through mock examinations and cross-examinations to fully equip him for trial.

The case went to trial on October 15, 2003, and IJM's Robert Earle was the only witness called on either side, though the false witnesses were present in the gallery. The courtroom was absolutely packed with interested parties from around the community. Robert even recognized some of the pimps he had met during his investigation, and they certainly had a vested interest in the outcome of this case. But it appeared as though the majority of the spectators were people from around the village of Svay Pak. They saw these suspects every day; they cut their hair and sold them food and generally got to know them as one would in a normal business setting. We knew, though, that everyone who worked in and around Svay Pak knew exactly what kind of business these people were in.

The trial now involved only seven defendants out of the original thirteen who had been arrested. One suspect had died in custody, and authorities had released the other five for insufficient evidence to charge them. We certainly didn't have any additional evidence on those five, so we didn't know if it was good or bad that they weren't on trial October 15.

The trial proved to be a landmark for young victims of sex crimes. Normally the victims would have to be produced and testify against the defendant. That is very difficult in Cambodia when you have child victims, because part of the strategy of both the corruption and the defense is to retraumatize the victims. We have heard horrific stories of girls being brought before their rapist in trial, being made to stand next to him and ask him, "Did you rape me?"

Of course the rapist answers, "No, I did not rape you."

Then the judge proceeds to yell at the girl. "You're lying! Don't you see? He just said he didn't rape you. You must be lying!"

The aftercare providers of the ten youngest girls in Svay Pak were very concerned about having the girls traumatized like this again, but they were willing to cooperate in any way they needed to in order to secure convictions for the perpetrators. However, if the girls needed to come to trial, they would need counsel, and they never were subpoenaed to testify. The twenty-seven older girls, living at another aftercare facility, had been subpoenaed to testify, though no one had informed us of this. But these twenty-seven girls had had no involvement with these four perpetrators, so they had no relevant contribution to make to the case. It was the younger ten children who had been victimized by these specific suspects.

On the morning of the trial, as Sharon was getting ready to enter the court, she saw a crowd of girls being taken off a truck, girls who had been rescued in March. At the moment she was on the phone with the Cambodian minister of women's affairs, who had called to wish IJM well in the trial and offer her assistance. Suddenly the twenty-seven girls burst into the room hooting and hollering, because they recognized Sharon and because they were happy to be out on a "field trip."

What are they doing here? Sharon wondered with dismay. She talked with the court monitor, who assists the judges, and explained that these girls were not involved in the case against these defendants; the girls could be of no assistance to the court; they would only serve as a disturbance in the courtroom. In short, these girls simply didn't need to be there.

"Where are the girls who could provide testimony in this case?" the monitor asked.

"They are in a separate aftercare facility from the one where these girls live. They were not summoned for court. I think there has been some confusion. Plus, because those younger girls weren't subpoenaed to appear, they don't have counsel, which they would need in order to appear."

There was a delay, during which Sharon and Robert discussed the option of bringing the younger girls to the trial that day. There was one good reason to do it: to aid in gaining convictions for the perpetrators. But there were so many reasons to not bring them in, including the trauma it could cause them and the lack of preparation of the girls. In the end, Sharon decided they could not bring the girls to the courtroom that day.

The monitor talked to the judge, who initially wanted someone to bring in the girls who were relevant to the case.

Then Sharon spoke to the monitor. "The little girls are too small to testify. They're just tiny little children. They aren't going to be able to testify. They don't have counsel; I can't represent them, and they cannot be produced today. The trial will have to be delayed."

Nobody wanted that, certainly not the judge. Not with a packed courtroom and all the attention this case was receiving. When the monitor called the judge back and explained Sharon's position on bringing the girls in, the judge agreed that the young victims were not necessary to testify.

The nongovernmental organization's staff escorted the twenty-seven older girls onto the truck and sent them home before the trial began.

"This was another incidence of God's intervention in this case," Sharon said. "Yes, it was a big deal that the little girls didn't have to be traumatized again by the suspects. But it was also significant in terms of setting a new standard. This decision of the judge could mark a turning of the tide in cases of sexual exploitation in Cambodia where the victims wouldn't be required to attend the trial if you had other evidence that was persuasive enough. It was a fantastic precedent for the girls."

———

Robert and Sharon brought a large TV monitor and a video player to the courtroom, so they could show the tapes as evidence against the four suspects we had identified.

Tension in the courtroom was running pretty high by the time Robert took the stand, and he testified extremely well. One defendant, then another, denied any wrongdoing. Then a video played, and everyone present saw the defendant doing precisely what he or she had denied only moments before—participating in the sale of children for sexual exploitation.

At lunchtime another surprise threatened to damage the testimony against Hay Kamlim, the trafficker who had earlier arranged for the five false witnesses to testify on her behalf. The court monitor came up to Sharon and said, "The tape of Hay Kamlim is missing. It was taken from the courthouse."

At first, the news was devastating because without the tape we had no case against the trafficker. Robert's testimony alone would not be enough to convict her. Now her tape, and hers alone, had disappeared from the court. This was a woman who was giving it everything she had to evade justice. She knew she was guilty, and she was leaving no card unplayed in hopes of undermining the proceeding.

Hearing the news about the missing tape, Sharon remembered the mini-digital-videotape she'd left back in her hotel room, "a video montage of the most compelling victim stories from Svay Pak," Sharon said. "On the front of the montage, although we never used it, were what we believed to be our strongest cases against the perpetrators. One of them just happened to be Hay Kamlim's case, and it was strong because it was so clear. She was obviously involved in trafficking, and you could see the little victims were so scared they were shaking."

Still on lunch break, Sharon and Robert went back to the hotel and retrieved the tape along with the small video camera required to play it for the court.

A video clip that was previously never used—"almost as a nuisance," according to Sharon—turned into the precise piece of evidence needed to bring accountability to a wicked person who bought and sold children like farm animals. If the tape of any of the other three defendants had been stolen, we wouldn't have had any evidence against them, because we weren't prepared to go to trial at that time.

Six of the seven tried that day were convicted, including all four of those IJM brought testimony against. Sok Chantha (whom we knew as "Kha"), the self-appointed village chief, received fifteen years; Hay Kamlim, the trafficker, fifteen years; Nguyen Chang Chouck, the man who posed as a police officer and offered protection for the sex party, five years; Nguyen Thi Viet, the woman who offered her house for hosting the sex-tourist party, five years.

Staff members of the NGOs that ran the aftercare facilities were happy about the verdicts; they were also happy that the girls didn't have to go through the ordeal of facing the defendants again. They hoped this would set a precedent and serve as the standard for future sexual exploitation cases. Our hope is that over time, as we work with the courts respectfully, we can help set up a system whereby girls can testify remotely or from behind a curtain or by some other technique that will protect the victims.

CHAPTER 55

A PIECE OF PAPER

In a different context, in the Philippines we discovered another local government in need of accountability in pursuing justice on behalf of victims, even when it's easier to give up or let the case die because of personal interests.

Cardela was born into grinding poverty on one of the more than seven thousand islands that make up the Philippine archipelago. Although public education is free in the Philippines, Cardela was forced to end her schooling after fourth grade because her parents did not have the money to pay for a school uniform, books, school supplies, and transportation.

In the summer of 1998, when Cardela was thirteen, her aunt Andrea Jo visited from Manila. Andrea Jo offered to take Cardela back to Manila, so Cardela could continue her education. The girl was very excited about the opportunity to continue her schooling and so, with her parents' consent, Cardela left her family and community and went to live with Andrea Jo.

Unfortunately for Cardela, her aunt did not have her best interests at heart. Although Andrea Jo did honor her promise to send Cardela to school, she required Cardela to do all the household cooking, cleaning, and laundry for Andrea Jo, her three children, and several others who lived in Andrea Jo's home from time to time. Cardela often worked until the early hours of the morning, washing clothes and hauling water so she could attend school the next day.

Cardela's living situation was further complicated: Every night Andrea Jo and her friends would abuse drugs in the living room until they passed out as Cardela and her cousin tried to sleep upstairs in the small home.

In December of that year, Marlon Abrigo, Andrea Jo's boyfriend—and the son of a local police officer—moved into Andrea Jo's home after his parents threw him out of the house for coming home drunk too many times from late-night parties at Andrea Jo's. Now, in addition to caring for her aunt's family, Cardela was forced to cook and clean for Abrigo as well.

On the evening of April 15, 1999, Cardela was at home with her cousin Sabrina and Abrigo. After dinner Abrigo sent Sabrina to the store to buy him cigarettes and then asked Cardela to go up to Andrea Jo's bedroom and get his towel. When Cardela went upstairs, Abrigo followed. As she turned to leave the bedroom, Abrigo pushed open the door, hitting her head and knocking her down. Despite her best efforts to escape and her fervent pleas for him to stop, Abrigo overpowered Cardela and raped her.

"If you tell anyone what just happened, I'll do it again, then I'll kill you," he told his petrified victim.

Cardela kept her terrible secret to herself for one month. Finally, after Abrigo moved out of Andrea Jo's home, Cardela mustered the courage to tell her aunt what Abrigo had done to her. Andrea Jo was not only sympathetic, she was furious. She took Cardela to the police station where she filed a complaint. After a brief investigation and medical examination that confirmed Cardela's allegation of rape, the case was referred to the city prosecutor, who filed charges against Abrigo in the Regional Trial Court. On July 21, the judge issued a warrant for Abrigo's arrest.

As happens far too often around the world, the warrant was never executed. Despite his being charged with raping a thirteen-year-old, the police never arrested him. Because of concerns for her safety, the court transferred Cardela to a Christian shelter for abused children. Her aunt Andrea Jo disappeared.

We learned about Cardela's case a year and a half later when Sean Litton, then IJM's Manila overseas field presence director, visited the shelter where she lived. Although it had been almost two years since the incident, and she was now fifteen, Cardela was still eager to pursue her case against Abrigo. Unfortunately, no one knew where Abrigo was, and a call to the courthouse confirmed that the case had been archived.

In February 2001, during the first operation run by IJM's office on this case, our staff located Abrigo using a fake contest ruse. We then referred his location to a high-ranking Christian officer in the Philippine National Police who immediately had him arrested and jailed.

Appointed by the court as Cardela's guardian ad litem, Sean Litton worked side by side with the prosecutor to build the case against Abrigo. The trial began in March 2001, and Cardela finally faced Abrigo in court as she told the judge what Abrigo had done to her almost two years before. Cardela's aunt Andrea Jo, whom our staff had also located, agreed to testify against Abrigo, as did the doctor who had examined Cardela and the police officer who had taken her complaint.

Several witnesses testified on Abrigo's behalf as well. In a startling twist, the accused claimed, and his friends affirmed, that it was not Abrigo but an uncle of Cardela's who had committed the rape. This evidence introduced a basis for reasonable doubt as to Abrigo's guilt; and because no one could find the uncle, there was substantial concern that the rapist would go free.

Sean and his team needed to find information on Cardela's uncle for two important reasons: He could offer proof that Abrigo and his friends were lying and, in providing an alibi, he would assure us that we weren't prosecuting an innocent man.

So Sean flew to the southern Philippines, where a local pastor helped him locate Cardela's uncle. Sean's interview with the uncle turned extremely frustrating, as the elderly seaman simply could not remember where he had been two years earlier at the time of the rape. Sean asked if he had any work documents that would show when he had been in or out of the Philippines. The uncle said he no longer had those documents.

Sean ended the interview terribly frustrated at the lack of progress made, and the pastor offered to drive the uncle home. As they rode together in the back of the pickup, the uncle asked Sean if he had ever been to Baltimore, Maryland.

"Yes, I have," Sean answered.

The old man opened his wallet to retrieve the card of a chaplain who worked at the seafarers' chapel in Baltimore. Just then, the wind blew a piece of paper out of the wallet. Sean quickly grabbed the paper before it could blow out of the back of the truck. As he began to hand it back to the uncle, Sean noticed that it was a U.S. immigration document given to seamen when they enter U.S. ports. Sean looked more closely and was stunned to see that the stamped dates and named ports indicated that the uncle had been in Seattle at the very time of Cardela's rape in Manila. We now had the proof we were looking for; Abrigo was lying and the uncle was innocent!

After several delays by Abrigo's counsel, the trial concluded on May 25,

2001. Litton assisted the prosecutor in preparing a final memorandum to the court, summarizing the case against Abrigo. Then our staff waited with Cardela for the judge's verdict.

On August 28, IJM staff called Cardela to deliver the good news: The judge had convicted Abrigo of rape and sentenced him to life in prison for the crime he had committed against her. When giving her decision from the bench, the judge noted that Abrigo was the son of a policeman and had remained at large for over a year and a half after the issuance of the warrant for his arrest. She said that "but for the intervention of International Justice Mission," Abrigo never would have been brought to justice. In addition to sentencing Abrigo to life imprisonment, she also ordered him to pay Cardela a substantial amount in civil liability and moral damages.

In October 2001, IJM staff invited Cardela, several of her friends, and the prosecutor who worked on her case to a dinner to celebrate the judge's verdict. It was an incredible opportunity to witness the redeeming hand of God's grace in a young woman's life. Cardela's joy-filled face that night was a beautiful picture of what justice looks like. She remained in the care of a Christian ministry for abused girls until she graduated from high school in April 2004. She is now looking forward to studying nursing or education.

CHAPTER 56

THE PAYOFF

With no local Cambodian field presence, we knew it would be very difficult to go back, find the girls we'd left behind, and get them out. You've seen what enormous force is required to pull off one raid-and-rescue operation. We couldn't continue to send over the required number of staff and spend the resources every time we decided to raid another brothel.

So we applied for a grant from the U.S. Agency for International Development (USAID) and, by the grace of God, we received that grant, almost $995,000 which opened the doors for us to be able to set up an office in Cambodia to continue fighting against sex trafficking. The new office director will move forward with the work we started, continuing investigations and interventions, managing the operatives and informants, building relationships with the police, championing that long-term change we aggressively pursue in the community of the criminals. With the seed money from USAID, we'll focus on applying ruthless pressure on traffickers 24/7. As we have resources, we will continue to train police officers in Cambodia, as many as 250 in the next few years, to fight trafficking. This will bring about the long-lasting change the children of Cambodia deserve. It will require persistence, investigative and legal expertise, continued cooperation from our friends in Cambodia, support from new friends, and lots of hard work. But the payoff is marvelous when you look into the eyes of one freed girl.

CHAPTER 57

A WAKE-UP CALL

As you've seen throughout this story, the plot in Svay Pak is full of twists and turns, villains and heroes. When Will Henry and Sharon Cohn went to Cambodia in May 2002, Will was walking down Svay Pak's dirt street when he spotted a Western man walking toward him.

They greeted each other, then Will asked him if he'd been here before.

"Is this your first time here?" the man asked.

"Yes, it is."

"Here, let's step over here a sec."

In a short, recorded conversation, Will learned that the man was Jerry Alton, a radiologist from Oklahoma. He said he often traveled to Asian countries on business but stopped off in Cambodia as part of his trip to seek out and have sex with minors.

Will interviewed him about his technique for ensuring he wasn't caught, which was getting more difficult now with the passage of regulations such as the Trafficking Victims Protection Act. Alton warned Will not to tell anyone where he was going when he came to Cambodia; people might figure out he was a sex tourist.

"If you have friends who are educated, who read, they may know this place has a reputation, and you don't want to implicate yourself in that," Jerry advised. "So you just tell them you're going to Bangkok, and you come here very discreetly. And you try to keep a low profile. That's all."

"How old are the girls you get?" Will asked.

"Fifteen, sixteen, and older. Maybe a fourteen-year-old might sneak in, if you can't tell the age," Jerry said with a smile. "But, you know, I don't take the really little ones back. That's just a little bit of discretion on my part."

"Do you get more than one?"

"For fifty bucks, I get three girls for the whole night," he said matter-of-factly. Then he added, "I think I'm gonna go cement a deal for tonight, so . . ." and he walked away.

In January 2004, Jerry would regret ever having that conversation. That's when these videotaped comments would be played for a national audience of millions on *Dateline NBC.*

While we were all in Cambodia preparing for the raid, guess who we ran into again? That's right. Dr. Jerry Alton. An IJM operative who had been assigned to look for Alton on a nightly basis spotted him seated comfortably in a bar called Martini's, a location where customers went to hook up with teenage prostitutes. A drink, a dance, then out the door with a fifteen-year-old girl or two or three. It was just that easy.

The *Dateline* guys did a little undercover investigation of their own and found out where Dr. Alton worked while in Guam and caught up with him there. They waited for him in the parking garage of that building and then walked up to him with cameras rolling as he approached the entrance. The reporter quickly recounted what he knew of Dr. Alton's escapades with minors in Cambodia. After he denied any wrongdoing, they showed him the undercover tape Will had shot almost a year before, the one where he admits to taking three girls for the night for fifty dollars.

He refused to comment about anything he had said on the tape because, "I might have been drunk, or someone could have slipped me a pill . . ."

Even the reporter thought that sounded ludicrous. "That's your defense?" he asked.

"Yes," answered Dr. Jerry just before he walked away.

Dr. Alton made careful statements to indicate that he had never traveled to other countries with the intent of engaging in sexual activity with children, thinking he was covered by the law that was written with that approach. However, a new law President George W. Bush had recently signed into effect removed the loophole. It said, in effect, that anyone who engages in sexual activity with children while in other countries is guilty of a crime.

We believe the media play an extremely important role in transforming the community of abusers—the global sexual exploitation and trafficking community. When major media outlets such as NBC and others will tell the stories of victims who otherwise have no voice, no defense, the public can become aware of the problem and take action. And equally as important, when they tell the stories of perpetrators caught, others in the same community must sit up, take notice, and stop their dark deeds.

So, we would be happy if the media plastered convicted criminals' faces across the front pages and throughout prime-time broadcast media, supplying the wake-up call to the abusers. Their time is up. It's not that we have a specific vendetta against this one man, though his actions are reprehensible and he needs to be subjected to the full scrutiny of the criminal justice system. As I've already written, it is to all victims' advantage when one perpetrator is brought to justice. And the wider the spread of the publicity for that case, the greater the deterrent for other perpetrators of all kinds of crimes of oppression.

The bottom line: We want the perpetrators to be as afraid as the children are. And in this case, it may be working. After the raid in March 2003, the convictions in October 2003 and January 2004, and the *Dateline* piece that unveiled Dr. Jerry Alton's secret life in Cambodia, Svay Pak would never be the same. Or so said the sex tourist community.

"Stay out of Svay Pak," read one Internet bulletin board, where pedophiles communicated with one another about the best, easiest, cheapest ways to find and abuse children.

"K11 [Kilo 11, another name for Svay Pak] is now over. . . . You stand a 99 percent chance of getting busted if you come here for the wrong reason," wrote another. "THE PARTY IS OVER. It will not EVER be like before."

I must hasten to add that one raid does not bring about an end to crime—not by a long shot. But a series of these kinds of results, with this message being sent loudly and clearly to the perpetrator community, can begin to chip away at the enemy's stronghold. That's why our Cambodian office is so important, so we can stay vigilant in our efforts to rescue victims and defend the oppressed.

CHAPTER 58

LANG PAYS

From the first trips into Phnom Penh in 2000, we were aware that Svay Pak wasn't the only place where minors were abused in brothels. When our investigators ventured out into the city's streets and casually asked the moto drivers where they could find "young girlfriends," the name of another establishment regularly came to the lips of the drivers: "Café 9999." So, along with our undercover trips to Svay Pak, we regularly went to Café 9999 in Phnom Penh to collect evidence and keep tabs on this operation.

We got to know the infamous Mamasan Lang, a powerful, well-connected brothel owner who had operated in Svay Pak for years, but who had grown weary of paying the fees for protection there required by her police friends. She then moved her operation into the city of Phnom Penh, where it was easier to blend into the hustle and bustle of the busy city's backdrop.

Because Lang had a large number of young girls at her service in the Phnom Penh brothel, we included her establishment in our plans for the day of the rescue/raid operation. We called her brothel by the code name "Whiskey," and we had hoped to pay Lang a surprise visit on the day of the raid, arresting her and freeing the fifteen or more girls under her control.

In preparation for that day, as Robert Earle gathered undercover evidence against the Svay Pak brothel keepers, he also paid visits to Lang under the same ruse, and captured on tape the brothel owner selling young girls for the purpose of sexual exploitation. Our tapes of Lang's business were unique, because of her flippant, carefree references to the girls' sexual experience and abilities. She showed off her girls like clothes or furniture, trying to make a good fit for each customer's needs and preferences: age, size, virgin, experience, types of sexual services performed, hotel or not.

When we visited her place with the *Dateline* crew, Lang smiled, laughed, and joked about our guys' taking away the virginity of one of her fourteen-year-old girls, as well as that of her ten-year-old sister. She was notorious for her cold, calculated, shrewd business tactics.

After the complicated raid in Svay Pak, it was too late in the day to go into Phnom Penh and Lang's brothel. Plus, we were fairly certain she would have heard about the raid by now, either from business associates in the village or friends on the police force. It was unlikely that we would find any girls there that night; we thought it best to let the situation cool a bit before going after Lang specifically.

What a great surprise, then, when we heard that the Cambodian National Police had conducted a raid of their own on location Whiskey on April 8, 2003. They arrested Mamasan Lang and her son, who served her as a pimp. We were contacted by the court and asked to testify at trial in Lang's case.

We readily agreed. When Sharon and Rebecca were in Cambodia in May 2003, they met with the judge in Lang's case and delivered reports and videos on the suspect, wanting him to have everything he needed to convict this perpetrator. Sharon and Robert cleared their schedules to be in Phnom Penh for the January 15, 2004, trial.

With what we knew of Lang, and as a result of the first trial, we had grave concerns for safety in the second trial. First, Lang had been running brothels in Phnom Penh since 1993, and she was extremely well connected, though we learned she had spent a short stint in jail during that time. Second, during the first trial we had shown our hand and our faces in court. We let people know who and what we were, and the brothel community had learned about some of our methods for gathering evidence. Many of those people were still on the loose.

So, for this trial, we had a lot more staff acting as eyes and ears around the courthouse, standing near doorways or in the halls of the two-story building, keeping watch. Each staff person wore a radio receiver in his or her ear, just in case something went wrong, and each had an assigned task for keeping everyone safe in the event of an emergency. The safety watch, though, started with each of them just being aware, being a little more cautious.

As for the case itself, the videotaped evidence we had against Lang was probably the strongest we had against anyone in terms of the number of times she was identified committing criminal acts on different occasions, her clear knowledge and complicity in the crimes, and her communication about the crimes in English.

The only potential complication was that we did not have any victims at hand, if the judge asked for them to appear. Only one who had worked for Lang had been rescued, and sadly she had run away from the aftercare facility. So if the judge had asked us to produce victims, we would not have been able to. But this time, the judge didn't ask.

The day of the trial arrived, and public and media interest was intense. Determined to demonstrate that it was an open and public trial, the court set up massive concert-sized speakers and strung cables outside into the streets so passersby and interested parties could follow the proceedings.

Once again Robert Earle was called as a witness in the case. As he stepped into the witness box, he turned to look at the suspects, Mamasan Lang and her son, who were being tried together. In their eyes he saw hatred, contempt, and malice. In spite of the evil looks intended to intimidate or influence him, Robert would not be deterred.

He testified extremely well, for several hours answering questions from the prosecution and being cross-examined by the defense. He played for the court the tapes of Lang's multiple offenses against children, stopping at several points to explain through the interpreter exactly what was going on.

The only real shot the defense had was to try to malign the credibility of IJM and malign Robert as an unwanted, uninvited foreign invader into the matters of Cambodia who had no business here. "Who gave you the right, the authority, to come here to pursue these cases?" the attorney asked him.

Robert replied calmly, slowly, allowing time for translation. "We were working with Cambodian authorities on these cases. The laws that were broken were Cambodian laws. Also, Cambodia was a signatory of the United Nations Rights of the Child proclamation, agreeing to protect children from such evils as sexual exploitation. We were simply operating according to the expressed wishes of the Cambodian government."

The trial progressed smoothly with no incidents, then the judge took a recess to decide the case and, we hoped, set a sentence for the offenders.

———

During the recess, Sharon stepped outside with a couple of other staff members. As Sharon fielded questions from a small group of reporters, the judge who had convicted and sentenced the four perpetrators in the first trial—and who had been the investigating judge in the Lang trial—walked up to her. After they pleasantly greeted each other, he asked how the trial was going. She answered briefly, and then he continued, going inside the building. His willingness to even dialogue with Sharon at that juncture was an encouragement to the team—that we would be able to continue to work cases through the judiciary.

It was a major victory for the children of Cambodia and those trafficked into the country when the judge returned and announced a guilty verdict for Mamasan Lang and her son. He sentenced Lang to twenty years in prison for her crimes—an unprecedented sentence that no doubt sent shock waves through the brothel community—and her son received five years for his role as her accomplice.

And we rejoiced.

In an e-mail to all staff, I wrote my reaction to the verdict:

The God of Justice granted a great triumph in Cambodia today as one of Phnom Penh's most notorious brothel keepers was sentenced to twenty years in prison for the brutal sex trafficking of children, based on video and testimonial evidence offered by IJM investigator Robert Earle in a Cambodian court. Congratulations to Cambodia team leader Sharon Cohn, who prepared the legal arguments and briefed the court in advance of the proceeding, and to IJM's fabulous team of Cambodian operatives. The brothel keeper's son was also sentenced to five years in prison as an accomplice to the sex-trafficking crimes. The judge publicly and specifically affirmed (1) the legitimacy of IJM's investigative personnel and operations, (2) that the live testimony of minor victims is unnecessary for conviction, and (3) that minors cannot consent to such offenses. Huge victories of great consequence. . . .

Sharon and Robert could describe many other great miracles (even as Sharon signed today the lease for our new IJM office space). Praise to our faithful God and thanks to everyone at IJM who worked so hard to see these offenders brought to justice so they cannot hurt any more children.

Let us not become weary in doing good, for at the proper time we will reap a harvest if we do not give up. (Galatians 6:9 NIV)

CHAPTER 59

WHERE IS GOD?

For many of us, the ugliness of abuse and oppression in our world leads us, quite understandably, to ask: Where is God in the midst of such suffering? Even if we have drifted to a place in life where we rarely address God, there is something about the rank cruelty of exploitation and the naked brutality of human violence that seems to lift our objection almost involuntarily to something larger and beyond ourselves. This was the cry that most resonated within my own heart while I struggled with the smell and mess and waste of genocide amid the mass graves of Rwanda. It was an appeal I heard echoing in an ancient cry of the psalmist:

> Why, O LORD, do you stand far off?
>   Why do you hide yourself in times of trouble?
> In his arrogance the wicked man hunts down the weak,
>   who are caught in the schemes he devises. . . .
> He says to himself, "God has forgotten;
>   he covers his face and never sees."
>   (Psalm 10:1–2, 11 NIV)

But over time, having seen the suffering of the innocent and the crushing of the weak all around the world, my plea has changed. More and more I find myself asking not, *Where is God?* but, *Where are God's people?*

There are still painful things of life I find myself arguing with God about, but these quarrels are less and less about injustice, and perhaps more about cancer or mental illness or rains that come too late or too hard. No, for me, the great tragedies of abuse and oppression in our world are so clearly man-made disasters that I find it difficult to keep blaming God. Not only because it is men and women, not God, who perpetrate the abuses, but also because God has so clearly given men and women the power to stop the abuses. The little girls of Svay Pak were not suffering because of vague and inexplicable forces of nature. They were suffering because men and women with names and faces chose to beat them, rape them, and terrorize them. They suffered because other men and women with names and faces chose to provide shelter and protection for the abusers. And at the end of the day, they suffered because the rest of us let it happen.

Given all the power and resources that God has placed in the hands of humankind, I have yet to see any injustice of humankind that could not also be stopped by humankind. I find myself sympathizing with a God who, speaking through the ancient prophet, told his people, "You have wearied the LORD with your words . . . by saying, . . . 'Where is the God of justice?' " (Malachi 2:17 NIV). Increasingly, I feel quite sure of the whereabouts of God. My tradition tells of a Father in heaven who refused to love an unjust world from a safe distance, but took his dwelling among us to endure the humility of false arrests, vicious torture, and execution. This is the God who could be found as "a man of sorrows, and familiar with suffering" (Isaiah 53:3 NIV). The more I have come to know him, the harder it has become for me to ask such a God to explain where he has been. In fact, surprisingly, I don't generally hear the victims of abuse doubting the presence of God either. Much more often I hear them asking me, "Where have *you* been?"

And it's more than a fair question. The victims instinctively sense, I believe, that humankind could, if it chose to, use the power and capacities that God has granted to overwhelm the forces of darkness that oppress them. Even the bullies and tormentors of our world know that they never have enough power or force to withstand even a fraction of what people of goodwill could, by God's grace, bring to bear against them. And thus the pain of the victims' question, for they suspect that their suffering is of the cruelest kind—the kind that is unnecessary. The deepest hurt comes not from the injury itself, but from the knowledge that they are so despised by some who would will their suffering and so unloved by others as to be unmoved by their suffering. And it all need not be so. Indeed, there is nothing I am more passionately convinced of through all of these travels through the world of brutal injustice than the simple truth that it need not be so. And there is no truth about our world that I am more eager to share, for I believe we all yearn for the joy that arrives when we decide to show up, when we find our own active place in the struggle against evil and discover the transforming power of life the Divine has granted to mere mortals.

Where are you? The question in the end is not an inquiry of obligation but an invitation—an invitation to the fundamentals of human joy for which we were made, a joy that our loving Creator refuses to hoard to himself.

I am reminded of the pastor who gathered with a group of friends to pray earnestly for a woman in Haiti who desperately needed a few hundred dollars for a lifesaving medical treatment that she could not afford. The group prayed to God to help this woman and to save her life. On and on the prayers went, until a thought came to the pastor. "Why," he asked, "are we asking God to do this when God has clearly given us in this circle more than enough money to just send her a check and stop her from dying?" The logic seemed unassailable and, as they thought about it, it also seemed like a lot more fun.

But many times we miss out on this joy by insisting that God do the work of goodness without us. We catch glimpses of the passionate exhilaration and beauty of confronting evil and doing good, but we lose heart, fearing the work too divine for us or the risks too great.

I remember when my twin daughters were of an age when they would beg me to take them horseback riding. They were thrilled to their toes by the beauty and power of horses. They each wanted a chance to be in the saddle, to grasp the reins in their hands and ride. Oh, how they begged. "Come on, Dad. Can we please go horseback riding? Please, Dad, please." On and on it went, with every horse spotted along the highway renewing the endless appeals.

Lacking the ready means to make their dream come true, it took great and elaborate arrangements for me finally to secure their date with destiny. We set aside a weekend and drove ten hours to visit generous family friends willing to share their horses and room to run. We borrowed some boots and unearthed two riding helmets. We engaged in endless preparatory conversations about what it would be like to actually ride the horses. As best I could, I responded to one excited question after another about what it would "really be like." Then the magical moment arrived. I rode up on a gorgeous steed primed and ready for this rendezvous with glory, and beckoned to whoever wanted to go first to join me in the saddle and grab hold of the reins. Both girls suddenly turned to me and said in perfect unison, "No, Dad, *you* do it."

"*You do it?*" I exclaimed. "What do you mean, '*You* do it'?" We laughed.

The whole reason for the journey and the provision and all the conversation was precisely so that *they* would do it with me. Of course, I *could* do it, as I had ridden horses before. But the whole point of our preparation together was so that *they* could know the joy and beauty and goodness of the ride *with me*. But when the moment came, they lost faith that such a thing was possible for them. Up close those horses looked so enormous. And by comparison, Dad looked so small and far away—even if he was up in the saddle. Fears took hold, and my girls wondered if the ride would really be such fun anyway. And all kinds of things could go wrong. They still wanted the glorious thing done, but they could think of only one thing to say: "You do it, Dad."

Eventually, with much reassurance, a boost into the saddle with me, and a few laps around together, they found that, indeed, they were made for such an exhilarating ride—to see triumph in difficult things.

Likewise, there are those moments when we sense the call to goodness. Our hearts are moved by the suffering of others, and we are drawn to engage the struggle for rescue and love and justice. It resonates not so much as a duty, but as an honor, a gift, and the deepest satisfaction of the soul. And so our Maker has prepared it for us. Not that such human suffering is prepared for our amusement. Never. But that even in such a fallen world of wickedness and pain as this, there is joy to be extracted by getting into the saddle with our Lord, gripping the reins, and riding into the battle. Indeed, it is the very reason for the journey and for our very being. We were created for good works, prepared beforehand that we might ride in them.

But drawing near the field, the clouds seem dark and the shadows long, and the challenge enormous. We doubt the joy and fear the risks. But wanting the good thing done, we ask, "Where is God?" We may even turn to him and say, "You do it!"

And lovingly our Father turns and beckons. "Come. I'll give you a boost to the saddle. We shall ride together." And as we have faith, we join him in that high seat and feel him place those rough, thick reins in our hands. A cool, fresh wind begins to rush past us as we gather speed and power beneath us, and soon enough we are off. We have a ride, with work and glory before us—a worthy struggle to engage alongside our Lord. A struggle for which we were made. A struggle to usher in the day "that man, who is of the earth, may terrify no more."

WHAT YOU CAN DO

As a global force, America and its people are able to generate wealth, exert governmental power, and impact the world in a way that's unprecedented in the history of nation-states. And we live here at a time when the world is full of massive and profound poverty, injustice, oppression, and suffering. Accordingly, the first step in good stewardship is to understand what God has given us by placing us here.

How can we, as good stewards of American influence and liberty, turn those blessings into action on behalf of the oppressed? It takes each one of us, faithfully offering what he or she has and allowing God to multiply it into something great.

Remember Mitchell, the NBC cameraman who dropped his camera to help rescue two victims during the Svay Pak raid? He had heard the stories, he had understood the gravity of the situation, and he was compelled to act. In doing so he saved two little girls, offering them a shot at a future and ending their horrific exploitation. Our hope at International Justice Mission is that you have been impacted in the same way by hearing these stories of rescue from a dark world of injustice. Our prayer is that you will see not just the enormous need, but also a wide-open opportunity for you to become involved. You may never have the chance Mitchell had to drop everything and literally whisk someone to freedom, but the other options for involvement are no less important.

I've told you how extraordinary my colleagues are. Of course, they don't view themselves as special. They are simply people doing the work God has placed before them and called them to do. We're all just ordinary people. We need more ordinary people who are willing to step forward and say, "I'm ready to go. Send me."

Here are some of the ways you can get involved to help seek justice:

Pray. At IJM we have a group of people called Prayer Partners who commit to pray daily for victims of oppression and their rescuers. After signing up on our Web site and agreeing to keep these requests in confidence, Prayer Partners receive weekly up-to-date requests for intercession.

Prepare. If you feel the call to get involved in a more professional capacity, begin to prepare to serve. IJM needs attorneys, caseworkers, and law enforcement and investigative specialists to work with us to seek justice. Other NGOs also are in need of well-trained social workers and counselors who can do the important work of aftercare. IJM has an excellent internship program that helps equip people to serve in many different areas of human rights work.

Volunteer. We often deploy volunteer investigative associates to help prepare information for interventions. If you have the background and expertise to help with this area of work, we'd love to hear from you. We also occasionally have the need for attorneys who can volunteer to research or handle a case or provide legal documentation.

Give. As worn out as this sounds, financial gifts are still one of the most needed areas of involvement. Although the work of justice is very doable, it is also costly in countries where we are paving new ground. It's time-consuming work that requires perseverance and professional excellence.

Tell others. You've learned about oppression, injustice, and suffering and now know these are not just big concepts but real problems. Take this information and share it with others. You may even want to read and discuss this book together with a small group. *The Justice Mission* is a video-based curriculum that walks students through a study of God's heart for the oppressed. Consider introducing student groups at your church or school to this study. You can be the start of a ripple effect as you use your influence to educate others.

You can learn more about the work of International Justice Mission at www.ijm.org.

LINCOLN CHRISTIAN COLLEGE AND SEMINARY 16010

306.742
H3714

3 4711 00187 5733